T0305602

Solarnomics

Solar power has come of age. Not only has it become one of the key alternatives to fossil fuels, it can now be deployed in a way that makes a viable business with a financial profit. This book shows industry professionals and students how to do just that.

Solarnomics describes the economics of building and operating a solar power plant today and provides a window into a future in which several technologies collaborate, and in which all participants in the electricity grid become smarter at scheduling both the supply and demand for electric power to give humanity a future that is sustainable, both environmentally and economically. The book shows how to estimate costs and revenues, how to tweak the design of a project to improve profitability, how to calculate return on investment, how to assess and deal with risk, how to raise capital, how to combine solar with wind and batteries to make a hybrid microgrid, and how to be prepared for future developments in the evolving smart electricity grid.

Solarnomics will enable professionals in the solar industry to assess the potential profitability of a proposed solar project, and it will enable students to add an extra dimension to their understanding of sustainability.

David Wright has a PhD from Cambridge University, UK and has experience in industry, academia and government in three continents. His university research in solar power has been conducted in collaboration with industrial partners in the Cleantech Sector and is published in top journals in renewable energy.

"Essential knowledge for the solar entrepreneur, *Solarnomics* is that rare book that discusses the technical and business aspects of solar power on equal footing. Wright succeeds in delivering the practical information needed to navigate today's solar market."

Chris Giebink, Head of Applied Optoelectronics and Photonics Lab, Penn State University

"*Solarnomics* provides a thorough and well-rounded perspective on the ins and outs of running a profitable solar business. As solar power becomes increasingly important as we move towards a low carbon economy, this book can act as a toolkit for the solar leaders of tomorrow as they look to understand the risks and returns made possible through solar business."

Katherine Arblaster, Senior Manager, Monitor Deloitte

"Professor Wright shows how evolving solar and green technologies can benefit established economic sectors. Solar energy financing is key to project success. This book provides financial options available to the reader in an engaging manner."

David Arenburg, President, DAI Inc

"Down to basics, straight to the core of the issue, yet insightful – a reading I recommend for anyone interested in solar economics who doesn't want to go to the trouble of getting a PhD in photovoltaics."

Yves Poissant, Research Manager and Senior Specialist in Solar Photovoltaic Technologies, CanmetENERGY

Solarnomics

Setting Up and Managing a Profitable
Solar Business

David Wright

Routledge
Taylor & Francis Group

LONDON AND NEW YORK

Cover image: © Getty Images

First published 2022
by Routledge
4 Park Square, Milton Park, Abingdon, Oxon OX14 4RN

and by Routledge
605 Third Avenue, New York, NY 10158

Routledge is an imprint of the Taylor & Francis Group, an informa business

British Library Cataloguing-in-Publication Data
A catalogue record for this book is available from the British Library

Library of Congress Cataloging-in-Publication Data
Names: Wright, David, 1941- author.
Title: Solarnomics: setting up and managing a profitable solar business / David Wright.
Description: Abingdon, Oxon; New York, NY: Routledge, 2022. |
Includes bibliographical references and index. |
Identifiers: LCCN 2021048619 (print) | LCCN 2021048620 (ebook) |
ISBN 9781032201450 (hardback) | ISBN 9781032201436 (paperback) |
ISBN 9781003262435 (ebook)
Subjects: LCSH: Solar energy industries—Finance. | Solar power plants—Management.
Classification: LCC HD9681.A2 W75 2022 (print) | LCC HD9681.A2 (ebook) |
DDC 333.792/3—dc23/eng/20220105
LC record available at https://lccn.loc.gov/2021048619
LC ebook record available at https://lccn.loc.gov/2021048620

ISBN: 978-1-032-20145-0 (hbk)
ISBN: 978-1-032-20143-6 (pbk)
ISBN: 978-1-003-26243-5 (ebk)

DOI: 10.4324/9781003262435

Typeset in Times New Roman
by codeMantra

To:
Mina, Leila, Norm, Rebecca, Allison, Ramin and Olwen

Summary Table of Contents

Detailed Table of Contents

Meet the Author

David Wright combines an Engineering PhD from Cambridge University with his current position as Professor at the University of Ottawa's Telfer School of Management to provide a business perspective on the Solar Power Industry. His recent work evaluates capital cost trends for solar deployment and identifies situations in which solar power can be profitable without government incentives. It is published in research journals with the top 2–3% of citations. Dr. Wright has experience in academia, industry and government in three continents and is cited in: *Who's Who in the World*, *Who's Who in Canadian Business* and *Who's Who in Science and Engineering*.

Preface

We can make a very large dent in global carbon emissions by generating electricity from renewable sources and using electric vehicles for transport. We have already started to do this with the help of government incentives that reduce the cost of generating solar power and subsidize the price of an electric car. Now governments around the world are phasing out those incentives because renewable power and electric vehicles can stand on their own feet, as economically viable technologies. We can deploy solar in a way that makes a financial profit, and this book shows how to do just that.

Why Solar?

I have been researching and publishing on solar economics for several years. It has been an exciting time. The profitability of solar has continuously improved, not just with reductions in the price of solar modules, but also with improvements in installation techniques. Now the cost of a fully operational solar generating plant is 79% less than it was a decade ago. The International Energy Agency says that solar is "the cheapest electricity in history[1]". Not everyone made money. Many companies, both large and small, that couldn't keep pace with the cost crunch fell by the wayside. Technologies that looked very promising five years ago were not profitable enough to be deployed, and now new solar technologies are emerging that could displace the modules that we are familiar with

> **Let's say "Modules" instead of "Panels".**
>
> Solar "panels" is the terminology a lot of people use. The industry, however, refers to solar "modules" which gives them a bit more dignity. After all, they may look like a panel, but a lot of semiconductor quantum mechanics went into their design, so let's use "module" in this book.

today. This book distills the experience that I have gained from working on a diverse range of projects in North America and the Middle East.

Of course, harnessing solar power is not the only way to generate renewable electricity. Hydroelectric and wind are the two major alternatives. What all three have in common is that they are all capital intensive. You spend a lot of money up front to build your power plant, and then, it sits there generating power for decades into the future. There are some relatively small operating and maintenance costs over the years, but no fuel cost – the economics depends largely on that initial construction cost. Due to the rapid pace of improvements in solar installations, the construction cost is declining at 12% per year. Hydro power is a very different story. The technology and its installation are well established and do not have much room left for further tweaking to reduce costs. We have already dammed the vast majority of the rivers that can be dammed easily, so new projects are in more challenging locations. Consequently, the average cost of hydro-electric power installation is *increasing* by 4.4% per year. Wind power tells a similar story. Although it is windier offshore than onshore, installation costs are very high for offshore wind turbines and there has been relatively little deployment except in shallow waters. With just modest technological advancement, costs of onshore wind farms are declining by only 2.7% per year, much more slowly than the 12% annual reductions for solar. For these reasons, this book focuses on solar and also describes some hybrid projects in which solar and wind are combined. We will almost certainly see a mix of solar, wind and hydro power deployment over the coming years and, because of the capital-intensive nature of all these technologies, many of the principles of economic analysis described in this book apply to all three.

As a result of these cost trends, the proportion of global new electricity generating capacity that is renewable increased from 50% in 2014 to 83% in 2020. Of those 260 GW of renewable capacity installed in 2020, solar had the largest share (Figure A).[2]

Renewable electric power is not much use by itself because it has a will of its own. The sun chooses when to shine and the wind decides when to blow. During a dry season, there may not be enough water in a reservoir to generate hydro-electricity. Unfortunately, humans are impatient and demanding creatures. They want electricity on their own schedule, not at the whim of nature. Can we switch on a solar power station when it is needed independent of whether the sun is shining? To make this happen, we need a means of storing electricity, for instance, a battery. Batteries are declining in cost at 11% per year, about the same rate as solar, but are currently expensive, eating into the profit margin on our renewable power plants. The industry

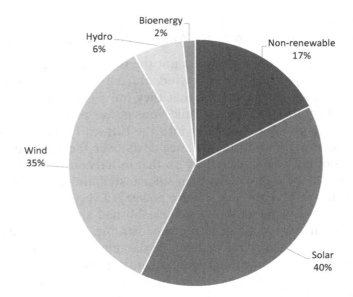

Figure A New electricity generating capacity added in 2020 worldwide.

is coming up with creative ideas to help speed up adoption – could we make our electric vehicle battery do double duty: to power a car and also to power our home after we have driven home? Solar is not just a stand-alone technology. It can be combined with something else to squeeze the maximum profit out of it. This book discusses the profitability of many technologies that mesh with solar to make a combo, not just wind and hydro, but also electric vehicles, hydrogen and a participative electricity grid in which the various players negotiate a balance between demand and supply.

Who Is the Reader?

This book is intended for anyone interested in the profitability of solar power, for instance:

- Business people and engineers currently working in the electricity industry.
- Business people and engineers currently working in the solar industry.
- Government planners working on energy supply economics.
- Government planners working on the energy transition to renewables.
- Students, graduate and undergraduate
    - Business students interested in how to apply what they are learning to the solar industry.

- Engineering students interested in a business angle on solar power.
- Students on multidisciplinary programs, e.g. environmental science, environmental engineering, sustainability, renewable energy, energy economics, and engineering management.
- The general reader interested in whether we can mitigate climate change and make a profit while doing so.

This book is NOT intended for someone who wants to know how to install a solar module on the roof of their house. There are plenty of books on that; this is not one of them. It is concerned with making a business out of solar and focuses on larger-scale projects.

The What? How? and Why? of Profitable Solar

This book provides facts and information in answer to the question "*What is the profitability of solar?*" It also answers the question "*How* do we assess the profitability of solar?" by providing a step-by-step process at the end of each chapter that shows how to implement what the chapter has covered. The question "Why?" is addressed by giving the reasoning behind everything described in these pages. The ultimate aim of the book is to provide an *understanding* of the profitability of solar power.

What Is the Writing Style of This Book?

In a word, the writing style is conversational, using active as well as passive voices. The page layout is varied, including diagrams, bullet lists and sidebars to break up the prose. Each chapter ends with four features to help understanding:

1. *Summary:* 100–200 words summary of the main points of the text.
2. *Takeaways:* More detailed summary in concise bullet format.
3. *Probe Deeper: The Why?* A why question and answer related to the content of the chapter.
4. *Process:* A flow diagram showing the sequence of steps you would follow to implement the content of the chapter.

What Are the Contents of This Book?

This book will show you how to estimate costs and revenues, how to tweak the design of a project to improve profitability, how to calculate return on investment, how to assess and deal with risk, how to raise capital, how to combine solar with wind, batteries, etc. to make a hybrid microgrid and how to be prepared for future developments in the evolving smart electricity grid. These topics are illustrated by examples from many different locations around the world and there is a separate geographical index at the back of the book.

It is in four parts. Parts 1 and 2 describe what the solar industry has done and is continuing to do: it is deploying solar in many diverse settings and estimating its profitability. Part 3 describes the new stuff it is doing now, building profitable microgrids that integrate solar with wind, batteries and other technologies. Part 4 provides a glimpse into the future, the new technologies and applications that are emerging and how we can make them mesh in a truly participative manner with both the public electricity grid and the microgrids on customers' premises.

Solarnomics describes the profitability of building a solar power plant today and also provides a window into a future in which several technologies collaborate and in which all participants in electricity grid become smarter at scheduling both the supply and demand for electric power to give humanity a future that is sustainable both environmentally and economically.

Notes

1 International Energy Agency, 2020, World Energy Outlook.
2 IRENA, International Renewable Energy Agency, 2021, Renewable Capacity Highlights.

Glossary and Acronyms

AC: alternating current

Agriculture-integrated photovoltaics: sharing of land area and sunlight between agriculture and solar electricity generation, also known as AgriVoltaics

AIPV: agriculture-integrated photovoltaics

AgriVoltaics: sharing of land area and sunlight between agriculture and PV electricity generation, also known as Agriculture-Integrated Photovoltaics

Aggregator: company that combines the offerings of other organizations to increase supply and/or reduce demand on the public electricity grid, to trade those offerings on the electricity market or the grid services market

Albedo: proportion of light scattered by the ground, also known as reflectivity

Aluminum: metal important to the electricity industry since it is extracted by passing large amounts of electric power through aluminum oxide

Ammonia: an input to the manufacture of nitrogen fertilizer that can be obtained by reacting hydrogen with nitrogen from air

Alternating current: electric current that alternates from flowing in one direction to the opposite direction; electricity from the grid is AC

Balance of system: the physical components of a solar installation other than the solar modules, includes the racking, wiring and other electrical equipment, e.g. the inverter

Battery cells: the parts of a battery that actually store electricity

Battery management system: the electronics that ensures that the battery cells are not overloaded and also maintains the battery within its range of operating temperatures

Battery pack: battery cells, casing, battery management system and other electronics

Behind-the-meter: a solar installation on a customer's premises, which feeds power into the customer's electrical system thus reducing the amount required from the grid

Bifacial: a solar module that can absorb light from both sides

Bifacial gain: the percentage of additional light absorbed from the back of a bifacial module

BIPV: building-integrated photovoltaics

Blue hydrogen: hydrogen made by reacting methane and steam at high temperature producing hydrogen and carbon dioxide and then removing the carbon dioxide using CCS

BoS: balance of system

BTM: behind-the-meter

Building-integrated photovoltaics: the incorporation of PV cells in building materials such as windows, facades, roofing tiles and shingles

Bulk generators: electrical generators that supply large amounts of electrical power into the grid; any large-scale generator can be regarded as a bulk generator, including coal, nuclear, hydro, solar and wind power

Capacity factor: amount of electricity actually generated in a year divided by the amount a system could potentially generate if it were operated 24/7. If a 250W solar module generates 350 kWh in a year, its capacity factor is (350*1000)/(365*24*250) = 0.16. Solar has a lower capacity factor than most other forms of electricity generation, since it only generates during daylight and does not generate at its full potential when the sun is low in the sky

Carbon capture and storage: removing carbon dioxide from a mixture of gases and storing it so that it does not escape into the atmosphere

Carbon equivalent: amount of carbon dioxide that causes the same amount of global warming; for instance, 1 ton of methane causes the same amount of global warming as 23 tons of carbon dioxide

Cash flow: income minus cost for a project in a specific year

CCS: carbon capture and storage

Compressed air storage: system for compressing and decompressing air to store and retrieve electrical energy, using an electric compressor, which also acts as a generator. Size ranges from a metal cylinder to an underground cavern

Concentrated (or concentrating) solar power: solar power system that uses mirrors to focus the sun's rays to the top of a tower, where the heat is used to power a steam turbine that generates electricity; also known as solar thermal power

Concentrating photovoltaics: system for optically concentrating sunlight on a small solar cell, e.g. a multijunction cell made of costly semiconductors

Counterparty: from the perspective of one company, a counterparty is another company in a financial contract for trade or investment

CPV: concentrating photovoltaics

CSP: concentrated (or concentrating) solar power

DC: direct current

Death spiral: as customers install BTM solar electricity because it costs less than grid electricity, the electric utility has to increase electricity prices to maintain its profitability. This produces even more incentive for customers to install more BTM solar modules

Demand charge: charge imposed by an electric utility on a customer's peak usage in a given month. Each month, the hour during which the customer's usage is at its maximum for that month is determined and the demand change is applied to the customer's consumption during that hour

Demand response: relationship between a customer and an electricity company in which the customer is paid to reduce demand

DER: distributed energy resources

Developer: company that constructs solar projects

Direct current (DC): electric current that always flows in the same direction; electricity produced by a solar module is DC

Direct normal irradiance (DNI): the power in the direct beam of light from the sun

Discount rate: parameter used for reducing the value of future cash flows to a present day equivalent value

Dispatchable: able to be switched on and off. A gas turbine is a dispatchable electricity generator, whereas a solar module is not since it can be switched off but not on if the sun is not shining. Solar module plus storage is dispatchable

Distributed energy resources: energy resources such as solar and storage, other than large, centralized installations; examples include solar installations that supply electricity directly to the distribution network, or installed behind-the-meter at a customer premises

Distribution: short-distance transport of electricity (e.g. within a city from transmission lines to customers)

Distribution company, also known as distribution system operator (DSO): company responsible for short-distance transport of electricity (e.g. within a city from transmission lines to customers)

Distribution system operator, also known as distribution company: a company responsible for short-distance transport of electricity (e.g. within a city from transmission lines to customers)

DNI: direct normal irradiance

DSO: distribution system operator

Efficiency of PV: the percentage of sunlight energy converted into electrical energy. The efficiency can apply to the PV cell, the PV module or the PV system. The efficiency of the cell is highest. Some energy is lost in the module, so the efficiency of the module is lower. More energy is lost in the wiring connecting the modules and in the inverter, resulting in a further reduction in efficiency when measured for the whole PV system

Electric energy: amount of electricity measured in kWh

Electric power: rate of flow of electricity measured in kW

Electricity charge: charge per kWh for electricity delivered by the grid to customers

Electricity market: (wholesale) market in which electrical energy (kWh) is traded

Electrolysis: process of separating water into oxygen and hydrogen by passing an electric current through it

Emissions trading system: The European Union carbon trading market

EPC: engineering procurement and construction

ETS: emissions trading system

Feed-in-tariff: tariff paid for electricity fed into the grid from solar installations on customer premises

Feeder line: electric power line in a city used by a distribution company to deliver power to many customers, each of which has a connection to the feeder line

Flexibility: tradeable commodity for balancing supply and demand on an electricity grid. Distribution and transmission companies can purchase "up" or "down" flexibility. Up-flexibility refers to increased supply of electricity or reduced demand. Down-flexibility refers to decreased supply or increased demand

Float-o-Voltaics: solar modules floating on water

Flywheel: spinning wheel, the speed of which can be increased or decreased to store and retrieve electrical energy using an electric motor, which also acts as a generator

Frequency sensing and regulation: ability of an electric load to sense the AC frequency of the electricity grid and respond by increasing/decreasing demand when the frequency is too high/low

Front-of-the-meter: solar projects that feed electricity into the public electricity grid as opposed to a customer site

FTM: front-of-the-meter

GHI: global horizontal irradiance

Gigawatt hour: a unit of electric energy $= 10^9$ watt hours

Global horizontal irradiance (GHI): the total solar power on a horizontal surface including the diffuse light from the whole sky plus the direct beam of sunlight, taking into account the angle of incidence

Gray hydrogen: hydrogen made by reacting methane and steam at high temperature producing hydrogen and carbon dioxide

Green ammonia: ammonia obtained by reacting green hydrogen with nitrogen from the air

Green hydrogen: hydrogen made by electrolysis of water using renewable electricity

Green steel: steel obtained by using hydrogen (instead of coke) to remove the oxygen from iron ore

Grid: network of generators, transmission lines and distribution networks operated by public utilities from which customers can purchase electricity

Grid balancing: ensuring supply balances demand on the electricity grid without variation in the AC frequency

Grid services market: market on which an electricity system operator can request an increase in supply or a reduction in demand at some time in the future

GW: gigawatt $= 10^9$ watts

GWh: gigawatt hour $= 10^9$ watt hours

Heat battery: device using electricity to convert a solid into a gel. When activated, the gel releases heat that can be used to heat water whenever needed, thus eliminating the heat loss from a hot water storage tank. The device stores electric energy and recovers it as heat, hence the name heat battery

HOMER: hybrid optimization model for electric renewables; commercial software for optimizing the design of a renewable energy system

Hurdle rate: the minimum IRR required for a project to go ahead

HVAC: heating, ventilation and air-conditioning

Hybrid: electricity generating system (e.g. a microgrid) that has more than one type of generator, e.g. solar, wind, tidal, and diesel

Hydrogen: gas manufactured conventionally by a process that emits carbon dioxide, but which can also be manufactured by using electricity to separate water into hydrogen and oxygen

IEA: International Energy Agency

Independent system operator: a company responsible for balancing supply and demand for electric power in the public electricity grid, e.g. by operating wholesale markets for power

Intermittency: variations in the level (applied to solar irradiance, wind speed, electric power, etc.); although the regular use of "intermittent" implies on/off characteristics, intermittency in the context of renewable energy implies variations in level (e.g. in MW)

Internal rate of return: financial profit from a project, defined as the discount rate for which NPV = 0

Internet of Things: sensors and actuators connected to the Internet

Inverter: Electronic device that converts DC electricity to AC electricity, e.g. electricity from a solar installation to the public electricity grid

IRENA: International Renewable Energy Agency

IRR: internal rate of return

Irradiance: a measure of the power of sunlight in kWh/m^2

ISO: independent system operator

kW: kilowatt = 10^3 watts

kWh: kilowatt hour = 10^3 watt hours

kilowatt hour: a unit of electric energy = 10^3 watt hours

LCOE: levelized cost of electricity

Lead: a toxic metal that is an essential component in some perovskites

Levelized cost of electricity: average cost of generating electricity over the lifetime of a project, discounting future costs and amounts of electricity generated

Load: (1) electrical device that consumes electricity, e.g. a domestic refrigerator or a conveyor belt used to transport rock in a mine, and (2) amount of electricity consumed by such a device

μm: micrometer = 10^{-6} meters

mCPV: microtracked CPV

Megawatt hour: unit of electric energy = 10^6 watt hours

Microgrid: electricity network consisting of several electrical components linked together, e.g. generators, storage devices and connections to deliver electricity to users and to the public electricity grid

Micrometer: 10^{-6} meters

Microtracked CPV: a form of CPV having the same form factor as PV, in which the concentrating optics are fixed and the CPV cell is moved behind the optics to maintain focus on the sun

Modules: also known as panels; mounted on racks, these are the building blocks of a solar installation. Each module consists of several solar cells covered with protective layers of plastic and held together in a metal frame. Solar modules typically produce 250–400 Watts of DC electricity and are 0.6–2 square meters in area

Multijunction solar cell: a solar cell consisting of multiple semiconductors on top of each other, each converting a different part of the solar spectrum into electricity

MW: megawatt = 10^6 watts

MWh: megawatt hour = 10^6 watt hours

Nanometer: 10^{-9} meters

Net-metering: a provision in an electricity tariff that allows customers to install generating systems on their premises that supply customers' electrical equipment. Excess power can be fed into the public electricity grid (turning customers' electricity meter backward) so long as at other times at least the same amount of power is purchased from the grid. The customer pays for the "net" amount measured by the meter

Net present value: total of all cash flows for a project, discounted back to a value today

nm: nanometer = 10^{-9} meters

NPV: net present value

Off-grid: generating systems not connected to the public electricity grid

Offtaker: a company that takes electricity off a solar project, i.e. a customer of a solar project who pays for the electricity supplied

Orange button: a standard for defining solar terminology that facilitates data exchange among different companies in the solar industry

Organics: a rage of semiconductors with a similar chemical structure that can be used for PV

P90: the amount of electric power that we can be 90% certain of generating (equivalent to the 10th percentile). P90 can also be applied to other things than power, e.g. revenue and profits

Participative market: an electricity market open to consumers and small businesses, in contrast to the wholesale market which is only open to large businesses

Pedestal: a vertical support for an array of solar modules that allows the modules to follow the sun by rotating about two axes: east–west and high–low tilt

Perovskites: a range of semiconductors with the same crystalline structure that can be used for PV

Photovoltaics: conversion of light (photo) into electricity (volt), which is the technology used in solar PV and is based on semiconductors, usually silicon

Power: rate of flow of energy; electric power is measured in watts, kilowatts or megawatts

Power purchase agreement: a contract to supply electricity to a customer, including the power required at different times of day and year and the price to be paid

PPA: power purchase agreement

Pumped hydro: a system for storing electricity by using it to pump water from a lower reservoir to a higher one; the pump doubles as a generator to provide electricity when the water flows back down

PV: photovoltaics

Racking: metal frames on which solar modules are mounted

Real-time price: the price of electricity on the wholesale market during a short interval of time, e.g. 5 minutes

ReFLEX: renewable energy flexibility, a participative energy market in Orkney Islands, UK

ReOpt: renewable energy integration and optimization; software for optimizing the design of a renewable energy system

Securitization: the process of bundling PPAs and loan agreements into a tradable security

SEIA: Solar Energy Industries Association

SEP: shared energy platform

Shared energy platform: an electricity trading platform at the Port of Amsterdam

Sky camera: a camera with software that monitors the passage of clouds across the sky to forecast solar electricity generation a few hours ahead

Soft costs: cost items in the development of a solar installation including land acquisition, obtaining permits, interconnection to the electricity grid, overhead and profit for the developer

Solar CSP: a solar power system that converts the energy of sunlight into heat that is used to power a steam turbine that generates electrical energy

Solar PV: a solar power system that converts the energy of sunlight directly into electrical energy

Solar thermal: a solar power system that uses mirrors to focus the sun's rays to the top of a tower, where the heat is used to power a steam turbine that generates electricity; also known as concentrated (or concentrating) solar power (CSP)

Space heating: heating the air in buildings

Spectrum: a range of wavelengths of light

Spot price: on the wholesale market for electricity, the average of the maximum real-time prices during several consecutive pricing intervals, e.g. 6 or 12 five-minute intervals

State of charge: amount of electric energy (kWh) stored in a storage device, e.g. a battery

Step tariff: a tariff that increases the charge ($/kWh) for electricity when the customers' monthly consumption exceeds a certain limit; also known as tiered pricing

Supercapacitor: a device for storing electricity by accumulating negatively charged electrons on a metal plate and positive charge on another plate connected by an electric circuit; electricity is recovered when the electrons flow away from the plate and positive charge flows in the opposite direction

Surety bond: an agreement between an insurance company and two parties, A and B, to a contract. If A fails to meet their contractual obligations, the insurer makes a payment to B. Surety bonds are widely used on solar construction projects, between a developer and a contractor, e.g. if an electrician fails to complete electrical work on time, a payment is made to the developer

Systems operator: company responsible (among other things) for balancing supply and demand in the public electricity grid

Tiered pricing: a tariff that increases the charge ($/kWh) for electricity when the customers' monthly consumption exceeds a certain limit; also known as a step tariff

Thin Film PV: solar cells made of a range of materials in very thin layers from a few nanometers to 10 micrometers on a substrate, manufactured by spraying, printing or vapor deposition

Time-of-use: an electricity tariff that charges different amounts per kilowatt of electricity depending on the time of day, day of the week and season of the year.

ToU: time-of-use

Tracker: a system that swings solar modules around so that they always point at the sun; single-axis trackers follow the sun from east to west; dual axis trackers also follow the sun as it changes altitude

Transactive market: an electricity market open to small transactions, in contrast to the wholesale market, which is only open to large transactions

Transmission: long-distance transport of electric power (e.g. from generating stations to cities)

Transmission company, also known as a transmission system operator: a company responsible for transporting electricity between generators and distribution companies in cities

Transmission system operator, also known as a transmission company: a company responsible for transporting electricity between generators and distribution companies in cities

TSO: transmission system operator

Utility-scale: large solar installations, usually feeding directly into the electricity grid, as opposed to powering customers' equipment directly

W: Watt

Watt: a unit of electric power

Watt hour: a unit of electric energy

YieldCo: a company that buys solar projects from a developer and operates them by selling electricity

Part 1
Deploying Solar: Costs and Revenues

Part 1 of this book puts the reader in the driving seat of a developer planning a solar project. As we drive down that road, we aim to answer two main questions. How much will it cost? How much revenue will it bring in? There will be twists, turns and obstacles on our journey. What factors are beyond our control that inevitably limit our revenues or add to our costs? But there will also be shortcuts that we can use to improve our profitability. In what ways can we tweak the design of our project to improve revenues or reduce costs? The end of the road in Part 1 will be the ability to assess and improve cash flows of a project at the planning stage. We will use these in Part 2 to answer two major questions. How much return will we get on our investment? Should the project go ahead?

Solar modules do one thing and one thing only: they use semiconductors to convert light into electricity. This is known as photovoltaics (PV): photo (light) to electricity (volts). There are many semiconductors that can do this trick and the solar industry has homed in on just one that is used in 96% of today's solar installations: crystalline silicon.

We have one semiconductor doing a single job, but its profitability depends crucially on how it is deployed. A few dozen solar modules on the roof of a school, serried ranks on the roof of a hospital or a vista of glistening modules in a desert stretching off to the horizon all use the same technology, but deployed differently. Part 1 of Solarnomics shows how diverse these deployments are when seen through the lens of profitability.

First the costs are different. The cost of the solar modules is the same but installing thousands of modules across a flat desert brings enormous economies of scale compared with a bespoke job on a residential rooftop. Second, the revenue streams are different, reflecting the value of electricity at different times of day. A residence may pay a flat rate price for electricity at

DOI: 10.4324/9781003262435-1

any time of day or year. An office building may pay a base price for electricity plus a charge that depends on the peak consumption of the building. If we can generate solar at that peak time, our solar is worth much more than at other times.

We will cover four different types of deployment of solar power in different parts of the electricity grid. This will allow us to choose which type of deployment gives us the biggest bang for our buck.

1. *Utility-scale*: large installations feeding directly into the electricity grid, the same way that a nuclear power station feeds into the grid. They benefit from more economies of scale than the other types of deployment.
2. *Commercial and industrial behind-the-meter*: medium-sized installations at a customer premises, mainly generating electricity that is used by the customer (rather than being fed into the grid, as with utility-scale deployments). At an office building, the installation is typically on the roof or as an awning over a parking lot. Mounting modules on the ground is less costly and is used at some industrial sites if there is sufficient space.
3. *Small business and residences behind-the-meter*: small installations on individual rooftops (e.g. on strip malls and houses) used primarily to reduce purchases of electricity from the grid (as with the commercial and industrial deployments). The layout of modules needs to be customized to individual roof architectures increasing the cost of these installations.
4. *Off-grid*: not just the iconic log cabin in the woods, but also villages in rural areas and mining operations in remote regions. The key issue here is how to provide electricity after the sun has set, so storage (e.g. batteries) and/or another power source (e.g. wind or hydro) is much more important here than in the previous three deployment scenarios.

A common element in each of the following chapters is facing the solar modules in the right direction. The sun rises in the east and sets in the west, and in the Northern Hemisphere, during the day, it passes through the southern sky, so we set up solar modules facing south. In the winter, the midday sun is low in the sky, and in the summer, it is high; the average altitude angle of the sun is 90° minus the latitude of our location. If we are installing fixed[*] solar modules, we tilt them at an angle approximately equal to our latitude to generate the most electricity during the course of a year. If we are near

---

[*] See Chapter 1 for reasons for installing ground-mounted modules that rotate so as to track the sun. See Chapter 2 for reasons for installing fixed modules on rooftops.

the equator, they are hardly tilted at all, facing almost straight up. In Perth, Western Australia, they should face north with a tilt of approximately 32°, and in Frankfurt, Germany, they should face south tilted at 50°. There are two basic reasons why we might *not* orient them in this way:

1. We might not want to. If the value of electricity is more in the afternoon than in the morning, we would angle them slightly west, where the sun is at the time when our electricity is more valuable.
2. We might not be able to. On the roof of an office tower, in a windy city like Chicago we might tilt them much less than the latitude (42° for Chicago), because a storm would cause undue stress to the modules themselves, the racking and possibly to the roof of the building. A flatter installation of 10° − 25° might be required by local building codes. Suppose we install them at 22° in Chicago, i.e. 20° away from optimal, we can expect a reduction in electricity output by about 6%.

This book is about the profitability of solar power for which we inevitably need a few engineering concepts, given in the boxes below. Also there is an extensive glossary that explains the terminology we use.

Electric Power

Solar modules usually have a power rating stamped on them (e.g. 250 watts (W) or 0.250 kilowatts (kW)). This measures the electric power output, which is analogous to the rate of flow of water from a pump in liters per second (L/sec). A kilowatt measures the *rate of flow* of electricity.

Batteries deliver electric power at a rate specified in kW. For instance, a battery with a capacity of 50 kWh that delivers power at a rate of 25 kW will last 50/25 = 2 hours. A tank holding 50 liters of water, which drains out at 25 L/sec will take 2 hours to drain.

Electric Energy

Electricity bills give prices in dollars per kilowatt hour ($/kWh). If your TV consumes 0.250 kW of power and you watch it for 4 hours, you consume 0.250 * 4 = 1 kWh of electric energy. A kWh of electricity is like a liter of water. It is an *amount* of electrical energy.

Batteries store electric energy, for example, an electric car battery might store 50 kWh, which would let you watch your TV for 50 / 0.250 = 200 hours.

Buying Solar Modules to Generate Electric Power

The cost of a solar module can be given in dollars per watt ($/W). What we are buying is the capability to generate a certain *rate of flow* of electricity measured in watts. It is like buying a water pump with a flow rate specified in liters per second.

Buying Batteries to Store Electric Energy

The cost of a battery can be given in $/kWh. We are paying for the capability to store an *amount* of electric energy measured in kWh.

We feed electric energy into the battery and get it back out again at a certain rate measured in kW. A 100 kWh battery capable of delivering power at 50 kW will cost more than one limited to 20 kW.

In case you are not familiar with the structure of the electricity grid, you may wish to take a look at Figure B and get a primer on the major players from the box below. Another box describes the structure of the solar power industry,[1] which is important for appreciating the costs of building and operating a solar project.

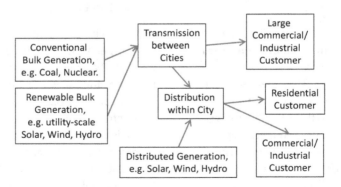

Figure B Structure of the electricity grid.

Players in the Electricity Grid

In some jurisdictions (e.g. SE USA), there is one vertically integrated company providing generation, transmission and distribution of electricity with its monopoly power controlled by a government regulator. To promote competition, many jurisdictions have split the electric power industry into five main components: generation, transmission, distribution, system operation and regulation.

- Bulk generators like natural gas, coal, hydro, nuclear and large solar farms compete with each other to supply electricity to the electricity grid. They are typically connected to the transmission network.
- Transmission companies (sometimes called transmission system operators (TSOs)) operate those lines of pylons we see straddling the countryside and delivering power to individual cities. Bulk generators including large solar farms feed power into the transmission network.
- Once electricity arrives at a city, it is transferred from the transmission company to the distribution company (sometimes called the distribution system operator (DSO)), which distributes it throughout that city to end-customers. Smaller-scale solar farms may sell directly to the distribution companies. Distribution companies are highly regulated since they are in a monopoly position, maintaining and controlling the wires and equipment that deliver power to customers.
- The independent systems operator (ISO) balances supply and demand in the public electricity grid (e.g. by operating wholesale markets for electric power), including day-ahead and intra-day markets; see also Chapters 11 and 12. Large consumers of power also have market access and can buy when the price is low. For instance, a cement factory may have its own natural gas generators and can switch them off and buy from the grid if the price is lower. It takes time to ramp up and down the power from nuclear and coal-fired power stations, so they cannot respond quickly to price fluctuations and instead typically provide baseload power under long-term contracts. In North America, there are nine system operators, and some of the larger ones, spanning several U.S. states, are known as regional transmission organizations (RTOs). In some jurisdictions, the ISO and TSO are the same organization.

- Government regulators control the prices charged to residences and businesses according to a published tariff, which includes many terms and conditions in addition to the prices themselves. For instance, if a customer has solar modules on their roof, the tariff specifies the conditions under which some of the power generated can be fed into the distribution company network. If a solar farm operator wants to sell power to retail customers, the regulator can require the distribution company not to charge those customers since they have contracts with the solar farm operator. The solar farm operator may pay the distribution company for use of the distribution network to transport its power. Railway networks are often regulated in a similar way with train operators selling tickets to customers and paying for use of railway tracks on which to drive their trains.

Structure of the Solar Industry

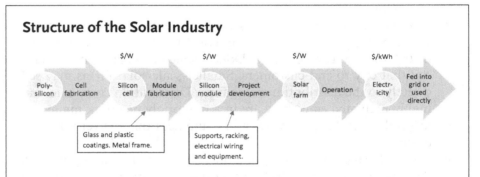

Figure C Major players in the solar industry.

The supply chain for solar power consists of four major players shown as arrows in Figure C. Each player has costs of purchasing items from the player upstream and from elsewhere. They also need to make a profit and allow some overhead to cover their fixed costs. As we will see in the coming chapters, the overhead and profit for one player is part of the cost for the next player downstream.

- Cell Fabrication: Cell fabricators take the raw material, polysilicon, melt it down, crystallize it and slice the crystals into wafers

0.1 – 0.2 mm thick and about 15 cm × 15 cm across. The wafers are processed into the cells that actually convert light into electricity. The cell costs just over half of the cost of the module or about $0.18/W.
- Module Fabrication: Solar modules come in many sizes and consist of solar cells arranged in a rectangular grid. For instance, a 250W module may consist of 60 cells arranged in six rows of ten each. Module fabricators attach electrical contacts to the front and back of the cells, coat them with polymers, glass and an anti-reflective coating and package them into a metal frame about 2 cm thick. Modules cost about $0.33/W.
- Project Development: Developers do the engineering design of a project and build it. Installers (often outsourced from the developer) mount modules on metal racks and install them on the ground or on the roof of a building. The development cost (in $/W) depends on the type of deployment and is given in each chapter in Part 1 of this book.
- Operation: The operating company, also called a YieldCo, is responsible for maintaining and running the solar installation. They clean the modules, replace defective ones and deliver the electricity to the public grid or to the end-user of that power. The revenue or savings from the electricity is measured in $/kWh.

Note

1 NREL, Solar Manufacturing Cost Analysis, https://www.nrel.gov/analysis/solar-manufacturing-cost.html.

1
Utility-Scale: Large Solar

Introduction

The aim of this first chapter is to set the stage for the profitability analysis of solar power by identifying the costs and revenues from utility-scale solar projects. These cash flows are then used in Part 2 of this book to come up with various measures of profitability for the project as a whole.

Utility-scale projects are the largest and include those vast solar farms stretching across the desert. They generate electricity and feed it into the public electricity grid also sometimes delivering it directly to a large consumer's premises. Let us define utility-scale projects to be at least 2 MegaWatts (MW) of capacity and many are in fact much larger, a few hundred MW. To get an idea of what a 2 MW system looks like, imagine 5,000 modules, each with a capacity of 400 W and a surface area of 2 square meters (m^2). To set 2 MW in perspective, the largest solar farm is at Bhadla, India with 2,200 MW, not far off the largest operational nuclear power station at Kori, South Korea with 7,500 MW. Countries do not have to be large to have large solar projects: Philippines has three projects of 1,200 MW each.

Costs

From coal to solar, generating electricity is a hugely capital-intensive business. The cost of building the generating plant dwarfs the annual costs we need to pay over the decades of its productive life, a statement that is particularly true of renewable power because we have no fuel to pay for in those annual costs. This section therefore focuses on the capital costs of a utility-scale solar installation.

DOI: 10.4324/9781003262435-2

Tracking Systems

Some installations use solar modules that are "fixed". This can be inefficient because the sun shines from a different angle in the sky depending on the time of day and time of year. It generates the maximum electricity when it is at right angles to the modules. The more oblique the angle, the less power is generated. When the sun rises in the summer, it may rise behind the solar modules, shining on their backs and not generating any power at all[*]. Eventually it comes round to the front, initially striking them at a very oblique angle, not generating much power. At midday, maximum power is generated, gradually tailing off as the sun sets. In the winter, the sun is low in the sky, and in the summer, it is higher, but this difference is only ±23.5° (reducing midday power output in mid-winter and mid-summer by only about 7%), whereas the sweep of the sun on the modules from morning to evening can be a full ±90° (reducing power output to zero when the sun is shining parallel to the module in early summer mornings and late evenings); see Figure 1.1. If we can angle our solar modules so that the sun shines at right angles to them all the time, we will generate the maximum power. Tracking systems do just that. They swing the solar modules around so that the sun is always shining directly at them. To track the sun from morning to evening, the tracker rotates the modules about one axis; see Figure 1.2 (center). If we also want to track the variations in altitude of the sun, we need a two-axis tracker.

With a pedestal-based, two-axis tracking system, we can make our solar modules follow the sun across the sky, always generating the maximum

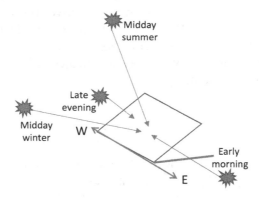

Figure 1.1 In early morning and late evening, the sun is at a very oblique angle to the solar module. At midday in the summer, it is high in the sky, and at midday in the winter, it is lower.

---

[*] In Chapter 13, we will discuss bifacial solar modules which generate electricity from sunlight on their fronts and backs.

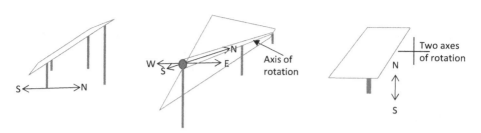

Figure 1.2 Fixed racking (left); single-axis tracking (center); and two-axis tracking (right) in the Northern Hemisphere. Fixed racking is south-facing in the Northern Hemisphere and north-facing in the Southern Hemisphere. Single-axis tracking is about a north–south axis swinging the modules from east to west. Two-axis tracking is mounted on a pedestal and tracks east–west and north–south.

power; see Figure 1.2 (right). But a two-axis tracker costs more than fixed racking and also has higher maintenance costs because of its many moving parts. Moreover, it consumes some electric power to operate. We could save on these costs by using a single-axis tracker to follow the sun from morning to evening, even capturing those early summer mornings when it would have been behind a fixed module. The power generated will be higher than for fixed modules but not quite as high as for a two-axis tracker since we are ignoring the variation in the sun's altitude in the sky.

It turns out that the extra electric power from a two-axis tracking system is usually not worth the additional cost. However, a single-axis tracker only adds 7% to the total cost and can pay for itself in extra electricity generated. It does this by capturing more of the early morning and late evening sun compared with a fixed racking system. In places with clear skies, this is worthwhile, but in locations near cities with hazy skies, or mist or cloud in the morning or evening, the additional electricity does not pay for the tracker. In the USA, about 70% of new utility-scale installations use single-axis trackers.

Single-axis trackers have two other advantages over fixed racking. It can be seen from Figure 1.2 that windstorms can blow underneath fixed racking, potentially destabilizing them. Single-axis trackers can orient the modules horizontal during high winds, reducing the risk of damage. On a cloudy day, solar modules generate electricity from the diffuse light from the whole sky. Fixed modules can only "see" part of the sky, whereas single-axis trackers can orient the modules horizontal so that they receive light from the whole sky.

Figure 1.2 shows the racking for individual modules, but in practice, there will be rows of them, potentially shading each other when the sun is low in the sky. Commercial software is available to estimate the electric energy yield from solar installations, taking shading into account. In deserts where land is zero-cost, spacing between rows can be used to reduce shading. Where there is a land cost, we need to make a trade-off between paying for space and reduced electricity generation due to shading.

Capital Costs

The industry uses capital costs in dollars per watt ($/W) of generating capacity. For solar, the generating capacity is the DC electric power generated by the solar module. The amount of AC electric power delivered to the grid will be slightly less due to losses in the wiring and in the inverters that convert DC to AC. Since the length of wiring differs from one installation to another, and each manufacturer's inverter has its own efficiency rating, we will refer to DC electric power by default. You may also see in the literature the notation $/W_{DC}$ and $/W_{AC}$.

For an average 100 MW system in North America, the split in terms of dollars per watt ($/W) is given in Figure 1.3. These costs are given as percentages, since the actual $/W figure ($0.83/W total in 2021) is declining at 12% per year, but the breakdown is relatively stable.

A couple of points stand out in this cost breakdown. First, we see that the guts of the system, the high-tech solar module, which actually generates the electricity, costs *less than half* of the total. Although reductions in solar module

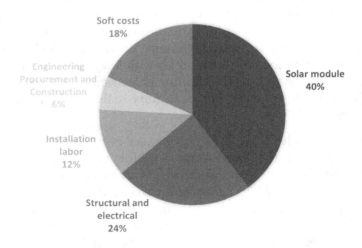

Figure 1.3 A breakdown of the cost of developing a utility-scale solar installation in the USA. Soft costs include land acquisition, obtaining permits, interconnection to the electricity grid, overhead and profit for the developer. Structural and electrical balance of system includes the ground supports, racking, wiring and other electrical equipment. Based on NREL.[1]

costs are welcome, reductions in the other components are more important in reducing total costs. Second, although these figures are for the USA, they are similar in other countries. Even in countries with lower labor costs, the figures don't change much since labor is only a small proportion of the total and qualified electricians with high wages are needed to install the wiring in any country.

We achieve considerable economies of scale during installation of a utility-scale solar project by automating parts of the operation. Robotic machinery drives metal piles into the desert to support the racks on which the modules are mounted. Another robot offloads modules, 8 at a time, from a truck and places them on the racking. By the time we have installed 5,000 modules this way, there are no additional economies of scale for the next 5,000, which is why, from a cost perspective, NREL classifies everything above 2 MW as utility-scale.

Operations and Maintenance Costs

In addition to the capital cost, solar installations have annual operations and maintenance (O&M) costs. The modules have to be cleaned of dust, sand and bird droppings, while failed modules need to be replaced. Many utility-scale plants are far away from urban centers and the travel time to the site is a major component of the maintenance cost. Module manufacturers provide 25–32 year warranties, but this generally covers a replacement module only – the cost of installing the replacement is left to the plant operator. Tracking systems have additional maintenance costs because of their moving parts. Operators of plants in remote areas schedule all maintenance in a single visit to the site accepting the fact that some power is lost due to faulty tracking systems or faulty modules that are not fixed immediately.

Summary

In a nutshell, the average costs[1] of utility-scale solar systems in 2021 in the USA were:

- Capital costs: $0.83/W fixed and $0.89/W single-axis tracked, declining at 13% per year.
- Operating and maintenance costs: $0.0163/W/yr for fixed racking and $0.0175/W/yr for single-axis tracked, with no appreciable trend up or down over time.

When assessing the profitability of a solar project, the operations and maintenance costs are small compared with capital costs. This is especially true when we consider the practice of discounting costs that occur in the future; more on this in Part 2 of this book.

Revenues

We now move on to discuss how we can make money by selling electricity to cover our costs. The first concept we need to understand is the capacity factor of an installation. After that, we can dive into how utility-scale deployments actually make money.

Capacity Factor

First let's see how much electric power we get from a 250 W solar module. If we set it up in the Moroccan desert on a sunny day, it will generate more than 250 W, and on a cloudy day in Norway, it will generate less. The rating on the module is measured under standard test conditions with 1 kW of simulated solar irradiance per square meter of surface area.

When we want to estimate how much power our module will *actually* generate when we install it in a specific location, we use solar irradiance measurements that are available for every hour of the year for most locations on Earth. Satellite observations of clouds are used to give good estimates of solar irradiance on the Earth's surface. Clearly, one year is different from the next, and some satellite observations go back 50 years so that these fluctuations can be smoothed out by averaging over several years. More accurate estimates can be obtained from ground-based equipment, but this requires expensive equipment at many locations around the world, and data may not be available over so many years. For instance, Saudi Arabia[2] installed 48 ground-based measuring stations throughout the country between 2013 and 2020, accurately recording irradiance every minute.

Using irradiance measurements for a specific site and commercial

---

Capacity Factor

Solar vs. Nuclear

Which generates more electricity in a year: a 1 MW solar installation or a 1 MW nuclear installation? The global average capacity factor for solar is 18%, whereas for nuclear it is 93%. Nuclear therefore generates 93/18 = 5.2 times as much electricity in a year as solar.

How would you compare $1/W_{AC}$ solar and $6/W_{AC}$ nuclear? Ignoring fuel, operations and maintenance costs, nuclear gives 5.2 times as much electricity for 6 times the capital cost.

software,[†,3,4,5,6] we can estimate how much electricity our 250 W solar module will actually generate each hour of the year and we can add these up to get the annual total, say 350 kWh. We can then compare this total with what we would have got if our 250 W module had been in standard test conditions for all 365*24 = 8760 hours of the year: 8760 * 250 / 1000 = 2190 kWh. Our location therefore has a "capacity factor" of 350/2190 = 16%, a number that takes into account the fact that it is not generating at night and it is generating below its full potential on cloudy days and when the sun is low in the sky. Solar has a low capacity factor,[7] between 10% and 25% depending on geographic location, with tracking systems achieving higher capacity factors than fixed systems. By comparison, the capacity factor of onshore wind is 25–50% and nuclear and coal, which run almost 24/7, have capacity factors approaching 100%.

Capacity factors can be used to estimate total annual electricity generated, from which annual revenues can be estimated if the price at which electricity is sold is flat rate. If the price varies with time of day or time of year, the hourly irradiance measurements need to be used, giving hourly electricity generation, mapped on to hourly prices to estimate annual revenues.

Wholesale Electricity Market

If the solar generator has access to the real-time market for electric power, it can sell at the going price. The marginal cost of solar is zero, since there is no fuel cost, and hence it does not make sense to switch off a solar farm just because the spot market price is low. Instead, solar generators that want to play in the market may store electricity until prices are high (e.g. by using a battery); see Chapter 9. Since the price on the wholesale market varies, there is a risk involved in selling electricity this way. We can mitigate that risk by using a power purchase agreement (PPA), which we discuss next.

Selling to the Electricity Grid Using Power Purchase Agreements (PPAs)

Large solar projects make most of their money from PPAs, which are contracts to supply electricity to the grid at a certain price determined by auctions. For instance, in Dubai in 2014, an auction resulted in a price of $60/MWh. The first thing to notice about this price is that it is a price per

---

† For example, some of the popular software packages at the time of writing are HOMER, PVSyst, SAM and REopt.

MegaWatt hour (MWh), whereas our capital costs above are measured per watt. Suppose we build a solar installation with a capacity of 100,000 watts and operate it at full capacity for ten hours, we would generate 100,000 × 10 watt hours of electricity = 1 MWh for which we would be paid $60 in Dubai in 2014. Using 2014 solar capital costs of $1.97/W, our installation would cost $197,000. With a capacity factor of 23% in Dubai, we need to operate our solar generator for 16 years[‡] to recover the capital cost, which looks good since solar modules come with a 25–32 year warranty. Part 2 of this book shows how to do a more detailed analysis of profitability.

$60/MWh was a low price for solar in 2014, reflecting the fact that Dubai is a very sunny city with a high capacity factor and more recent projects are described here.[8] Even in 2019, with solar capital costs 51% lower, PPAs in Hawaii were over $60/MWh. In 2020, in Southern California, solar PPAs were around $30/MWh.[9] We auction off PPAs because we need more electricity on the grid, and one advantage of solar is that it can be built fast (e.g. within a year compared with 5–8 years for nuclear). The PPA contains a clause stating when the project should be operational. In the early days of writing PPAs, some contracts in Spain and Japan omitted these clauses with the result that developers could wait until the capital cost had declined significantly before building the project. Another way of ensuring that the company that wins the PPA auction actually builds the project is to require a deposit at the time of signing the PPA which is refunded when the project is operational.

Some PPAs include escalation clauses specifying a rate of increase of price over future years, which is important to take inflation into account and also because the energy yield of solar modules declines at 0.5–1% per year. The escalation rate may be specified in the PPA contract or may be linked to inflation.

Another important factor that is included in some PPAs is price variation, reflecting different levels of demand for electricity at different times of day and year. For instance, in Western Australia, South Africa and Southwest USA, where air-conditioning constitutes a major proportion of demand during the summer, the base price is increased by, say, 20% during summer afternoons. This is to the advantage of solar, which generates well at those times.

An example PPA incorporating all these factors is in the sidebar on the next page. Looking at this from the perspective of a solar developer, you may regard the conditions as onerous. You have to put in a lot of up-front leg work and cash to play in this game. This is intentional and the history

---

‡ $(10/0.23)*(197000/60) = 142750$ hours = 16 years.

of PPAs internationally is littered with stories of small inexperienced companies winning PPA auctions and being unable to deliver an operational project within a realistic time frame.

A PPA is a contract with clauses that determine penalties if the solar generator fails to supply the amount of power specified in the daily/annual schedule. Since the sun does not shine at night and is intermittent on cloudy days a solar generator therefore needs to incorporate storage for electric power to avoid these penalties. Chapter 9 covers many different types of storage, including batteries. In the example PPA above, the peak requirement of 10 MW could be provided by a 12 MW solar installation with excess power being stored for use at times of low solar irradiance. The capacity of the storage depends on how certain we want to be of not having to pay penalties for failing to meet the power production schedule. Solar irradiance is very well documented over several decades so that intermittency is known and commercial models are available to optimize the amount of storage to install. More on this in Chapters 9 and 10.

Corporate PPAs

Instead of selling to the grid, some solar projects sell to corporate customers (see sidebar for examples). Datacenters are a growth market for electricity and examples from Sweden, Quebec and Iceland are also described in another sidebar. There are four different types of PPA. The first

Example PPA

Bidders should bid a base price, which would be increased by 25% from 1 p.m. to 5 p.m. during June–August. A schedule determines the amount of power to be delivered at different times of day and year. For instance, it could require 10 MW peak power with 30% of the peak being required between 10 p.m. and 7 a.m. To qualify as a bidder in the auction, a company would have to show that they have the right to purchase adequate land and also that planning permission is available. A deposit of $5m is required on signing, which will be refunded in $1m increments for each 2 MW commissioned (i.e. made operational) within 18 months. The PPA price will be escalated at 1% below the electricity price index for the region in future years.

Large Corporate PPAs

In 2020, Amazon and Total bought the largest corporate solar PPAs with 3GW each, spread over multiple PPAs. Taiwan Semiconductor Manufacturing Co. (TMSC) signed a single PPA for almost 1GW at a fixed price over 20 years.

Datacenters

The backbone of cloud computing, datacenters have thousands of electricity-devouring servers providing processing and storage. Where should we put them: close to electricity generation or close to the users of the cloud computing service? It costs more to transport electricity over transmission lines than to transport data over optical fiber (and the delay is negligible). Facebook has a datacenter in northern Sweden in a disused paper mill using hydroelectricity from the local river. Datacenters are largely automated and require minimal local staff. Ericsson has a datacenter in a disused aluminum smelter in Quebec using that province's low-cost hydroelectricity. Iceland, with its ample geothermal and hydroelectric resources, finds it costly to export electricity to Europe using undersea electric power cables; instead, it exports datacenter services using undersea optical fiber cables.

Utility-scale solar projects are typically some distance from cities because of their extensive land requirements, and need to pay for transmission lines to take the electricity to their customers (corporate or grid). Attracting a datacenter to locate at the same site would add to the market for the electricity generated, so long as the solar was combined with wind and a battery (see Chapter 10) since datacentre operation is 24/7.

three are "physical" PPAs since the corporate customer takes ownership of the electricity generated by the solar project. The fourth is a "virtual" PPA, which is a financial agreement between buyer and seller, although no electricity changes hands between them.

Physical PPAs

1.   *On-Site PPA*: The simplest type of corporate PPA is when a customer contracts for a solar project on the customer's premises to provide them with electricity. Each month, the customer pays the project the amounts specified in the PPA.

2.   *Off-Site PPA*: If the customer does not have space at their site for a solar project, it can be built elsewhere with the electricity being transported across the public grid to the customer for a fee. Assuming the amount of electricity specified in the PPA is actually fed into the grid by the solar project, the customer pays the project the amounts specified in the PPA.

3.   *Sleeved-PPA*: Building on the off-site PPA, the grid operator provides additional functionality with a sleeved-PPA. If the solar project is not generating as much as specified in the PPA, the grid operator makes up the difference and supplies the customer with additional electricity. Conversely, if excess electricity is generated, the grid operator absorbs that excess. Clearly the grid operator is paid an additional sum in the PPA for providing these energy services.

Virtual PPA

4. *Virtual PPA (also known as Financial PPA and Synthetic PPA)*: Figure 1.4 illustrates a virtual PPA. The solar project sells electricity to the public grid and is paid the wholesale market price. The customer purchases electricity from the public grid and pays the wholesale market price. If the market price is higher than the PPA price, the solar project makes a balancing payment of the price difference

> **Green Beer For All**
>
> Heineken, based in the Netherlands, produces beer at 31 European sites and has negotiated a ten-year virtual PPA with Neoen, which generates renewable electricity in Finland. During the course of this contract, green electricity will contribute to producing one bottle of beer for each adult on Earth.

to the customer. Conversely, if the market price is lower than the PPA price, the customer makes a balancing payment of the price difference to the solar project. The net effect of this arrangement is that the solar project sells and the customer buys electricity at the PPA price independent of price on the wholesale market. Virtual PPAs are a purely financial agreement between the solar project and the corporate customer. The grid buys and sells the actual electricity. They can even operate between companies in different countries; see sidebar for an example between the Netherlands and Finland. If renewable energy certificates are part of the deal, they are the only commodity that changes hands between the solar project and the corporate customer.

When a customer has multiple sites, an on-site solar project at each site lacks the economies of scale of a single large off-site project, which is facilitated by PPAs of types 2, 3, and 4 above. Off-site projects can also be located where land is low cost so long as the grid has sufficient capacity to receive the power generated.

The features of PPAs between a solar generator and the electricity grid can be incorporated in corporate PPAs, including varying amounts of electricity and prices at different times of day and year, escalation of pricing for future years and penalty clauses.

Customers are usually motivated to sign solar PPAs to reduce their carbon emissions. If the project is obtaining renewable energy certificates (RECs), they are transferred to the customer as part of the PPA contract. However,

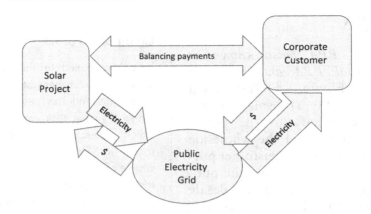

Figure 1.4 Payments and electricity flows in a virtual PPA.

RECs require certification by a third party and some corporate customers want more than a certificate that they are using renewable electricity. They want to be able to say that the solar project would not have been built without the PPA that they signed. This is known as "additionality". It is the action of the customer that has resulted in additional renewable electricity being generated. The solar project was not going to be built anyway. Additionality is important in greenhouse gas accounting since it demonstrates that reductions in carbon emissions would not have happened with business-as-usual, and are due to the corporate customer signing the PPA. It is important in this case that the PPA is signed before construction starts on the solar project.

International agreements between governments can be regarded as a special type of PPA. Jordan has vast land area suitable for solar but lacks water, whereas Israel has less land to spare for solar but has access to salt water in the Mediterranean Sea. Israel and Jordan could negotiate for solar electricity to be imported from Jordan to Israel in exchange for desalinated water going the other way. Ecopeace Middle East sees such "Green-Blue Deals" as more than trade but also contributing to "conflict resolution and peace building" in the region[10].

A PPA, whether for providing electricity to the grid or to a corporate customer, provides a regular stream of revenue to a solar project and therefore reduces risk; see Chapter 8. If financing is needed to cover the capital cost of project development (see Chapter 7), the PPA should preferably be signed when a project is at the planning stage, and then used to negotiate financing.

Feed-in Tariffs (FITs)

Finally, there is the option for the government to decide on a price that it will pay for electricity. This was done in the early days of solar, when governments wanted to stimulate the development of a solar industry in their jurisdiction. These Feed-in Tariffs (FITs) had to have prices high enough to cover the costs of solar at a time when harnessing solar energy was not profitable at market rates. Guess who the government had to ask to estimate solar costs. Answer: the solar industry. I will leave you to guess whether the solar industry overestimated its costs when it replied to the government's requests. FITs were successful in Denmark at stimulating the growth of the wind turbine industry, but elsewhere (e.g. Canada), they became bogged down in a plethora of regulations and low caps on the amount of power that could be sold via the FIT. Many customers criticized FITs as being the reason why their electricity bills were increasing. In Spain, the government reneged on payments on some FIT contracts. Most FITs have been phased out now as the cost of solar has declined to the point where it is economically viable without government support.

Summary

This chapter has shown how to estimate the costs and revenues for a utility-scale solar installation. This information is used in Part 2 of this book to assess profitability. The major cost component for utility-scale projects is the capital cost. Single-axis tracking significantly increases the amount of electricity generated while not adding much to this cost. The capacity factor for a given location allows us to estimate the total electricity that can be generated in a year. This can be converted to a dollar value if the selling price of the electricity is flat rate. If not, we use satellite observations and ground-based equipment that give hourly measurements of the amount of solar radiation throughout the year from which commercial software estimates the electricity generation each hour of the year. This can be mapped on to the time-varying value of that electricity either from a PPA or from the wholesale market price to estimate the annual revenue to be expected from a solar project.

Takeaways

- Costs of utility-scale solar
  - Solar module costs constitute only 40% of the total installed capital cost ($0.83/W) of a utility-scale system.

- The capital cost is declining at 13% per year.
- This capital cost is the major determinant of profitability since operating and maintenance costs are much smaller ($0.0163/W/yr).
- Single-axis trackers are widely used in high-irradiance locations to capture early morning and late evening sun at only a 7% increase in capital and operating costs compared with fixed modules.
- Capacity factors and irradiance measurements
  - An estimate of the amount of electricity generated over the course of an entire year can be obtained using capacity factors that are specific to the geographic location.
  - This can be used to estimate revenue if the selling price of the electricity is flat rate.
  - More detailed estimates of electricity generated each hour or minute of the year can be calculated from satellite estimates or ground-based irradiance measurements using commercially available software.
  - This can be used to estimate revenue if the selling price of the electricity is not flat rate.
- How solar power is sold
  - Solar operators can participate in a market for wholesale electric power, including a spot market for the current price and also hour ahead and 24 hour ahead markets.
  - Solar operators can bid a base price in an auction of a Power Purchase Agreement (PPA) with the electricity grid. The PPA may specify how this base price is increased at certain times of day or year, and also how it increases in future years.
  - Solar project developers can negotiate a PPA with a corporate customer. The project can be developed at the corporate site or off-site with electricity transported across the electricity grid. Alternatively electricity is bought and sold by the grid, and the solar operator and the corporate customer make balancing payments so that the net payment corresponds to the PPA price.

Probe Deeper: The Why?

Why generate electricity from solar which is only available for a few hours per day compared with nuclear which generates 24/7? Because solar costs less, can be built faster, and can be combined with a battery to provide power 24/7.

Process

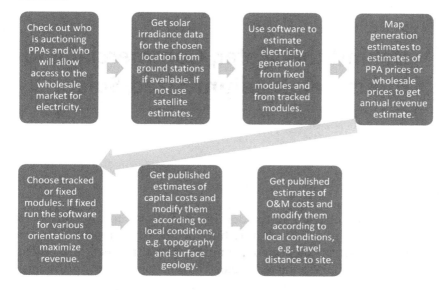

Notes

1 NREL, U.S. Solar Photovoltaic System and Energy Storage Cost Benchmark, 2021 National Renewable Energy Laboratory, USA
2 Renewable Resource Atlas, Saudi Arabian National Renewable Energy Data Centre, https://www.energy.gov.sa/en/FutureEnergy/RenewableEnergy/pages/renew2.aspx
3 HOMER, Distributed Generation and Distributed Energy Resources, Homerenergy.com
4 PVSyst, Software for Solar Power Systems, www.pvsyst.com
5 REopt, Renewable Energy Integration and Optimization, reopt.nrel.gov
6 SAM, System Advisor Model, National Renewable Energy Laboratory, sam.nrel.com
7 US Department of Energy, Generating Capacity, https://www.energy.gov/ne/articles/what-generation-capacity
8 Mohammed bin Rashid Al Maktoum Solar Park, https://www.dewa.gov.ae/en/about-us/media-publications/latest-news/2019/06/solar-park-phase-5
9 Utility-scale Solar PPA Prices for PV, Berkeley Lab, https://emp.lbl.gov/pv-ppa-prices
10 Ecopeace, Green-Blue Deal, https://ecopeaceme.org/gbd/

2

Behind-the-Meter, Commercial and Industrial: Medium-Sized Solar

Introduction

The purpose of this chapter is to identify cash flows in and out of a solar project, as we did in Chapter 1, but specifically for projects on a commercial or industrial customer premises. These projects are called "behind-the-meter" (BTM) since the electricity is generated on the customer side of the electricity meter and the aim of the project is to reduce the customer's electricity bill. By contrast, the utility-scale projects we dealt with in Chapter 1 are sometimes called "front-of-the-meter" (FTM).

It's nothing new for organizations to generate their own electricity. By law, hospitals must have back-up power generators in case of a black-out. Somewhere in the basement, they probably have a gas turbine that an engineer checks out every month but which is very rarely used. At the other extreme is aluminum smelting, a process that extracts aluminum by passing enormous amounts of electricity through aluminum oxide. The Kitimat smelter[1] was constructed at the end of a fjord in Northern British Columbia because of the hydroelectric potential of this mountainous region. It has its own hydroelectric power station and is also connected to the electricity grid of British Columbia to buy power when needed and to sell power when excess is generated.

Heavy industrial sites such as metal refineries, petrochemical plants and cement factories consume a lot of electricity and many of them do not have a lot of space to install solar modules; see sidebar for an example from Bahrain.[2] In this chapter, we focus on commercial buildings such as shopping malls and offices instead of industrial sites. Commercial buildings consume less power per square meter and have space to install solar modules on the roof and on awnings over adjacent parking lots. However, the

DOI: 10.4324/9781003262435-3

principles in this chapter would apply to an industrial site if it had similar characteristics. For instance, waste-water treatment plants often have space around treatment ponds where solar modules can be installed.

This chapter deals with medium-sized installations and the next chapter deals with smaller installations. The distinction is not just the size of the project itself, which results in more or less economies of scale but primarily the electricity tariff. In many jurisdictions, medium-sized

The Alba Aluminum Smelter

The world's largest aluminum smelter outside China is in Bahrain and has a footprint of 2.2 square kilometers. It consumes 3.5 GW of electricity, which is generated on site from natural gas 24/7. To generate the same power from solar would require a site 40 times as large, even in sunny Bahrain (plus a very large battery).

customers are subject to a tariff that incorporates a "demand charge". Each hour of each month, the customer's electricity purchases from the grid are recorded and the demand charge is applied to the hour during which the demand was highest for a given month. For instance, suppose that in August, the customers demand was highest between 2 p.m. and 3 p.m. on August 10. The demand charge will be applied to grid purchases during that hour. Demand charges can be quite high (e.g. $10/kWh, compared with $0.05/kWh for electricity), and are designed to provide an incentive for customers to flatten their load profile. The distribution company must install and maintain equipment with sufficient capacity to deliver the peak load demanded by customers. A flatter load profile means less cost for expanding grid capacity plus a reduced maintenance cost for grid equipment. In Chapter 3, we will see different mechanisms in the electricity tariff for incentivizing a flatter load profile for smaller customers. The point at which demand charges kick in depends on the jurisdiction and can be around 25–100 kW. Customers whose peak consumption is above this level are subject to demand charges and are dealt with in this chapter.

Two other types of installation are worth mentioning here, medium-scale projects that feed directly into the grid, typically to the distribution company. These are not BTM operations but are mentioned in this chapter because the scale of the project and hence its costs are similar to others discussed here. In one type of grid-connected project, power is sold directly to the distribution company similar to the utility-scale projects described in Chapter 1. The other type is known as "community solar" and is described in the box.

Community Solar

A developer buys some land close to a city, builds a solar installation and feeds electricity into the grid. However, the electricity is not sold to the distribution company, instead the developer negotiates contracts with customers to sell them "green" electricity at a price comparable with the distribution company price. The developer may pay the distribution company to transport the electricity from the solar installation to the customers.

The term "community solar" implies not only services offered by solar installations to residential communities but also to commercial customers, i.e. any customer within the local community, typically within the same city. Transporting power to another city may involve additional costs to the developer. The advantages of selling to commercial customers is that long-term contracts can be negotiated. The customer acquisition cost for residential customers is high, distributing flyers and knocking on doors costs $300–$400 per customer who signs up. Residential contracts are short term since courts generally regard it as exploitative to convince residential customers to sign a long-term contract for electricity. They should have the freedom to switch suppliers. It is generally low/medium income customers who sign up for community solar since electricity constitutes a large proportion of their total income and offering a discount of 10–15% to the price from the distribution company is very welcome. These customers are likely to move house or default on their payments. Although higher-income customers may be attracted by the environmental benefits of solar power and might pay more, they have been found to be in the minority in practice. A major factor in making community solar successful with residential customers is very smooth back office operations during the switchover from the distribution company to the community solar provider. Glitches at this time annoy customers and lose them. Another factor is ensuring that the solar project is commissioned and operating before signing contracts with customers. People lose confidence if there is a delay. If everything is transparent to the customer, there is more chance that they continue with the community solar provider even beyond the original contract term and the customer acquisition cost can be spread over a number of years.

Costs

Capital Costs

Solar installations at commercial sites are custom jobs. Even if we are installing on a flat roof, we need to avoid obstacles such as vents and elevator motor houses and we must also take into account possible shading by other buildings and trees. We need a structural evaluation of the roof to confirm whether it can support the modules taking into account wind speeds in the area.[3] Ideally the modules should face South in the Northern hemisphere and North in the Southern hemisphere but if the building is oriented differently, we need to choose between mounting modules diagonally across the roof and aligning them with the building at a slight reduction in power output. Most of these issues also arise when we are installing awnings over parking lots, and we have the additional cost of mounting the modules high enough for vehicles to park underneath. Figure 2.1 shows an installation that is not aligned with the shape of the roof and also one on a parking lot. Many building owners are hesitant to have holes drilled into their roofs for solar modules to be bolted on and ballast is often used instead, e.g. sandbags holding the module racking down.

These complexities add not only to costs, but also to risks, so that the engineers and installers need to allow additional overhead for contingencies. Figure 2.2 shows the breakdown of costs and compares it with the utility-scale system we analyzed in Chapter 1. The additional overhead in the

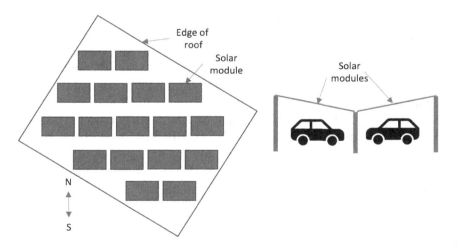

Figure 2.1 South-facing solar installation on a non-south facing roof (left). Parking lot solar awnings tilted to catch rainwater (right).

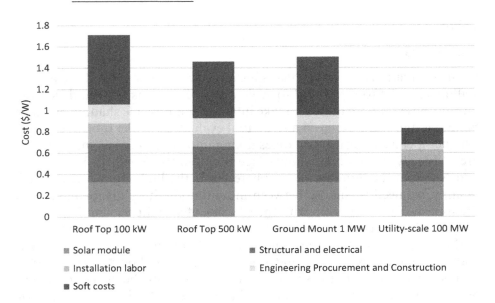

Figure 2.2 Breakdown of average costs of developing commercial rooftop and ground-mounted systems compared with the much larger utility-scale system discussed in Chapter 1. Soft costs include land acquisition, obtaining permits, interconnection to the electricity grid, overhead and profit for the developer. Structural and electrical balance of system, includes the ground supports, racking, wiring and other electrical equipment. Based on NREL.[4]

commercial systems is evident in the Engineering Procurement and Construction (EPC) and soft costs, which are considerably higher than for a utility-scale system. Customization of the design to the specifics of a commercial site also adds to the balance of system costs and installation labor. Gone are the economies of scale from robotic installation that we saw in Chapter 1, so there is no surprise that the total cost of an installed system is higher, $1.46/W for a 500 kW rooftop system in the USA, compared with $0.83/W for a 100 MW utility-scale system. The 500 kW commercial system has some economies of scale in the labor, EPC and soft costs compared with the 100 kW system. The soft costs are the major component for commercial rooftop systems, with the solar module itself constituting only 19% of the costs of a 100 kW system.

Distributed energy systems that sell power to the distribution company and community solar systems are typically ground-mounted. For these, Figure 2.2 shows a slight reduction in EPC costs, since there is no engineering design necessary related to the layout of the roof and the installation cost is slightly higher due to the need to mount the supports deep in the ground.

Operations and Maintenance Costs

Operating and maintenance costs are slightly less than for utility-scale systems at $0.013/W/yr. One reason for this is that systems in commercial areas are more accessible than utility-scale systems for which there is a significant travel cost to get to the site.

Summary[4]

- The average capital costs are:
  - 100 kW rooftop $1.71/W
  - 500 kW rooftop $1.46/W
  - 1 MW ground mount $1.50/W
  - On average, costs are declining by 9% per year.
- The average O&M costs are $0.013/W/yr.

Savings

The amount of financial savings achieved by BTM solar depends on the electricity tariff that the customer is subject to,[5] and this section discusses the major alternatives.

Net-Metering

To offset the above costs, a BTM system reduces the electricity bill paid by the commercial customer. A natural question is whether the electricity bill can become negative as a result of a large system generating more power than is consumed by the building. The answer is that it depends on the tariff in that jurisdiction. Some tariffs allow "net-metering" in which the electricity meter does run backward during times of excess power production, so long as there are other times when power is purchased from the grid. Over the course of a year, the net power purchased should be positive. The reason for this restriction is two-fold:

1. If a building is a net supplier of power to the grid, it is in the business of generating power and should be taxed on that business operation, rather than simply have its meter run backward.
2. The distribution and transmission companies have built a grid to transport electricity from a generating company to the customer. The tariff it charges that customer (say $0.15/kWh) represents the cost of generation (say $0.04/kWh), transmission (say $0.04/kWh) and distribution

Giant Battery

With net-metering, solar uses the electricity grid like a giant battery, pumping power in during the day and taking it out at night; pumping power in during the summer and taking it out in the winter. This is great for the solar operator, but not necessarily for the grid operator.

(say \$0.07/kWh). It is economically inefficient to allow a customer to feed an unlimited amount of power into the grid and receive \$0.15/kWh, when other generating companies are receiving only \$0.04/kWh.

Net-metering is designed to allow self-consumption of power generated BTM, without allowing office buildings to generate excessive revenues by operating as generating stations. Solar installations benefit from net-metering since excess power can be fed into the grid during the summer when solar is generating well, so long as more power is purchased from the grid in the winter. This allows building managers to build larger solar systems than if they had to consume all the power they generate every hour of every day. Under net-metering, the electricity fed into the grid is valued at the retail price of electricity purchased from the grid. Some jurisdictions offer net-billing instead, in which the customer is paid less for electricity than they are charged, to take into account point 2 above.

Not all jurisdictions allow net-metering, but some go one step further and allow "virtual net-metering". Imagine a distribution company with a feeder line delivering electricity to a commercial area of the city with several business parks. A single customer may operate several office buildings in that area, some low, flat, pancake-style buildings and some high-rise skyscrapers. Solar on the roof of a pancake building generates more electricity than the building consumes, whereas the reverse is true of a skyscraper. A multi-site customer can use *virtual* net-metering to total the net annual power consumed over all the buildings it operates. With *plain* net-metering, each building would be treated separately, so that the full roof space on the pancake building could not be used for solar as it would generate too much, making the net annual consumption negative. Virtual net-metering therefore allows developers to achieve economies of scale by building a few large projects at selected sites instead of many smaller projects. Virtual net-metering also makes sense to the distribution company so long as all the buildings are supplied from the same feeder line. Electricity fed into that line by the pancake building is used by the skyscraper. If the pancake building was on a separate feeder line, it might overload that line. Virtual net-metering is therefore only available among a group of buildings within certain geographical areas of a city.

To decide whether our building needs net-metering, we ask a simple question that is tough to answer precisely. If I put solar on the roof of my office building, how many floors of the building can it provide with power? The answer clearly depends on how sunny the location is and what goes on in that building. If it houses a data center with racks of servers crunching through machine learning algorithms 24/7, the answer is that rooftop solar is a drop in the bucket of total power consumption. However in a typical office, used from 9 a.m. to 6 p.m., with laptops, LED lighting and HVAC*, the answer is from two floors with air conditioning to six floors without air conditioning on an average day. Buildings taller than this can benefit from rooftop solar even if net-metering is not available in our jurisdiction.

Demand Charges

A major distinguishing feature of the customers we are considering in this chapter is that they are subject to demand charges on their peak consumption each month. These charges provide an incentive for customers to flatten out peaks in their consumption of power from the grid, thus reducing the need for the distribution company to increase the capacity of its grid.

Suppose an office building's peak consumption in September was 100 kW on September 8 from 1 p.m. to 2 p.m., and we install solar on the roof generating 51 kW at that time of day, how much do we save on the demand charges of $10/kW? The answer is almost certainly less than 10*51 = $510. If we reduce the peak at one time of day, another peak often pops up at another time of day as shown in Figure 2.3. In this case, the new peak is 68.5 kW from 9 a.m. to 10 a.m., and our savings on demand charges is 10*(100–68.5) = $315. However, the new peak depends very much on the consumption profile of the building and the generating profile of the solar modules, each of which will be different on other days of the month.

The office building consumption in Figure 2.3 has a peak in consumption at a time that is aligned with the peak solar generation. If the peak is flatter or if there is less alignment, the reduction in demand charges could be much less. In the case of a building with evening use, such as a shopping mall, the consumption profile can be much flatter from, say, 9 a.m. to 10 p.m. when it is in use. Peak load can occur after sunset because of evening use of the facility, so that solar needs to be combined with a battery to reduce demand charges: see Chapters 9 and 10, and see examples in the sidebar from Kansas City, Lancaster, Modesto and Las Vegas.

* HVAC: Heating, Ventilation and Air Conditioning.

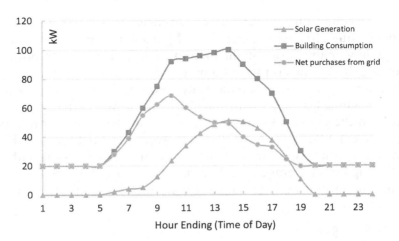

Figure 2.3 Peak building consumption of 100 kW at 1–2 p.m. is reduced by 51 kW of behind-the-meter solar producing a new peak of 68.5 kW at 9–10 a.m.

The bottom line on demand charges is that they may contribute significantly to savings on the electricity bill, but we need to do a detailed calculation including the consumption profile of the building and the solar generating profile to estimate how much.

System Peak Charges

Another way to incentivize a flattening of the demand profile for electricity purchased from the grid is to impose a charge based on peak demand for the entire grid instead of peak demand of the individual customer. Some jurisdictions impose these system peak charges on grid purchases during the peak hours of the entire year. In Ontario, Canada, they apply to the five peak hours and are about $25/kW. Five hours at $25/kW is 5×25 = $125/kW and is comparable to a demand charge of $10/kW per month for 12 months, or 12×10 = $120/kW. System peak charges were originally applied to large commercial and industrial customers, consuming over 5 MW, for instance, a university campus or a cement factory. At first glance, it may seem unfair that a customer has to pay an additional charge based on the time at which *all the other* customers are consuming a peak amount of electricity, but in fact $25/kW provides an opportunity to reduce electricity bills and many smaller companies lobbied successfully to be allowed to use this tariff. Now any customer consuming more than 1 MW has a choice between demand charges and system peak charges. A whole consulting industry has grown up around predicting when the five peak hours will occur and advising customers how to reduce demand at those times. The system operator gladly offers a wealth of data and publishes its own predictions, and a lot of equipment upgrades have been avoided as a result of shaving peaks off the demand curve. System peak charges can be 50% of the total electricity bill and some customers have been very successful at reducing their bills significantly.

Can solar help reduce system peak charges? The answer depends on when those peak hours occur. When this tariff was introduced in Ontario in 2010, the system peak was due to air conditioning and averaged 2:00–4:00 p.m. in July and August, when solar is very productive. Over the years, though, companies have done exactly what the tariff was designed to achieve; they have reduced their consumption at these peak times, resulting in the system peaks being pushed later in the day. They now average 5:00–7:00 p.m. in July and August, when the sun is lower in the sky. What will happen next? Will system peaks get later still or will they flip back to match the early afternoon air conditioning usage? In 2015, two of the five peak hours occurred in January and February, not good months for solar power.

The Ontario experience underlines a major source of risk in solar power. A system optimized for the situation in 2010 would have seen a gradual decline in savings over the next decade and would have been particularly hard hit in 2015. Risk is discussed in more detail in Chapter 8. One way of mitigating the risk of summer peaks moving to different times of day is with the use of batteries which give flexibility in when electricity is provided. They can be discharged at the times when we forecast the system peaks will occur in each individual year. Batteries are discussed in detail in Chapter 9.

Maximizing Savings

To maximize *electricity generation*, we would face our solar modules south if we are in the Northern Hemisphere and north if we are in the Southern Hemisphere. We would tilt them just below the latitude of our location. Maximizing *savings* is a different issue. If we are aiming to reduce demand charges or system peak charges that occur in the afternoon, we should orient our modules towards the West facing them more to where the sun is at the time these charges occur. In a study[6] for the University of Ottawa in Canada, which is subject to system peak charges, we found an increase in savings of 19% when solar modules were oriented 54° West of South.

The tilt on many rooftop modules is low, about 10°, not because these installations are close to the equator, but because the wind load would be too high during a storm if the tilt were closer to the latitude, say 40°. This reduces the amount of electricity generated by the modules and hence the savings obtained, but is necessary to comply with building codes. Many solar modules themselves are certified to withstand winds of up to 220 km/hour; it is the racking and the ballast that is of concern during a storm.

This issue of wind load also means that tracking systems are not suitable for rooftop installations. The vertical supports in Figure 1.2 (center) of Chapter 1 would cause localized stress on the structure of the roof. This further reduces the savings that can be obtained from a rooftop system.

Shading by trees and other buildings is a particular concern in urban locations. Software is available to analyze photographs taken from the site to estimate the hours and months during which the site will be shaded and take that into account in calculating the amount of electricity generated.

Carbon Reductions

Solar modules do not produce greenhouse gases when they generate electricity. However, their manufacture and installation do, just the same as building any other power plant. A study by the Potsdam Institute for Climate Impact Research, published in Nature Energy,[7] combines construction and operation into life-cycle carbon equivalent costs for a range of different electricity-generating technologies. A quote from their report is in the sidebar showing that, taking everything into account, the carbon cost of solar power is very small compared with other generating technologies.

A company with solar modules on its office building may be able to claim

> **Life-Cycle Carbon Costs, from the Potsdam Institute**
>
> "We project life-cycle emissions from fossil fuel carbon capture and sequestration plants of 78–110 gm CO_2 eq. per kWh, compared with 3.5–12 gm CO_2 eq. per kWh for nuclear, wind and solar power for 2050. Life-cycle emissions from hydropower and bioenergy are substantial (similar to 100 gm CO_2 eq. per kWh), but highly uncertain".

carbon credits, renewable energy certificates, renewable obligation certificates or whatever is available in the local jurisdiction. Each scheme operates differently, but credits and certificates are generally tradable with the price set by a market mechanism.

The number of carbon credits that can be claimed depends on how much carbon the electricity grid produces. France is about 70% nuclear, Ontario is almost 85% nuclear and hydroelectric, so installing solar there does not reduce carbon emissions as much as in many US states, which are almost 50% coal, or in Nigeria, which is over 80% natural gas.

Intangible Benefits

Solar modules on a building or parking lot are highly visible, adding to the environmentally friendly image of the company, which may result in some intangible benefits such as attracting customers and employees. Another indirect benefit of solar module awnings over parking lots is that they shade the cars from the sun so that employees do not come to a baking hot car after a day in the office.

Summary

This chapter has shown how to estimate the costs and savings for behind-the-meter commercial and industrial solar installations for customers subject to demand charges on their peak monthly electricity consumption. Most of these projects are on rooftops and parking lots, but can be ground-mounted if there is enough space. Capital costs benefit from economies of scale and larger rooftop installations cost less than smaller ones. For the same reason, rooftop costs are substantially higher than for the utility-scale systems we discussed in Chapter 1. Operating and maintenance costs are slightly less than for utility-scale systems, because of the travel cost involved for large utility-scale projects distant from the city. High demand charges and system peak charges provide the opportunity for good savings if solar is generating well at the times when those charges are applied.

Takeaways

- Costs
  - Solar module costs constitute only 19% of the total installed capital cost of a 100 kW rooftop system, which costs $1.71/W, on average, about double the cost of a 100 MW utility-scale system.

- The operating and maintenance costs are $0.013/W/yr, on average, slightly less than for a utility-scale system.
- These capital and O&M cost estimates need to be modified for each local situation.
- Savings
  - The amount of electricity generated may be reduced from the maximum possible because (i) modules may need to be aligned with a roof or parking lot; (ii) building codes in windy areas may require modules to be mounted without the use of trackers and at a low tilt; and (iii) the site may be shaded by other buildings and trees.
  - Savings on the customer's electricity bill can be increased if net metering is available. Virtual net metering can produce further savings for multi-site customers.
  - The reduction in demand charges depends on the customer consumption profile and on the solar generation profile.
  - Some customers opt for tariffs including a charge at times of peak grid consumption, but these times vary from year to year, making the use of a battery important in conjunction with a solar system.
  - The benefit of a solar installation may be increased if carbon credits are available and if the grid uses a significant percentage of fossil fuel generation.

Probe Deeper: The Why?

Why build a solar project on the roof of an office building when it costs far less to build a much larger one in a desert? Because the savings on rooftop projects come from the retail price of electricity whereas utility-scale projects sell electricity at the lower wholesale price.

Process

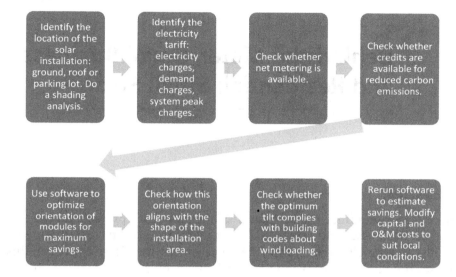

Notes

1 Kitimat Aluminum Smelter, British Columbia, Canada, https://www.riotinto.com/en/operations/canada/bc-works
2 Alba Aluminum Smelter, Bahrain, https://www.albasmelter.com/Pages/default.aspx
3 Gambone, S., How Safe Are Your Solar Panels in Severe Weather? Paradise Energy Solutions, https://www.paradisesolarenergy.com/blog/how-safe-are-your-solar-panels-in-severe-weather
4 NREL, U.S. Solar Photovoltaic System and Energy Storage Cost Benchmark, 2021 National Renewable Energy Laboratory, USA
5 Wright, D.J., Ashwell, J., Ashworth, J., Badruddin, S., Ghali, M.R., Robertson-Gillis, C., 2021, "Impact of Tariff Structure on the Economics of Behind-the-Meter Solar Microgrids", *Cleaner Engineering and Technology*, 2: 100039, https://doi.org/10.1016/j.clet.2020.100039.
6 Haysom, J.E., Hinzer, K., Wright, D.J., 2016, "Impact of Electricity Tariffs on Optimal Orientation of Photovoltaic Modules", *Progress in Photovoltaics: Research and Applications*, 24(2): 253–260.
7 Pehl, Michaja, Arvesen, Anders, Humpenöder, Florian, Popp, Alexander, Hertwich, Edgar G., Luderer, Gunnar, 2017, "Understanding Future Emissions from Low-carbon Power Systems by Integration of Life-cycle Assessment and Integrated Energy Modelling", *Nature Energy*, 2(12): 939–945.

3
Behind-the-Meter, Small Business and Residential: Small Solar

Introduction

This chapter identifies the costs and savings for solar projects on the sites of small businesses and residential customers. To incentivize flattening the profile of electricity demand for these customers, the electric power industry uses time-of-use (ToU) and tiered pricing instead of the demand charges and system peak charges discussed in Chapter 2.

ToU pricing is an electricity charge that depends on the time of day and also on the month of the year. Clearly, the idea is to charge more at times of high usage of the electricity grid. In Chapter 2, high usage applied to an individual business or to the entire grid. For residential customers, high usage applies to a residential area. For instance, residential usage is high from 5 p.m. to 10 p.m. when people are cooking their dinners, recharging their electric vehicles and playing their video games. However, this is not a peak time for the city as a whole as many workplaces are closed for the day. A high ToU charge in the evening therefore reduces the need for the distribution company to upgrade grid equipment in residential areas of the city but does not have so much impact on the rest of the distribution grid or on transmission companies.

Tiered pricing applies a higher price if a customer's monthly usage exceeds a certain limit and is also known as a step tariff. It is designed to reduce electricity consumption overall independent of time of day or time of year.

The size of business for which ToU and tiered pricing are available depends on the electricity tariff in the local area and generally applies to customers whose power requirement is below 25–100 kW. Examples of small businesses discussed in this chapter include small shopping centers with up to about ten retail stores, restaurants, farms and car repair shops.

For the purposes of this chapter, residences are single-family homes or buildings with a few apartments in which the owner can use the roof and/or

DOI: 10.4324/9781003262435-4

adjacent land to install solar modules. Larger apartment buildings and condominiums often pay for electricity to the distribution company and resell it to occupants of individual units and would therefore count as medium-sized businesses as described in Chapter 2.

The average residential solar installation costs about $20K, almost as much as a new car. Not many people pay cash for a car, most take out a car loan and some lease the car. The same options are available for residential solar installations. Car loans are sometimes offered by car manufacturers and some solar developers offer solar loans. One business model for residential solar is that the homeowner makes loan payments to the developer and owns and operates the system. Another business model is that the developer owns and operates the system and sells electricity to the homeowner at a price lower than the price of purchasing from the grid. This is attractive to homeowners who do not want to be responsible for generating their own electricity and brings the developer a regular stream of revenue in return for their capital outlay for installing the system. When this latter model is applied to small businesses, they sometimes charge the developer a rent for use of the roof space, but the rent is usually quite low since there are not many other competing uses for a small business's roof.

Costs

Capital Costs

The range of architectural designs of single-family homes means that rooftop solar is very much a custom job. The design needs to deal with chimneys, skylights, vents, dormers and gables. It is unusual to find a home with a straightforward installation as in Figure 3.1 (top). Also some residential installations are quite small as in Figure 3.1 (bottom), not allowing any economies of scale.

Residential roofs in different parts of the world are made of slates, tiles and shingles. Slates and tiles usually last the lifetime of the building and are common in Europe, but shingles typically have a 20–25 year warranty and are used widely in North America. It therefore makes sense to install solar modules on a shingled roof toward the end of the shingle warranty so that they can be replaced at the same time as installing the solar modules. Installing on slates or tiles costs more than installing on shingles but can be done at any time.

It is no surprise therefore that the cost of solar installations on residences is higher than any other type of deployment. This is not only due to the customization and lack of economies of scale but also to a new cost, which is less relevant to commercial deployment: sales and marketing. Homeowners

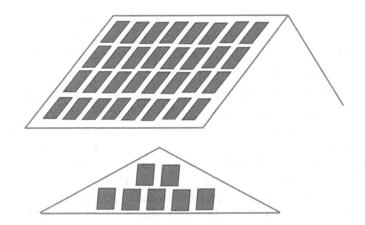

Figure 3.1 Large and small residential rooftop installations.

need to be educated about the costs and economic benefits of solar power and convinced that they will see a return on their investment. Salespeople waste time if they pitch to homeowners who are environmentally motivated to install solar modules, but whose roof design is not suitable or whose shingle warranty will expire in ten years' time. Sales and marketing adds significantly to the cost as shown in Figure 3.2, bringing the total to $2.65/W for a residential customer.[1] This cost is declining by 3% per year. Costs for a small business are in between the two examples shown in Figure 3.2.

The costs given above are for retrofitting on an existing building and would be less for new construction. Some jurisdictions, for instance, California, require all new homes to have solar installed on their roofs. One way of doing this is to use solar shingles that look similar to black asphalt shingles. The solar cell is part of the construction materials for the building and hence this design is referred to as Building-Integrated Photovoltaics (BIPV); see Chapter 14. Solar shingles can be based on silicon semiconductors in which case they are rigid, or alternatively they can be flexible, similar to regular shingles, based on a thin film solar technology using, for instance, a cadmium telluride semiconductor; see Chapter 13. At the time of writing (2021), the installed cost of solar shingles is more than that of solar modules. In their favor, some people prefer them aesthetically and they avoid the cost of installing regular shingles.

Operations and Maintenance Costs

Homeowners typically clean their own solar modules. In residential areas of a city there is less road traffic than in commercial and industrial areas so

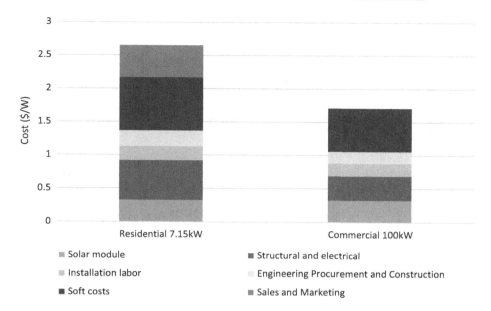

Figure 3.2 Cost comparison of an average (7.15 kW) US residential installation with a 100 kW commercial installation showing the cost of additional customization and lack of returns to scale for the residential installation together with the cost of sales and marketing. Soft costs include land acquisition, obtaining permits, interconnection to the electricity grid, overhead and profit for the developer. Structural and electrical balance of system (BoS) includes the racking, wiring and other electrical equipment. Based on NREL.[1]

that there is less particulate pollution from car exhausts and modules don't need much cleaning anyway. Rain also washes the modules clean naturally. If a module fails, the developer replaces it under warranty so that there is no identifiable dollar O&M cost for residential installations. For small business installations, O&M costs are similar to those for medium-sized businesses discussed in Chapter 2: $0.013/W/yr.

In summary, the capital costs of residential solar designs are $2.65/W with no dollar value associated with O&M costs.

Savings

The savings from behind-the-meter solar comes from the reduction in the electricity bill and therefore depends on whether the electricity tariff uses ToU pricing or tiered pricing. An example of ToU pricing is presented graphically in Figure 3.3 for Ontario, Canada, showing higher charges during summer afternoons. Solar is generating well during these air-conditioning

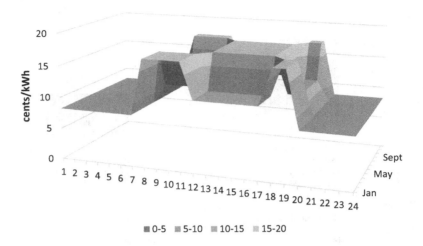

Figure 3.3 Residential time-of-use pricing in Ontario, Canada (cents/kWh) by hour ending and month.

peaks and can reduce electricity purchases from the grid at a time when the price is high.

Tiered pricing does not depend on time of day or time of year but increases in steps according to total monthly usage. Heavy users of electricity can therefore save more from solar than lighter users, since their grid price is higher.

Net-metering, as discussed in Chapter 2, is generally not available with ToU pricing, to discourage customers from purchasing a battery, charging it when the price is low and discharging it back into the grid when the price is high. However, net-metering can be used with tiered pricing if enough roof space is available to sometimes generate more power than is being consumed.

These savings apply to the business model in which the customer owns the solar installation and also to the model in which the developer owns the installation and sells electricity to the customer. In the latter case, the revenue for the developer is the payments for electricity by the customer.

Small business customers with flat roofs may be able to orient their solar modules so as to achieve maximum savings by angling them toward the position of the sun when ToU prices are high. An analysis of the ToU tariff for Modesto, CA, together with hourly solar irradiance measurements, results in an optimum angle 34° west of south and an optimum tilt of 30°. A flat rate tariff would result in south-facing modules with an optimum tilt just below the latitude, which is 38° for Modesto. The ToU tariff has not had much effect on the optimum tilt, but angling the modules 34° west of south is significantly different from pointing them due south; see other examples from SW USA in the sidebar.[2]

For residential customers with sloped roofs, the modules need to be mounted flat on the roof and are therefore oriented according to the architecture of the roof. This can lead to non-optimal orientation of the solar modules, and even two different orientations on a single roof as in Figure 3.4. Commercial software is used to estimate the hourly electricity generation given the angle of the roof. This hourly amount can then be mapped on to the grid price at that time to get the dollar savings for a whole year.

Residential and small business electricity prices can apply to an entire country (e.g. England), an individual province (e.g. Ontario) or a single city (e.g. Modesto, California). Modesto is just 75 miles drive from Sacramento but its average electricity price was 43% higher in 2021. The savings derived from a solar installation are higher if the electricity price is higher. The climate including

Author's Experience

In a study of SW USA, we calculated the optimum angle for small business customers with ToU tariffs and obtained the following results:

Tucson, AZ: 6° E of S
Bakersfield, CA: 36° W of S
Fresno, CA: 30° W of S
Los Angeles, CA 34° W of S
Sacramento, CA 20° W of S
San Jose, CA: 36° W of S
Denver, CO: 22° W of S
Las Vegas, NV: 52° W of S

Are Savings Higher in Sunnier Locations?

The *amount* of electricity produced is higher in a sunnier location. For behind-the-meter installations, the *value* of that electricity depends on the electricity tariff.

Figure 3.4 Solar modules at different angles on a residential roof.

the solar irradiance is very similar in Modesto and Sacramento so that the amount of electricity generated from comparable solar installations is also similar, but the dollar value of that electricity is on average 43% higher in Modesto than in Sacramento. Developers choosing cities in which to install residential solar designs choose a combination of sunny locations and high electricity prices.

Summary

This chapter has shown how to estimate the costs and savings for behind-the-meter residential and small business solar installations for customers subject to ToU or tiered electricity charges. We have seen how the cost of solar installations for residences and small businesses is higher than for larger installations, due to the need for customization, lack of economies of scale and sales and marketing costs. We discussed how to take advantage of ToU pricing to orient the modules toward the position of the sun when the ToU price is high. This may be possible for small businesses with a flat roof but the sloped roofs of single-family homes mean that savings are more limited.

Takeaways

- Costs
  - Average residential installations in the USA cost $2.65/W, the highest of all the systems considered in Part 1 of this book. However, there is no dollar O&M cost since homeowners clean the modules themselves.
- Savings
  - With ToU pricing, customers with flat roofs may be able to orient the solar modules to face the position of the sun when prices are high so as to maximize savings.
  - For residential installations, the amount of electricity generated may be reduced from the maximum possible because the slopes of different parts of the roof are not optimal for solar installations.
  - Net-metering may be available with tiered pricing and can allow excess power to be fed into the grid at some times of the year.
- Business Models
  - Residential customers may get a loan or lease from the developer in much the same way they would get a car loan from the car manufacturer.
  - Alternatively the developer may own a solar installation on a customer's roof and sell them the electricity at a price below the grid price.

Probe Deeper: The Why?

Why would a homeowner or a small business owner who knows nothing about solar power spend several thousand dollars to install solar modules on their roof? A developer will front the capital, be responsible for the installation and maintenance and sell electricity to the building owner (or tenant) for less than they would pay the electricity distribution company. Investors fund developers who focus on locations with high electricity tariffs and high solar irradiance.

Process

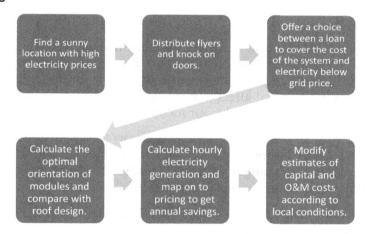

Notes

1 NREL, U.S. Solar Photovoltaic System and Energy Storage Cost Benchmark, 2021 National Renewable Energy Laboratory, USA
2 Tomosk, S., Haysom, J.E., Hinzer, K., Schriemer, H., Wright, D.J., 2017, "Mapping the Geographic Distribution of the Economic Viability of Photovoltaic Load Displacement Projects in SW USA", *Renewable Energy*, 107 (July 2017):101–112, http://dx.doi.org/10.1016/j.renene.2017.01.049.

4
Off-grid: Small to Large Solar

Introduction

In this chapter, we describe a variety of solar installations ranging in size from small to utility-scale, in areas that are not served by the public electricity grid. In many respects, these projects differ from those described in Chapters 1–3 in ways that affect how we calculate their economic viability. It is these differences that will be our focus in this chapter.

A key issue with all off-grid solar projects is how to supply electricity after the sun has set. Two options are available: combining solar with storage, e.g. a battery and/or combining it with another form of electricity generation, e.g. wind or diesel. More on this in Chapter 10.

Another major issue is how to supply reliable power from solar and wind, which are inherently intermittent. If diesel or hydroelectric generation is available as a back-up, we can get by without the cost of a battery. If there is no such back-up, not only do we need a battery, but we also need a solar plus wind capacity that is larger than our load. This additional capacity is needed so that we can supply our load and charge the battery at the same time. If the battery is already charged, then we will be generating "excess" power, which has to be "curtailed", i.e. discarded without being used. This type of off-grid project is therefore significantly more expensive than a grid-connected project or a project with back-up hydro or diesel. To provide reliable operation 24/7, it requires that we invest in extra capacity and then discard some of the power generated.

We will divide off-grid projects into two types:

1. Remote Industrial Operations,
2. Remote Communities and Small Islands.

DOI: 10.4324/9781003262435-5

Remote Industrial Operations

Most industrial operations are connected to the public electricity grid. Only those in very remote regions are off-grid, of which the classic example is mining. Much mining is done away from populated areas and requires a lot of energy including electricity. It often makes economic sense to generate electricity on site instead of building a transmission line to extend the grid to the mining site. An example of a much smaller off-grid operation is a mobile network base station (also known as a "tower"). Many rural areas of the world have mobile phone service but no electricity, hence the need to generate electricity locally at each base station.

Mining

Mining is an energy-intensive operation and, in particular, uses a lot of electricity. The electricity cost can be up to 50% of the total operations cost of the mine. A survey of open pit mines in Canada[1] showed that energy-use varies considerably from mine to mine, but on average, 75% of the total energy used was split 50/50 between electricity and diesel. The rest included propane, explosives, natural gas and fuel oil. Underground mining uses a higher proportion of electricity to operate elevators and the ventilation system. A successful solar project at a mine in Chile is described in the sidebar.[2]

Solar at a Large Copper Mine in Chile

In the summer of 2020, in the middle of the Covid-19 pandemic, Sonnedix built a 171 MW solar installation at the Collahuasi copper mine in Northern Chile. At an altitude of over 4,000 meters, it is even higher than the Atacama Desert. With little atmosphere above it to absorb solar radiation, it is one of the world's most productive locations for solar power. Protecting the 500 workers from the ultra-violet radiation at this altitude involved face coverings that did double duty as protection from viral infections. All employees were given Covid tests, and 2 meters of distancing was maintained at work, in the canteen and on buses used to bring staff to the site. The mine operates 24/7, which is reflected in a 24/7 requirement in the power purchase agreement (PPA). This is the fifth largest copper mine globally and 171 MW constitutes only 12% of the mine's electric power requirements. Assuming this project is successful, there is plenty of scope for more to follow at the same site.

Most electricity in off-grid mines is generated on site using diesel or fuel-oil generators, with the fuel being trucked to the site. In assessing the economic viability of solar generation, our benchmark for cost comparison is therefore not only the cost of diesel or fuel-oil generation (which is high to start with) but also the cost of trucking the fuel to the site, which can add considerably to the cost. From this point of view, harnessing solar energy is an attractive option, particularly in sunny locations like Africa, Australia and South America. The more remote the location, the further the fuel has to be trucked and the better the business case for solar.

On the other hand, there are three downsides to solar installation at an off-grid mining site:

1. Its high capital costs. With its zero fuel cost and low operations and maintenance costs, harnessing solar energy is more capital-intensive than diesel and fuel-oil generation, where the cost of fuel is a high proportion of the total cost. Some mining companies are reluctant to invest so much up front capital in solar power, particularly when it is a new technology for them.
2. Solar only generates during the day and most mines have 24/7 operations. One option is to use batteries, adding to the complexity of the project from the viewpoint of the mining company. A second option is to use diesel or fuel oil when the solar is not generating, which adds the cost of the fuel to the operation.
3. Solar installations generate power for 25–32 years, whereas some mining operations are shorter term. If an ore deposit will be exhausted in ten years, the economic viability of the solar installation needs to be assessed over that time horizon (see Part 2 of this book). Some solar developers specialize in supplying the mining industry and may be able to salvage the modules and racking from one site after ten years and install them at another site. However, there is a labor cost associated with this, and Chapters 1 and 2 have shown us that the modules do not necessarily constitute a large proportion of the total cost of a solar installation.

The solar industry has adopted two strategies to facilitate the transition to renewable electricity for off-grid mines. First, they make the transition gradual, with initial pilot projects generating a small proportion of total electricity from solar, say 10%. This allows mining companies to gain confidence that solar power can be reliable 24/7 with the use of batteries. Second the solar developer finances the capital cost of the project and operates it for the mining company. The mining company can then focus on mining and the solar company can focus on generating electricity. They can negotiate a Power Purchasing Agreement (PPA) stating how much electricity will be supplied, at what price and for how many years. Alternatively, the mining company can rent the solar facility from the solar developer. If the life of the mine is projected to be less than the life of the solar installation, the PPA price or the rent will be higher than for a longer-term contract.

In assessing the profitability of solar for off-grid mining, it is important to distinguish two situations: a new mine or an existing operation. In the case of a new mine with 20% of the electricity coming from solar plus a battery, we need 20% less diesel-generating capacity thus saving on the capital cost of diesel, plus we save 20% on fuel cost. If we are installing 20% solar generation at an existing mine, where the diesel generators are already in place, we only save on fuel cost. In this latter situation, we do not need to aim for 24/7 solar electricity and can therefore avoid the cost of a large battery. Instead, we operate more of the existing generators during the night.

Some mining operations expand their need for electricity during the course of their operation, see example, in Tanzania in the sidebar.[3] They may be expanding or they may have exhausted the ore that can be mined from a surface operation and are moving to underground operation with its additional electricity requirements for ventilation and elevator operation. Expanding capacity is similar to starting a new mine. Solar plus battery can reduce the number of diesel generators required as well as reducing the fuel cost.

There are therefore two distinct ways of calculating the profitability of solar from the point of view of a mining company:

- *Existing mine.* The capital cost of solar compared with the savings from reduced fuel cost.
- *New or expanding mine.* The capital cost of solar plus battery compared with the savings from the reduced cost of diesel generators plus fuel.

If the mining company outsources the solar generation to a solar company under a PPA or if they rent the solar installation from the developer,

Solar at a Small Gold Mine in Tanzania

At Shanta Gold's New Luika mine in Tanzania, 60% of the processing cost is electricity. In 2018, it switched from surface to underground mining increasing its electricity requirement from 3.3 to 6 MW. In addition to diesel generators, it rented a 0.7 MW solar installation from Redavia, a German company specializing in solar rentals. The rental allows Shanta Gold to control its solar facility without having to front the capital cost.

the mining company compares the PPA price or the rent with the cost of fuel and/or diesel generators. The solar developer compares the PPA price or the rent with the capital cost of harnessing solar energy and (if necessary to fulfill the requirements of the PPA or rental agreement) batteries.

Mobile Network Base Stations

At the other end of the scale from the megawatt-sized solar projects at mining sites are the kilowatt installations at mobile network base stations. Tiny though they are, there are vast numbers of them and 5G and 6G networks need many more base stations than 3G or 4G. Moreover, successive generations of wireless technology involve more computation and hence more electricity.[4] The future looks bright for solar installations at base stations.

Base stations, sometimes called "towers", receive the wireless communications from mobile phones and relay them on to the mobile operator's core network where they are routed to the required destination. People use their mobile phones when they are in remote areas, living in villages away from the wired telephone network, hiking in the wilderness and driving down highways through forests and deserts. The public electricity grid often does not extend to these locations and electricity needs to be generated at the base station site, often using diesel. As with mining sites, there is the additional cost of delivering fuel to the site, enhancing the business case for solar, see sidebar.[5] Base station sites typically have little security and suffer from the problem of theft of fuel from the storage tank. Solar and wind generation can solve these problems, with the solar modules and small wind turbines mounted on the tower out of the reach of thieves, whereas the heavy fuel tank needs to be on the ground.

An off-grid base station site is typically in an area remote enough that it would be costly to install telecommunication cables to connect it to the mobile operator's core network. The base station uses another radio channel to relay mobile phone traffic, separate from the channels used to communicate with customers' mobile phones. This adds to its electricity needs, since wireless communications requires more power than the wired alternative. It is therefore completely wireless, having no wires for telecommunications or for electricity from the grid.

Base stations use about 50% of their electricity for user communications and the rest for internal processing and cooling of electronics. When a mobile phone is far from the base station, more power is needed for communications than when it is closer. Mobile phones come within range of the base station, get closer and then they move on to the next base station. The electricity demand at an off-grid base station therefore varies considerably and is less at night when fewer people venture into remote areas. The profile of solar power, generated during daytime, matches this usage pattern well reducing the size of the battery needed for nighttime and cloudy days. An exception to this is base stations by highways crossing deserts where many people prefer to travel at night to avoid the heat and glare of the day.

Wind turbines are also used at base stations. Towers are often built tall in remote areas to increase the range of communications and wind turbines mounted high on the tower benefit from higher wind speeds than lower down. Wind blows at night and can complement solar, but a battery is still required because of the intermittency of both wind and solar. Reliability is an important performance measure for mobile phone companies and a dependable electricity supply is essential to maintain base station operation.

> **Solar Base Stations in South Africa**
>
> A comparison of a base station powered by diesel and by solar with batteries was conducted by Cellstrom in South Africa, a country with some of the highest solar irradiance in the world. They showed that, although the initial capital cost of the solar was much higher, the cost of diesel fuel over the 20-year life of the system resulted in the solar system costing half the cost of the diesel system.

Base stations consume between 1 and 12 kW depending on their capacity and in remote areas are at the low end of that range. A 4 kW base station consumes less than 4 kW most of the time due to the variability in user telecommunications traffic. However, it may need a solar generator capable of generating more than 4 kW to recharge the battery for nighttime use and for cloudy days. This can be very successful economically; see an example from South Africa in the sidebar. The capacity of the solar and battery depends on the local traffic profile, the local irradiance profile and how sure the mobile phone company wants to be that the base station will be operational. Maintaining service during a week of cloudy days in winter requires large solar and battery capacity. Software such as HOMER[6] and ReOpt[7] is used to optimize system design for local conditions.

Solar is also used at urban base stations to supplement the grid electricity. There are three reasons for this:

- Base stations account for 80% of total electricity costs for a mobile network operator. In areas where the price from the grid is high, there is a considerable incentive to investigate alternative options like solar.

- In areas where grid electricity is generated from fossil fuel sources, carbon credits may be available for using solar power.
- In areas where the grid is unreliable such as in Africa and India, solar power enables mobile phone service to continue during a brown-out or black-out.

It should, however, be born in mind that, in cities, mobile phone traffic peaks in the late evening and therefore larger batteries are required than in remote areas with predominantly daytime traffic.

Remote Communities and Small Islands

UN High Commission for Refugees (UNHCR)

Refugee camps in general do not have access to the electricity grid and the UNHCR uses solar microgrids with batteries and diesel generators to provide electricity to support construction, agriculture, telecommunications, health care, education and household applications.

People living in remote off-grid communities face issues similar to those described above for mining sites: reliance on legacy-generating technologies, notably diesel generation, the cost of transporting fuel and the need to provide power at night. The solution is to combine solar with wind, batteries and/or the existing diesel generators, see sidebar for an example at refugee camps.[8]

In this section, we will describe the specifics of some remote communities and islands in both very cold and very hot countries to get a feel for the diverse range of issues that arise when installing solar at a site previously served by diesel generation.

Northern Canada

In Northern Canada, there are 170 remote first-nation communities using diesel generators, with the diesel fuel brought in by truck, boat or air; see Arctic example in sidebar.[9] Not only does this increase the cost of diesel generation, but it also increases the capital cost of a solar installation since the solar modules, racking and cement for the footings need to be brought in by the same mode of transport. In particular, fly-in communities with planes landing on local lakes need to think outside the box to create a solar design that reduces the weight of construction materials.

Northern communities experience high winds in the winter resulting in the danger of tilted solar modules being lifted off the ground. One solution is to tilt modules at a very shallow angle, as was shown for rooftop installations in Chapter 2. However, the optimum tilt on solar modules is approximately equal to the latitude, so that a high tilt is needed in Arctic areas like Nunavut (see the sidebar) where the latitude is over 60°. One solution is to mount the modules back to back, facing East and West, forming a "tent" shape that reduces the wind load on the modules, Figure 4.1. This reduces the amount of cement needed in the footings and hence reduces the cost of transporting cement by air.

Some Northern communities live on permafrost and geotextiles and drainage tile need to be installed to prevent water from getting into the soil, adding to the construction cost.

Another important factor is heating people's homes and businesses. Some communities have a district heating system using the waste heat from diesel generators. If diesel is replaced by solar power, it is important to include the cost of the additional heating required.

Saudi Arabia

Saudi Arabia, famous for its oil reserves, also has abundant wind

Arctic Solar

The Vuntut Gwitchin First Nation (VGFN) living inside the Arctic Circle in Canada has installed 900 kW of solar plus 350 kWh of batteries in a microgrid linked to its diesel generator. VGFN believes in living symbiotically with the environment and is motivated to reduce its greenhouse gas emissions. The project also saves CDN$400K per year after servicing the loan used to pay for the solar installation.

Price of Diesel-Generated Electricity in Northern Canada

Nunavut, a territory in Northern Canada, with five times the land area of Germany, has a population of 38,000 people living in 25 communities. The electricity utility, Qulliq Energy Corp. (QEC), does not have a grid; instead, it operates diesel generators in each of the 25 communities with microgrids distributing the power to the homes and businesses. The price at which it sells electricity is very high, CDN$0.60–1.20 per kWh. However, residents pay CDN$0.06 with the difference taken up by the Nunavut Housing Corporation as a subsidy. As of 2021, one community had a 500 kW solar installation operated by QEC.

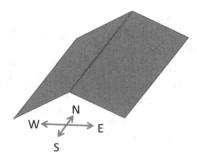

Figure 4.1 Tent-shaped solar module installation reduces upward wind load on modules.

resources in the North and East of the country and solar resources, particularly in the West, bordering the Red Sea. Electricity is currently generated largely from oil and natural gas, and demand is rapidly increasing. In 2019, there was about 2 GW of solar and 1 GW of wind power installed.

Many villages in Saudi Arabia are off-grid and use diesel generators, for which the fuel cost is very low, being based on the internal price in Saudi Arabia, not the international market. However, because of concerns to reduce greenhouse gas emissions, Saudi Arabia is interested in transitioning to renewable energy sources.

We conducted an analysis of off-grid villages in seven locations around Saudi Arabia to investigate the cost of generating electricity from a combination of solar, wind and battery, using HOMER software to optimize the configuration.[10] The load profile of a typical village has a summer peak from June to September from 11 a.m. to 5 p.m. due to air conditioning, which matches solar generation well. In the winter, the peak usage is in the evening from 5 to 10 p.m. for which a battery and/or wind turbines are necessary. Although these villages are off-grid, they are not as remote as those in Northern Canada described above. There is therefore no additional cost of transporting diesel or solar construction materials to the site and the analysis uses the cost estimates given in Chapter 2.

For five of the seven sites, the cost of electricity is lowest using a solar/battery combination. For the other two sites, Yanbu, a windy coastal location, and Sharurah, a windy Southern location, a combination of wind/solar/battery is optimal. The prices of solar and batteries are projected to decline faster than the price of wind turbines, so that if the project start date was postponed to 2025, wind would not be necessary even in Yanbu and Sharurah, so that a solar/battery combination would be optimal for all seven sites.

The solar capacity needs to be higher than customer demand so that there is sufficient electricity to charge the battery for nighttime usage. The variability of customer demand and of solar generation means that there will be times when solar power is generated when the battery is already fully charged and the needs of customers are already satisfied. This "excess" electricity is lost in an off-grid system and amounts to up to 30% of the total electricity generated over the course of a year at the seven locations we studied. It is optimal to produce excess electricity sometimes so that we are sure of having enough at other times.

We did a detailed analysis of the optimal orientation of solar modules for villages near Riyadh, the capital city. The optimum tilt is 24° just less than the latitude of 25°. The afternoon sun is more intense than that in the morning, resulting in angling the modules 20° to the West of South. More surprising is the result of optimizing for summer and winter separately. In the winter, the optimum tilt is 47°, very different from the summer optimum of 9°. We can increase annual energy yield by 3–4% by changing the tilt of the modules in Spring and Autumn. This is a labor-intensive operation and requires adjustable racking but could be efficient if costs are low enough.

Small Islands

Most inhabited small island states, for example, in the Caribbean or Western Pacific Ocean, have several towns and villages and hence larger populations than the communities we have discussed in Northern Canada and Saudi Arabia. Nevertheless, many of them are too small to justify a nuclear power station and hence they generate electricity from diesel and natural gas, so that the retail price is high. A wish to reduce foreign exchange spent importing fossil fuels combined with a desire to reduce greenhouse gas emissions is leading to interest in solar power as an alternative.[11] The Pacific Islands Framework for Action on Climate Change has goals for almost 100% renewable power in many islands as an example to the world to treat climate change seriously, since shorelines of some islands are being eroded by rising sea levels and storm surges. On islands with hydroelectric power, it is easier to achieve 100% renewable power, but with intermittent solar and wind only, large batteries are needed to satisfy demand 24/7.

Antigua installed 3 MW of solar in three months during 2020 and plans for a further 7 MW, which will bring the total to almost 20% of peak load. All Caribbean islands have abundant sunshine year round. They are also prone to hurricanes that knock out parts of the electricity grid causing blackouts. A move to solar energy could be done in two ways. The first option is to build a utility-scale solar farm to supplement the present centralized diesel or natural gas generators. A second option would be for the electric power company to distribute many smaller solar farms around the island and/or for residences and businesses to install their own behind-the-meter solar. Although the second option would have less economies of scale and therefore be higher cost, it would provide more resilience than centralized infrastructure that could be knocked out by a storm.

Puerto Rico relies on bulk oil and natural gas generation with transmission lines taking electricity to cities, mountain villages and around the coast. Hurricane Maria exposed the vulnerability of this centralized system in 2017 and over 3 million people were without power for weeks or more. One of the main power plants was damaged by an earthquake in 2020. Many people have advocated for distributed solar and wind generation instead of repairing the aging legacy system, yet progress has been slow.[12]

Small islands, by definition, have a limited land area and solar installation takes up a considerable amount of space. A single-family home typically has enough roof space to power itself from solar, but apartment buildings and businesses need additional land to deploy solar installations. Some islands are hilly and/or forested, limiting the area available for solar. But one resource all islands have is the water surrounding them, and floating solar is emerging from a research concept to a commercially viable option. Regular modules or flexible thin-film solar* can be supported horizontally on floating structures with cables bringing the electricity ashore, see Chapter 13 and an example from Spain's Canary Islands in the sidebar.[13]

Canary Solar: Float-o-Voltaics

Tenerife, one of the Spanish Canary Islands, has achieved 42% of its power coming from wind and 18% from solar. An innovative project is a floating solar installation off the coast of another island. The initial stage involves 250 kW of horizontal solar modules surrounded by a circular boom to protect them from waves which can reach 10 meters in height during storms.

Summary

This chapter has provided a diverse range of examples of solar installations that are not connected to the public electricity grid. In these off-grid applications, solar needs to be combined with another electricity generation technology such as wind, gas or diesel or with an electricity storage option such as a battery to supply electricity 24/7. We have seen how the local conditions can

---

* See Chapter 13.

affect the economics of solar and how some innovative ways of improving profitability have been found. Some remote communities in Northern Canada can only be accessed by air and design solar installations to reduce the amount of concrete that needs to be flown in. Islands with insufficient land to deploy solar installations use floating solar in the surrounding ocean. A reason for using solar instead of diesel to power remote mobile phone base stations is that it deals with the problem of diesel fuel being stolen from the storage tank.

Takeaways

- Mining
  - Electricity is a large proportion of the operating cost of a mine.
  - Most off-grid mines generate electricity from diesel and operate 24/7.
  - The cost of installing solar power at an existing mine can be offset against the cost of the fuel plus the cost of trucking the fuel to the mining site. The cost of a battery can be offset against the cost of running existing generators at night.
  - At a new or expanding mine, the cost of solar plus battery can be offset against the cost of diesel generators plus their fuel and its transport.
  - Solar is more capital-intensive than diesel. Solar developers can lease a solar installation to the mine, or operate the installation themselves and sell electricity to the mine.
- Mobile Network Base Stations
  - Electricity consumption at base stations is a large proportion of the total electricity costs of a mobile phone company.
  - Off-grid base stations are typically powered by diesel generators and have suffered from theft of fuel from the tank.
  - Solar modules, supplemented by small wind turbines and/or batteries can be mounted on the tower out of easy reach.
  - Mobile phone traffic at off-grid base stations is mainly during the day, matching solar generation well.
  - Mobile phone companies need high availability of their services and wind turbines and/or large batteries are needed to cover several consecutive cloudy days.
- Remote Communities in Northern Canada
  - In Northern Canada, remote communities generate electricity from diesel locally, bringing the fuel by sea, road or air. The cost of electricity is up to $1/kWh.
  - Solar power can reduce this cost and is being introduced gradually.
  - At communities accessible only by air, innovative solar designs reduce the weight of structural materials and cement needed for construction.
  - Waste heat from diesel generators is used for district heating. Part of the cost of solar is the provision of alternative heating.

- Villages in Saudi Arabia
  - Many villages in Saudi Arabia use diesel generators with low-cost fuel, which is available locally.
  - Transitioning to solar is part of government policy to reduce greenhouse gas emissions.
  - At many sites, wind only marginally complements solar, which matches usage patterns well. Batteries supply power at night.
- Small Islands
  - Diesel generators currently used require import of fuel.
  - Many islands suffer from storms that can knock out large parts of a centralized electricity grid.
  - Distributed solar power can reduce electricity prices and provide more reliability.
  - If suitable land area is limited, floating solar in the surrounding ocean can be used.

Probe Deeper: The Why?

Why install solar off-grid when it has to be supplemented with diesel, gas, wind and/or batteries, all of which add to the cost? Because the alternative, typically diesel alone, costs more because of the cost of transporting the fuel to the site.

Processes

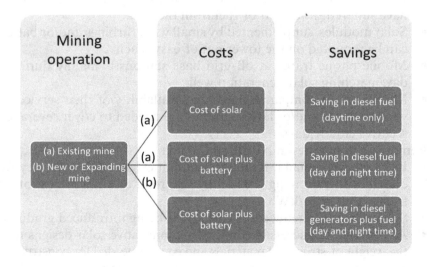

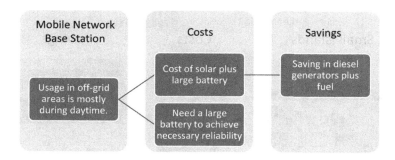

Mobile Network Base Station
- Usage in off-grid areas is mostly during daytime.

Costs
- Cost of solar plus large battery
- Need a large battery to achieve necessary reliability

Savings
- Saving in diesel generators plus fuel

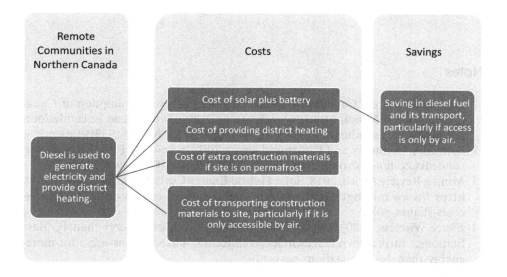

Remote Communities in Northern Canada
- Diesel is used to generate electricity and provide district heating.

Costs
- Cost of solar plus battery
- Cost of providing district heating
- Cost of extra construction materials if site is on permafrost
- Cost of transporting construction materials to site, particularly if it is only accessible by air.

Savings
- Saving in diesel fuel and its transport, particularly if access is only by air.

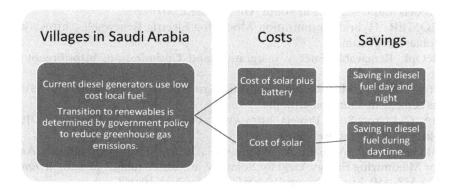

Villages in Saudi Arabia
- Current diesel generators use low cost local fuel.
- Transition to renewables is determined by government policy to reduce greenhouse gas emissions.

Costs
- Cost of solar plus battery
- Cost of solar

Savings
- Saving in diesel fuel day and night
- Saving in diesel fuel during daytime.

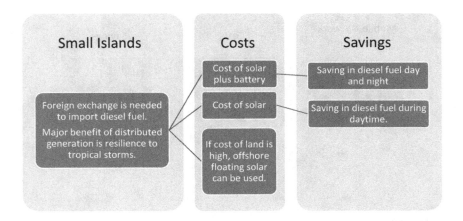

Small Islands	Costs	Savings
	Cost of solar plus battery	Saving in diesel fuel day and night
Foreign exchange is needed to import diesel fuel.	Cost of solar	Saving in diesel fuel during daytime.
Major benefit of distributed generation is resilience to tropical storms.	If cost of land is high, offshore floating solar can be used.	

Notes

1 Natural Resources Canada, Benchmarking the Energy Consumption of Canadian Open-Pit Mines, https://www.nrcan.gc.ca/sites/www.nrcan.gc.ca/files/oee/pdf/publications/industrial/mining/open-pit/Open-Pit-Mines-1939B-Eng.pdf

2 Sonnedix, Sonnedix and Collahuasi sign a 100% renewable PPA, https://www.sonnedix.com/news/sonnedix-and-collahuasi-sign-a-100-renewable-ppa

3 Mining Review Africa, 2018, Solar Hybrid Energy Curbs Costs for Shanta Gold, https://www.miningreview.com/news/solar-hybrid-energy-tanzania-curbs-costs-shanta-gold/

4 Fierce Wireless, 2020, 5G Base Stations Use a Lot More Energy than 4G Base Stations, https://www.fiercewireless.com/tech/5g-base-stations-use-a-lot-more-energy-than-4g-base-stations-says-mtn

5 Banjo, A., Aderemi, S.P., Chowdhury, Daniel, Olwal, Thomas O., Abu-Mahfouz, Adnan M., 2017, "Solar PV Powered Mobile Cellular Base Station: Models and Use Cases in South Africa," *IEEE Africon*.

6 HOMER, Hybrid Optimization Model for Electric Renewables, https://www.homerenergy.com/

7 ReOpt, Renewable Energy Integration and Optimization, https://reopt.nrel.gov/

8 https://microgridnews.com/when-microgrids-mean-hope-powering-refugee-settlement-in-shimelba-ethiopia/

9 BA, Old Crow Solar Project, https://www.bba.ca/wp-content/uploads/2019/07/oldcrow-en-spread-web.pdf

10 Al Garni, H.Z., Awasthi, A., Wright, D.J., 2019, "Optimal Orientation Angles for Maximizing Energy Yield for Solar PV in Saudi Arabia," *Renewable Energy*, 133:538–550, https://doi.org/10.1016/j.renene.2018.10.048.

11 IRENA, International Renewable Energy Agency 2018, Transforming Small-Island Power Systems: Technical Planning Studies for the Integration of Variable Renewables.

https://www.irena.org/-/media/Files/IRENA/Agency/Publication/2019/Jan/IRENA_
Transforming_SIDS_Power_2018.pdf
12 Gallucci, M., 2020, Privatization of Puerto Rico Power Grid Is Mired in Controversy, *IEEE Spectrum*, https://spectrum.ieee.org/energywise/energy/policy/-
the-privatization-of-puerto-rico-power-grid-mired-in-controversy
13 Garanovic, A., 2021, Floating Solar Power Off Canary Islands, *Offshore Energy*,
https://www.offshore-energy.biz/floating-solar-power-set-for-trials-off-canary-
islands/

Part 2
Solar Profitability

In Part 2 of this book, we cover the "big picture" profitability analysis of solar projects, how to measure it (Chapters 5 and 6), attract investment (Chapter 7) and de-risk it (Chapter 8). We add some ways to improve this big picture in Part 3.

The basic issue is that we have a very large capital cost for constructing a solar project, followed by a stream of annual revenues and operations and maintenance costs for the lifetime of the project, probably about 30 years. Right at the end there will be a cost of dismantling the system and some revenue from recycling the metal structure and glass from the solar modules. Figure D shows these cash flows for an example of a 32-year commercial rooftop project[1] starting in 2020. The vertical axis is scaled to show the annual costs and savings, by comparison with which the initial capital cost is way off the bottom of the graph and is therefore indicated by a thick downward arrow. The items shown in the graph are:

- Solar installation in 2020 with 32-year warranty on solar modules.
- The inverter, which converts the DC electricity from the solar modules and the battery into AC electricity to feed into the commercial building's electricity system, must be replaced in 2036. The cost of the initial inverter is included in the 2020 installation cost.
- Battery installation in 2020. The lifetime of the battery depends on how often it is charged and discharged, and in this case, it is projected to last 16 years. In 2036, there is going to be a replacement cost for the battery cells only. The casing, battery management system and other electronics do not need replacing.
- The operations and maintenance costs, which are the same each year.
- At the end of life of the system in 2052, there is a net cost for recycling, that is, the cost of dismantling the system is more than the value of the recycled glass and metal.[2]

DOI: 10.4324/9781003262435-6

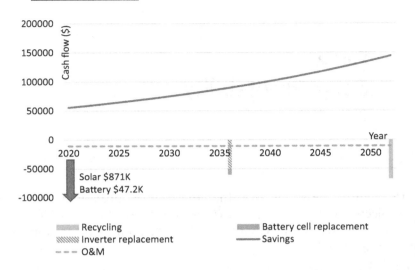

Figure D Example of cash flows for a commercial rooftop solar project starting in 2020.

- The annual income from the electricity generated is projected to increase over the life of the system, due to a projected increase in electricity prices in the installation area. In fact solar modules degrade over time, but the rate of increase in electricity prices more than compensates for this degradation.

Of course there are many assumptions in projections 32 years into the future, which we will discuss in the following chapters.

Notes

1 Wright, D.J., Ashwell, J., Ashworth, J., Badruddin, S., Ghali, M.R., Robertson-Gillis, C., 2021, "Impact of Tariff Structure on the Economics of Behind-the-Meter Solar Microgrids," *Cleaner Engineering and Technology*, 2(2021): 100039, https://doi.org/10.1016/j.clet.2020.100039.
2 Di Francia, G., 2013, The Impact of Recycling Policies on the Photovoltaic Levelized Cost of the Electricity," *International Conference on Renewable Energy Research and Applications*, Madrid, Spain. pp. 979–983, DOI: 10.1109/ICRERA.2013.6749894

5
Net Present Value and Internal Rate of Return

Introduction

In this chapter, we describe how to reconcile a large initial capital cost of solar with a stream of operations and maintenance costs and income over the subsequent years. We combine these costs and income into a single measure of the profitability of a solar project using discounted cash flow analysis.

Net Present Value (NPV)

Discounting attaches a lower value to money in the future compared to its value today, reflecting what is sometimes referred to as the "time value of money". If I have $100 today and invest it at 10% for one year, I will have $100 * (1 + 0.1) = 110 in one year. Assuming there is no risk in this investment, we can say that $110 in one year is equivalent to $100 today. If I had kept the capital and interest invested for two years, I would have $100 * (1 + 0.1)^2 = 121. If someone offered me $100 today or $121 in two years, I would have no preference between the two, assuming that I can obtain a risk-free rate of return of 10% per year. I am discounting the future amount of $121 in two years at a discount rate of 10% per year to obtain its value today: $121/(1 + 0.1)^2 = 100.

In the case of a solar power project with income, I_n, and operations and maintenance costs, O_n, in year n, the equivalent amount in year zero is $(I_n - O_n)/(1+d)^n$, where d is the discount rate. This is referred to as the net present value (NPV) of the future income minus costs for that year. The NPV of the whole project is obtained by summing over each year of the life of the project and subtracting the initial capital cost, C, which does not need discounting since it occurs in year zero:

$$\text{NPV} = \sum_{n=0}^{N} \frac{(I_n - O_n)}{(1+d)^n} - C$$

DOI: 10.4324/9781003262435-7

This is a standard calculation in discounted cash flow analysis with which some readers may already be familiar and which is included in many software packages for solar analysis. The cash flows are the income less the costs (in year zero, this includes both operations and capital costs). Let us now look at the details of its application to a solar project. We also include electricity storage, for example, a battery, which is discussed in more detail in Chapters 9 and 10.

• The life of the project, N years, is typically taken to be the length of the warranty on the solar modules, say 32 years. This will give a conservative estimate of the NPV. In fact the solar modules don't suddenly stop working just because their warranty has run out. We can squeeze some more electricity out of them in the ensuing years even though it will be heavily discounted in the NPV calculation. In fact, the project manager, 20–30 years from now, may have other options for increasing profitability, for example, by replacing the modules with new ones using a future more efficient solar technology. The reason we are calculating the NPV at the planning stage of a project is to convince investors to front the capital to pay for the construction. They do not want a proposal that depends on a future technology or on extending the life of the modules beyond the manufacturer's expectations. They want an estimate of the NPV, which does not involve undue risk. Hence we use the module warranty period as the life of the project.
• The income, I_n, in year n is the revenue from the sale of electricity for utility-scale projects, or the savings for behind-the-meter projects. We estimate income in the first year of operation and then project it into the future taking into account two factors. First, the efficiency of solar installations degrades by 0.75% per year for utility-scale and commercial/industrial projects and by 1% per year for residential projects.[1] The amount of electricity generated in kWh per year therefore declines at those rates, reflecting not just the degradation of the solar cells over time, but also the accumulation of dust on the modules if they are not cleaned often and the microscopic scratches if they are. Second, the price of electricity in $/kWh will change in the future. For projects with a power purchase agreement (PPA), the price paid per kWh is specified in the PPA together with an escalation rate determining how that price increases in the future.

The Math for Income

The income in year n is:

$$I_n = I_0 (1+r)^n (1-D)^n$$

where:

r is the future escalation rate of electricity prices

D is the degradation rate of the solar installation

For behind-the-meter projects, we need to estimate future trends in electricity prices. One way to do this is to extrapolate past trends. For projects subject to demand charges, we need to take into account the fact that the trend in demand charges may be different from the trend in electricity prices. The same is true of the individual levels in time-of-use pricing and tiered pricing; they may be trending at different rates.

- The operations and maintenance costs, O_n, in year n, includes not just the regular operations and maintenance costs given in Chapters 1–3, but also replacement costs for the inverter and battery cells. A rule of thumb is to replace the inverter after about 15 years and inverters cost $0.098/ W.[2] The entire battery does not need replacing; it is the battery cells that actually store the electricity that gradually lose their efficiency, so we get less power out than we put in. Some battery suppliers recommend replacing the cells after a certain number of charge/discharge cycles, for example, 5,000. If we have one battery cycle per day, we would replace the battery cells after 5000/365 = about 14 years. Inverters and battery cells do not have to be replaced at a precise date. If the solar module warranty is 32 years, it would make sense to replace the inverter and battery cells at year 16, getting the same 16-year life out of the replacement as the original. Another factor to include in O_n is the end-of-life costs, decommissioning the installation and recycling the glass from the solar modules and the metal from the support structure. An estimate is a net cost of $18.25 per square meter,[3] which may not be very accurate since very few solar installations have reached the end of their lives and been decommissioned. However, accuracy is not essential since the cost will be heavily discounted by multiplying by $\dfrac{1}{(1+d)^N}$.

- The capital cost, C, is the capital cost of the solar installation (from Chapters 1 to 3) plus the cost of the battery (see Chapters 9 and 10).
- The discount rate, d, depends on the company doing the solar project. It represents a risk-free rate of return on investment. The yield on government bonds is one choice for d. However, if the company has other projects that it could fund, we could take d to be the rate of return on those other projects. No project is as risk-free as a government bond, but it is important that our comparator projects have about the same level of risk as solar. For instance, a commercial building manager, considering rooftop solar, may also be able to achieve a good financial return by upgrading the furnace or the cooling system. The rate of return on those other projects could be used as the discount rate in calculating the solar NPV. In practice, many published studies have used a wide range of discount rates for solar projects, ranging from 5% to 10%.

The NPV is used at the planning stage of a solar project to answer the question. "If I invest C today in solar, what is today's value of the return that I can expect?" This is an important question to address, but its answer depends on the discount rate used. At year 16, that is, halfway through a 32-year project, cash flow is multiplied by 0.46 at a 5% discount rate and by 0.22 at a 10% discount rate, a very substantial difference.

It would be good to be able to do a discounted cash flow analysis without having to worry about what discount rate to use. Enter the internal rate of return (IRR).

Internal Rate of Return (IRR)

The IRR is the discount rate at which the NPV = 0, that is, the entire future stream of cash flows over the whole life of the project just covers the initial investment and no more.

$$\sum_{n=0}^{N} \frac{(I_n - O_n)}{(1 + \text{IRR})^n} = C$$

At the start of this chapter, we had an example of investing $100 for two years at 10% interest rate and getting $121 in two years. In this case, the IRR equals the interest rate of 10%, since the NPV = $121/(1 + 0.1)^2 - 100 = 0$.

The IRR is essentially the interest rate that the project is equivalent to and is calculated in software packages for solar economics. If we estimate the IRR from our solar project to be 2% and we can get 3% from a (risk-free) government bond, forget about solar. It is less profitable and more risky. If our rooftop solar IRR is 8% and we can get 10% from installing robots in our factory, first we need to assess which project is less risky. If the robots are less risky, go for the robots since they are also more profitable.

Calculating the IRR for each project a company is considering enables them to rank projects from high IRR to low IRR. However, projects with high IRR may well also have a high risk. The IRR for a solar project should be compared with the IRR of projects with a similar level of risk. Some companies have a "hurdle rate" that they use as a benchmark for all projects of similar risk. If the project IRR is higher than the hurdle rate, the project looks good. If not, it is unlikely to go ahead. Risk assessment for solar is described in detail in Chapter 8.

The IRR is also useful for government planners considering policy options for renewable power. Clearly, they don't want to have to ask potential developers what discount rate they use for their internal decision-making. Instead, they can estimate an IRR for wind or solar without having to assume any value for a discount rate. Freedom from having to choose a discount rate is a major benefit of using IRR.

Examples of Internal Rate of Return

IRR varies considerably from one geographic location to another, not only because the solar irradiance is different, but also because the value of the electricity generated is different. In the case of utility-scale projects with PPAs, the PPA price is often similar within a given geographical region. However, the savings obtained from behind-the-meter projects depends on the electricity tariff. Figure 5.1 shows the highest irradiance area of Canada, in the Prairies, spanning three provinces, Alberta, Saskatchewan and Manitoba. The solar energy yield is highest in Southern Alberta and in South Western Saskatchewan. We calculated the IRR for behind-the-meter projects for small businesses in 18 cities in these provinces and the results are shown in the map on the right.[4] Projects in the highest irradiance region of Alberta are not profitable, having a negative IRR, because the electricity price in Alberta is too low for enough savings to offset the capital cost of solar. By contrast, projects in the medium-energy yield area of South Eastern Saskatchewan have an IRR over 10%, since electricity prices there are higher. Each province has its own electricity tariff and IRR declines as we move North within a province due to reduced irradiance and hence lower energy yields.

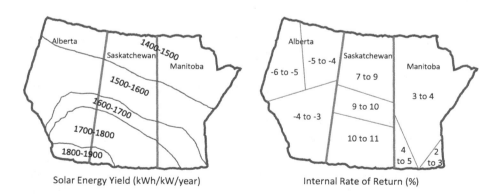

Solar Energy Yield (kWh/kW/year)   Internal Rate of Return (%)

Figure 5.1 Electric energy yield due to variations in solar irradiance in Alberta, Saskatchewan and Manitoba, Canada (left). The IRR of behind-the-meter solar projects in the same region, showing little correlation with energy yield due to different electricity tariffs in each province (right).

We also studied the effect of a 2% annual rate of decline in the capital cost of solar installations. In Saskatchewan, the most profitable province, the effect of a 10% (five years) and 20% (ten years) reduction in capital costs was to increase the average IRR in the province by 15% and 34% respectively showing the impact of capital cost in the IRR calculation.

IRR varies considerably across different countries influenced mainly by electricity tariff and solar irradiance. One study of residential solar projects[5] found that the median IRR was highest in Australia, India and Italy, with intermediate values in Brazil, China, Germany, the USA (Hawaii) and the UK.

Summary

This chapter has shown which factors to take into account when applying discounted cash flow analysis to a solar power project. The fact that the appropriate discount rate varies from one developer to another leads us to use the IRR as our measure of economic viability since it does not involve any assumption about a discount rate. In practice, IRR for behind-the-meter projects varies from one jurisdiction to another dependent on the solar irradiance and the electricity tariff. For utility-scale projects, the determining factors are the PPA and the solar irradiance. When comparing alternative projects using IRR, it is important that the projects have a similar level of risk.

Takeaways

- Definitions
  - The Net Present Value (NPV) of a solar project is the discounted value of the stream of cash flows over the lifetime of the project including its capital cost.
  - The Internal Rate of Return (IRR) is the discount rate at which the NPV is zero.
- Factors needed for IRR calculation
  - Lifetime of the project, income in year zero, rate of increase in electricity prices in the future, rate of degradation of solar modules, operations and maintenance costs, inverter replacement cost, battery cell replacement cost, capital cost of solar plus battery, end-of-life recycling costs.
- Main factors that determine whether a location has a high IRR
  - Solar irradiance, electricity tariff or power purchase agreement.

- Use of IRR
  - When we do not have a discount rate available, the IRR can be used to rank projects of similar risk level in order of profitability.
  - When we do know the discount rate, it can be used as a yardstick against which to compare the IRR of various projects. Projects whose IRR is less than the discount rate should not go ahead.

Probe Deeper: The Why?

Why use IRR to compare among alternative projects? Because it avoids having to assume a value for the discount rate. However, it should not be used to compare projects with different levels of risk.

Process

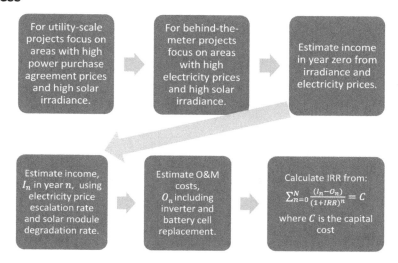

For utility-scale projects focus on areas with high power purchase agreement prices and high solar irradiance.

For behind-the-meter projects focus on areas with high electricity prices and high solar irradiance.

Estimate income in year zero from irradiance and electricity prices.

Estimate income, I_n in year n, using electricity price escalation rate and solar module degradation rate.

Estimate O&M costs, O_n including inverter and battery cell replacement.

Calculate IRR from:
$$\sum_{n=0}^{N} \frac{(I_n - O_n)}{(1+IRR)^n} = C$$
where C is the capital cost

Notes

1 Deceglie, M.G., Jordan, D.C., Nag, A., Shinn A., Deline, C., 2019, "Fleet-Scale Energy-Yield Degradation Analysis Applied to Hundreds of Residential and Nonresidential Photovoltaic Systems," *IEEE Journal of Photovoltaics*, 9(2), DOI: 10.1109/JPHOTOV.2018.2884948.
2 NREL, U.S. Solar Photovoltaic System and Energy Storage Cost Benchmark, 2021. National Renewable Energy Laboratory, USA.
3 Di Francia, G., 2013. "The Impact of Recycling Policies on the Photovoltaic Levelized Cost of the Electricity," *International Conference on Renewable*

Energy Research and Applications, Madrid, Spain. pp. 979–983, DOI: 10.1109/ICRERA.2013.6749894

4 MacDougall, H., Tomosk, S., Wright, D.J., 2018, "Geographic Maps of the Impact of Government Incentives on the Economic Viability of Solar Power", *Renewable Energy*, 122:497–506, doi.org/10.1016/j.renene.2017.12.108

5 Rodrigues, Sandy, Torabikalaki, Roham, Faria, Fábio, Cafôfo, Nuno, Chen, Xiaoju, Ivaki, Ashkan Ramezani, Mata-Lima, Herlander, Morgado-Dias, F., 2016, "Economic Feasibility Analysis of Small Scale PV Systems in Different Countries", *Solar Energy*, 131:81–95, https://doi.org/10.1016/j.solener.2016.02.019

6
Levelized Cost of Electricity

Introduction

This chapter and the previous one describe alternative approaches to assessing the profitability of solar power. The previous chapter focused on the internal rate of return from a solar project, whereas this chapter focuses on the cost of the electricity produced. To compare among different generating options, this chapter equips us with a measure known as the levelized cost electricity (LCOE) from each alternative.

What LCOE is for

The aim of LCOE is to come up with a single measure of the cost ($/kWh) of all the electricity generated over the life of a generating system. This is useful if we are comparing among several alternative generating systems. For instance, if a mining company is expanding an off-grid mining operation and is considering a diesel generator or solar plus battery, they could calculate the LCOE of each option and compare them from a cost perspective. There are four major points to take into account before using LCOE:

1. LCOE is a "levelized" cost. It is levelized or, in a sense, averaged over all years of operation of the solar installation. The cost of generating electricity may be more in some years than others, for example, the years in which we need to replace battery cells. The amount of electricity generated may be more in some years than others, for example, years at the start of the project when the solar modules have not had much time to degrade. These variabilities are leveled out in the LCOE.
2. LCOE deals with annual totals, that is, total electricity generated and total cost in a year. LCOE assumes that enough electricity is being generated to meet requirements at all hours and months throughout the year.

DOI: 10.4324/9781003262435-8

3. The costs in LCOE need to be applied to electricity that is actually used, not to excess. If there is a possibility that solar output will be curtailed during the course of the project, the electricity output in the LCOE calculation should be net of curtailment.

4. There is nothing in LCOE that considers the price at which the electricity is sold or the savings on the electricity bill for behind-the-meter applications. LCOE deals only with cost, not with income.

Points 1–3 are also true of the internal rate of return (IRR) that we discussed in the previous chapter. IRR is a rate of return "levelized" or averaged over the whole life of a solar installation, based on annual cash flows.

It is point 4 that really distinguishes IRR and LCOE and makes IRR useful for grid-connected projects where we have a dollar value for the power generated. On the other hand, LCOE is more suited to off-grid projects when electricity is generated and used within a single business operation without any payment being made. For instance, a mobile phone company may operate its own solar modules to supply power to off-grid base stations, but there is no actual dollar payment involved. The way to compare between solar plus battery and wind plus battery for this application is to compare costs, i.e. the two LCOEs.

Even if there is a dollar payment, LCOE is useful at the planning stage when we are choosing which generating technology to use. If we are supplying electricity to an island or to a rural community, we can calculate the LCOE of solar plus battery, wind plus battery and diesel and use the results to compare those options from a cost perspective. When one is selected and electricity is flowing, customers will almost certainly be paying for it, but those payments would be the same whichever technology was selected, and are not therefore relevant to choosing among our three options.

How to Calculate LCOE

In year n, we have operating costs O_n (\$) and we generate E_n (kWh) of electricity. In year n, the cost of generating electricity is therefore O_n/E_n (\$/kWh).

The aim of LCOE is to average out these costs over the lifetime of the solar project. To do that, we total up the discounted values at our discount rate, d, giving:

$$\text{LCOE} = \frac{\sum_{n=0}^{N} \dfrac{O_n}{(1+d)^n} + C}{\sum_{n=0}^{N} \dfrac{E_n}{(1+d)^n}}$$

where C is the capital cost in year zero.

As with the net present value (NPV) in Chapter 5, the LCOE depends on the discount rate.

Relationship between LCOE and IRR

Suppose we were to sell the electricity we generate at a price equal to the LCOE. We would not be making any profit since we are selling at cost, but we would be making an IRR. The Mathbox shows that this IRR is equal to the discount rate.

This result applies to a situation where we know a discount rate and have used it to calculate an LCOE. The result says that, if we sell electricity at a price equal to the LCOE, then our IRR will equal the discount rate. This gives two ways of looking at a project that is borderline as to whether it is profitable or not. It is borderline if the price we get for our electricity equals the cost of producing it. Alternatively,

> **Mathbox: LCOE and IRR**
>
> In Chapter 5, we used the notation I_n to represent the income. We analyze the case where that income is derived from selling E_n kWh of electricity at a price equal to LCOE:
>
> $$I_n = \text{LCOE} * E_n$$
>
> Using this in the equation above that defines LCOE, and flipping the denominator to the left side, we have:
>
> $$\sum_{n=0}^{N} \frac{I_n}{(1+d)^n} = \sum_{n=0}^{N} \frac{O_n}{(1+d)^n} + C$$
>
> Combining the two summations and comparing with our definition of IRR in Chapter 5:
>
> $$\sum_{n=0}^{N} \frac{(I_n - O_n)}{(1+\text{IRR})^n} = C$$
>
> we see that $\text{IRR} = d$.

it is borderline if the IRR equals the discount rate. A project is profitable if the selling price is higher than the LCOE or if the IRR is greater than the discount rate. Thus, the LCOE approach in this chapter is consistent with the IRR approach in Chapter 5.

If we know the discount rate, we can use it to calculate LCOE and we can also use it as a yardstick against which to compare IRR. If we do not know a discount rate, we cannot calculate LCOE but we can calculate IRR and compare the IRRs of different alternative projects to choose among them.

Examples of LCOE

In this section we give a case study of how to use LCOE for a comparison among generating technologies and also for a comparison among alternative locations.

Figure 6.1 Locations for LCOE analysis in Saudi Arabia. The number in brackets indicates the ranking of the locations for solar plus battery.

Saudi Arabia is planning a transition to renewable energy for off-grid villages currently using diesel generators and is interested to know which locations are most suitable. We used HOMER[1] to calculate the LCOE for seven locations distributed around the country[2] as shown in Figure 6.1. The results are given in Table 6.1 for solar, solar and wind and wind power.

Table 6.1 LCOE ($/kWh) for seven locations in Saudi Arabia for three different electricity generation options

	Solar and battery	Solar, wind and battery	Wind and battery
Al-Jouf	0.12	0.123	0.251
Al-Wajih	0.118	0.132	
Hafr-Batin	0.129	0.131	0.375
Jeddah	0.12	0.132	0.341
Riyadh	0.124	0.135	
Sharurah	0.121	0.119	0.207
Yanbu	0.12	0.112	0.146

HOMER optimizes the size of each component and in each case, a battery was included since these are off-grid projects.

It can be seen that solar gives a much lower LCOE than wind. Two locations, Al-Wajih and Riyadh, were not windy enough for a realistic LCOE calculation. A third option is to combine wind and solar, which does in fact marginally reduce the LCOE in Sharurah and Yanbu, but the other five locations have lower LCOE using solar without wind. Adding solar to wind significantly reduces LCOE, but adding wind to solar has only a marginal impact on LCOE.

The results can be used to rank the locations in order of LCOE and Figure 6.1 includes that ranking for solar without wind. It should be noted that there is not a very large difference in LCOE among these locations.

Summary

This chapter has described the circumstances in which it is useful to calculate the LCOE and has given the calculation necessary. LCOE is a weighted average of the costs incurred over the life of a project divided by a weighted average of the amounts of electricity generated. Calculating the LCOE requires an assumption of the discount rate. We have also shown that the LCOE approach and the IRR approach are equivalent from the point of view of recommending whether a project is sufficiently profitable to go ahead. A case study from Saudi Arabia shows how to use LCOE to compare between solar and wind and also to rank possible project locations in order of LCOE.

Takeaways

- Definition
  - LCOE is the sum of the discounted costs ($) divided by the sum of the discounted amounts of electricity generated (kWh).
- Factors needed for LCOE calculation
  - Lifetime of the project, discount rate, operations and maintenance costs, inverter replacement cost, battery cell replacement cost, capital cost of solar plus battery, end-of-life recycling costs, annual electricity generation.
- Use of LCOE
  - LCOE can be used at the planning stage of off-grid projects where we are choosing among alternative generating technologies or among different locations for an installation.

Probe Deeper: The Why?

Why calculate LCOE for a solar project? Because we want to compare the cost of solar electricity with the cost of electricity from an alternative generating technology, for example, wind. Because we are not selling the electricity we generate but using it internally within our company, so that there is no revenue that can be used to calculate IRR or profitability.

Process

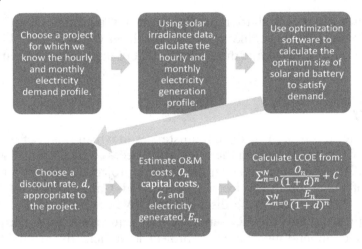

Choose a project for which we know the hourly and monthly electricity demand profile.

Using solar irradiance data, calculate the hourly and monthly electricity generation profile.

Use optimization software to calculate the optimum size of solar and battery to satisfy demand.

Choose a discount rate, d, appropriate to the project.

Estimate O&M costs, O_n capital costs, C, and electricity generated, E_n.

Calculate LCOE from:

$$\frac{\sum_{n=0}^{N} \frac{O_n}{(1+d)^n} + C}{\sum_{n=0}^{N} \frac{E_n}{(1+d)^n}}$$

Notes

1 HOMER, https://www.homerenergy.com/
2 Al Garni, H.Z., Mas'ud, A.A., Wright, D.J., Design and Performance Assessment of a Hybrid Solar-Wind System in Saudi Arabia using HOMER, Sustainable Energy Technologies and Assessments, Vol. 48, https://doi.org/10.1016/j.seta.2021.101675.

7
Solar Finance

Introduction

Electric power generation is a capital-intensive business and solar is no exception. The purpose of this chapter is to identify ways of attracting investors to fund the capital cost of solar installations.

Finding Roofs or Finding Capital?

In 2012, a solar developer explained his job to me. "My job is to find roofs. I have an investor who will front the capital for any rooftop solar project. I just have to convince building owners to let me use their roofs". Things were different in 2012, investors saw the profits available from the feed-in-tariffs (FITs) but, for building owners, solar was very new. There was a lot of money chasing a few projects. Today FITs have been largely phased out, but the cost of solar has dropped to the point where developers see many great project opportunities. Now we have a lot of projects competing to attract money.

There are two sources of capital: debt and equity. For small- to medium-sized projects in the solar industry, debt means a bank loan and equity means private equity. The bank finances the construction of a solar project and is repaid with interest at a time specified in the future. The private equity company injects some capital in return for partial ownership of the solar company and sometimes an ongoing return on their investment in the form of dividends.

For large projects, a company can issue tradable securities on the bond market, which is lower cost than a bank loan. Issuing shares on the stock market is less expensive than dealing with private equity companies and is also suited to raising large amounts of equity financing. In this chapter, we will see how these two basic models are being used to provide the solar industry with large amounts of capital at low costs.

DOI: 10.4324/9781003262435-9

We can divide the solar industry into two parts: (i) developers building solar projects and (ii) operating companies, called YieldCos, running the solar projects once they are built and selling the electricity generated. Constructing a solar project is riskier than operating one. Construction projects are subject to cost overruns, delays, supply chain issues, etc., and solar projects are no exception. By contrast, operating a solar project involves less uncertainty. The solar modules sit there generating electricity, which has a well-defined dollar value. They need regular cleaning and occasionally failed modules need replacing under warranty – relatively small and mostly predictable costs. These differences in risk level are a major reason for companies in the industry to focus on one or the other part of the business. Another reason is the type of financing they need.

A developer is typically set up by investors who buy shares representing the proportion of the company each investor owns. This equity financing is leveraged by borrowing a larger amount to finance the cost of a solar construction project. Debt financing is typically used for construction projects since the debt can be secured against a real asset, namely the solar project. Smaller companies can take out a bank loan and larger ones can issue debt in the form of a tradable security, which is sold on the bond markets, for instance, to institutional investors. In each case, the loan has to be repaid at maturity and interest has to be paid to the lender. Since solar projects generate power for 30 years, it seems at first sight that the only type of loan that is appropriate would have a term of around 30 years. This is very restrictive and many lenders want to see their money back faster than that. Enter the YieldCo.

YieldCos buy solar projects from developers after they are constructed, commissioned and are generating electricity. They get the capital needed for this either from private equity investors or by issuing shares on the stock market (i.e. they use equity financing). Investors purchase shares and receive a dividend corresponding to the value of the electricity generated by the YieldCo less the costs of operating the projects. When a YieldCo's shares are listed on a stock market, it is very easy to trade them, generating liquidity for the YieldCo and the opportunity to invest in solar power generation for retail investors as well as institutional investors.

When a YieldCo purchases a project from a developer, the developer is able to repay their loan, issue more debt and start building their next project. Figure 7.1 summarizes the relationship between a developer and a YieldCo and we now move into more detail on each of these companies, for which we first need a look at "securitization", the process involved in creating a tradable security.

Figure 7.1 Characteristics of a developer and a YieldCo and the relationship between them.

Securitization

Let's follow a developer for a few years of its life starting when it has some capital from its investors for constructing solar projects. The first project is utility-scale and sells electricity to the grid under a power purchase agreement (PPA), and is followed by behind-the-meter projects that are smaller and are constructed on commercial or residential rooftops under contract to the building owner. Upon completion of each project, the developer hires an independent consulting company to provide an assessment of the amount of electricity being generated by the project. They also hire an engineering firm to inspect the installation for quality of construction. These third-party evaluations are useful later, when the developer wants to sell the project.

When a behind-the-meter (BTM) project is completed, some building owners purchase electricity from the developer under a PPA, others pay for the project outright and yet others negotiate a loan from the developer. The loan agreement specifies the amount lent by the developer and a schedule of repayments by the building owner to the developer. Both projects with PPAs and also loan agreements involve outlays of capital by the developer and there is a limit to the amount of capital available. Eventually, the developer needs an inflow of investment to finance the construction of their next project. One option, stated above, is for the developer to sell a project and its PPA to a YieldCo, but suppose no YieldCo wants to buy. A second option is to assemble a bundle of PPAs and loan agreements into a tradable security that can be sold on the bond market. To attract institutional investors, the total value should be at least $100m. The process of bundling PPAs and loan agreements into a tradable security is called securitization. Both PPAs and loan agreements specify a future stream of income, exactly the sort of thing institutional investors are looking for. However, the typical pension fund does not have the expertise to evaluate the riskiness of solar PPAs and solar project loans. Enter rating agencies such as Moody's and Standard and Poor's, as shown in Figure 7.2.

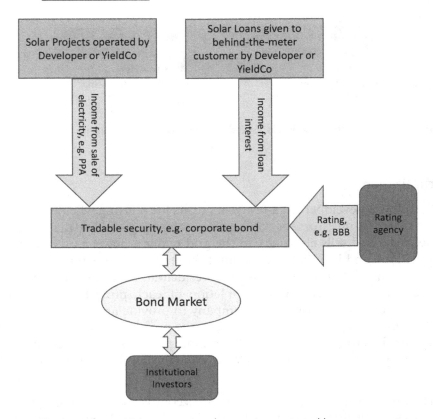

Figure 7.2 Process of securitizing power-purchase agreements and loan agreements.

To assess risk, ratings agencies do not spend much time on the details of each individual project, since third-party assessments have already been obtained. The rating agency is more interested in the mix of types of projects in a security. The greater the diversity in the types of project, the more the risk is spread. A bundle of solar projects on the roofs of office buildings in Northern California would not be attractive because all these projects are subject to the same risk of a downturn in the local economy causing defaults, a change in the electricity tariff affecting profitability, a change in environmental regulations, an earthquake, etc. A more attractive bundle would consist of some solar, some wind, and some hydro in different climate zones in different countries. A few projects may fail, a few borrowers may default but there is no single source of risk that could impact a large number of projects.

Once the rating agency has given its rating (BBB and above is "investment grade"), the security can be offered, for example, on the bond market for institutional investors to purchase. The purchase provides the developer with funds with which to finance its next solar project.

Bonds issued by solar developers can be purchased by any institutional investor. They can also be designated as "green" bonds to target two focused groups of investors. First are "thematic" investors who pursue specific types of investment, for example, solar or renewable energy in general. The second are ESG investors who invest in companies with high ratings for environmental, social and governance (ESG) performance. In Europe, green bonds are particularly well established compared with other jurisdictions. Certifications agencies such as Sustainalytics and Climate Bonds Initiative can be employed to certify that a bond meets their environmental requirements.

This process of securitization is summarized in Figure 7.2, and we now explore more detail about the workings of developers and YieldCos.

Developers

There are four ways for developers to raise capital to finance the construction of their next project:

1. Bundle PPAs from existing projects into a tradable security.
2. Bundle loan agreements from existing BTM customers into a tradable security.
3. Obtain a bank loan: good for small projects, but with a high interest rate. The bank will usually choose a consulting company to perform an independent risk assessment. The consultant will typically be paid by the developer.
4. Sell an existing project to a YieldCo: good if a YieldCo can be found that will offer an acceptable price.

In this section, we will focus on the securitization options 1 and 2. There is not much to say about bank loans and the relationship with YieldCos is discussed in the last section of this chapter.

Bundling Power Purchase Agreements into a Tradable Security

The main reason for issuing tradable securities is for the developer to access large amounts of capital from institutional investors ($100m and up) at interest rates lower than bank loans. A single, large project could meet that minimum. According to the costing in Chapter 1, the capital cost of a utility-scale project is about $1/W, so that a 100 MW project needs about

$100m of capital to construct. However, investors prefer to invest in multiple projects to spread their risk, so that it would be better to bundle a $100m project with other projects to make a larger security, say $500m. The bundle can consist of utility-scale, commercial/industrial and residential projects so long as there is a contract for sale of electricity specifying a future stream of income for the developer. PPAs are normal for utility-scale projects selling to the grid. They are also used for supplying electricity to industrial customers like a data center of a cloud computing provider, and for selling electricity from rooftop installations to building owners, for example, office buildings or residences. What institutional investors are interested in acquiring is the future stream of income from these PPAs.

The diversification in the portfolio of projects from a single developer may be limited. They may operate in a certain geography and specialize in a certain type of project. Also they may not have enough projects to make up a $100m minimum. In these cases, they can employ the services of a company such as Mosaic Solar that makes tradable securities by bundling together projects from several different developers.

Once a bundle of projects has been assembled, it needs to be rated by a rating agency and the security needs to be underwritten by an insurance company. For this, they can employ the services of kWh Analytics, a company that has accumulated a database of solar projects including the amount of electricity that they have generated to date. They sell access to this database to insurance companies underwriting securities so that they can check whether forecasts of electricity generation are reasonable and can reliably provide the projected future streams of income from PPAs.

Bundling Loan Agreements into a Tradable Security

For commercial and industrial solar projects, the developer is building the project for the commercial or industrial client. In this case, the client may pay for the project outright or may pay over time by having the developer loan the project capital to them. Developers perform due diligence on the credit-worthiness of the borrowers to avoid defaults of the loans. They need capital of their own to provide these loans, and ultimately, there is a limit on how much the developer has available. At some point, they can bundle together a large number of project loans to make a tradable security, which they can offer to institutional investors. Again, about $100m of projects is needed and these projects can come from a number of different developers. Because the risk of investing in multiple projects is lower than investing in a single project; developers will typically receive more attractive interest rates from lenders when they can securitize loans from multiple projects. Institutional investors are familiar with securitized car loans and leases, and had a bad experience[*] with securitized mortgages in 2008–2009, so they need an assessment of the risk of the borrowers defaulting, as well as the risk of the projects themselves failing. They have available credit-checks on borrowers and independent assessments of the quality of the projects themselves. As with PPAs, the security is assessed by a rating agency, to check how the risk of default of individual loans is spread over a diverse mix of loan types.

Residential projects can be financed in a similar way to commercial and industrial projects, and here the analogy with a car loan is particularly relevant. Using the capital costs of $2.85/W for residential projects from Chapter 3, an 8 kW project on a residential roof costs approximately $2.85*8*1000 = $22,800, comparable with buying a car. Only 10–20% of people pay cash for a car, while most of the rest take out a car loan and some lease the vehicle. People are used to getting loans for large capital outlays and expect the same to be available for a solar installation. The developer can initially provide the loans to the customers and then bundle a large number of residential solar projects in with other renewable energy projects to make a tradable security. Car manufacturers do this for car loans and institutional investors are familiar with the resulting securities, lending over 90% of the total value of the individual loans. This ratio, known as the "advance rate", is much lower for securitized residential solar loans (around 75%) since this is a new asset class in the investment industry.

Investors purchasing securitized loans are interested in the future stream of loan payments specified in the loan agreements, similar to the streams of future payments in securitized PPAs.

YieldCos

The YieldCo purchases projects and operates them, obtaining revenue from sale of electricity and incurring some operations and maintenance costs. From the net income, it then pays dividends to investors, retaining some income for contingencies and for purchasing more projects.

This is a low-risk business. PPAs provide utility-scale and some BTM projects with a predictable stream of revenues, and maintenance costs on solar modules generally amount to regular cleaning. YieldCos spread their risk

---

[*] Due to low creditworthiness of many individual borrowers, thus combining high risk with low diversification.

by diversifying into wind and hydro as well as solar and also may purchase projects in multiple geographies and even internationally.

In UK, YieldCos have been successful, generating 8.1% annual return compared with the Financial Times Stock Exchange All-Share Index of 8.2% but with much lower volatility, according to a report from Imperial College, London.[1]

There are two ways for YieldCos to raise capital to finance the purchase of their next project:

1. Sell shares to a private equity company
2. Issue shares on the stock market

Private equity is an expensive way to raise capital and is used when a YieldCo is too small to list on the stock market. Private equity investors in large solar projects need to keep track of how their investment is performing and therefore need access to data on electricity generation, O&M costs, equipment failures, etc. Some investment agreements have a clause allowing investors to access the operating company's database using standard data exchange protocols.

When a YieldCo lists on the stock market with an initial public offering (IPO), the sale of its shares brings in investment that it uses to purchase renewable energy projects from developers. A company needs to be a certain size to issue an IPO, and hence many of the solar projects it purchases are utility-scale, although it may also purchase bundles of commercial rooftop projects that generate revenue from selling electricity to the building owners or to the grid under PPAs.

YieldCos do not provide the excitement that day traders relish, but risk-averse investors are attracted to the very long-term and regular stream of dividends that shares in a YieldCo should provide, without expecting much capital gain. If investors need money for some other purpose, they can sell their shares, benefiting from the liquidity that the stock market provides. A stock market listing also provides transparency and the YieldCo is required to provide investors with quarterly reports on its finances and future plans.

Retained earnings remaining in a YieldCo after paying operations and maintenance costs and dividends can be used to buy more projects. A major purchase, such as buying a large utility-scale project or purchasing another YieldCo, may require more shares to be issued.

The options available to developers and YieldCos for raising capital are summarized in Figure 7.3.

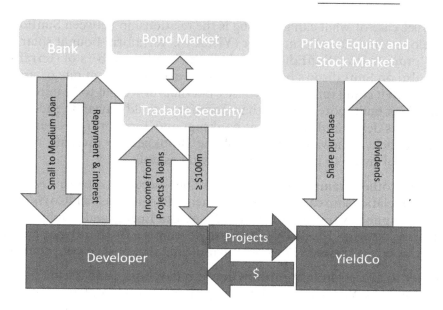

Figure 7.3 Solar industry sources of financing.

Developer – YieldCo Interaction

Some companies operate as both a developer and a YieldCo. For instance, SolarCity (now part of Tesla) installed solar modules on residential rooftops and sold the electricity to the homeowner at a discount to the price from the distribution company. SolarCity retained ownership of the project, even though it was on someone else's roof, and hence needed to front the capital costs for thousands of installations. Some homeowners took out a loan from SolarCity to own part of the installation. In 2016, it bundled 64 MW of residential installations together with the stream of income from loan interest and electricity sales into a security that was rated BBB (investment grade) by Standard and Poor's and sold for $185m. This was the first time an institutional investor had invested in residential solar in the public markets. Since then, the installed cost of solar has dropped and more homeowners are interested in owning their own projects.

YieldCos buy projects from developers and it is clear that there is a potential conflict of interest if they are not independent of each other. For instance, if a holding company owns both the developer and the YieldCo, or if the developer sets up the YieldCo as an investment vehicle controlled by itself, the issue arises as to whether the projects are transferred from the developer to the YieldCo at a fair price. This issue is very important to the investors who buy shares in the YieldCo.

A classic case of what can go wrong is the relationship between SunEdison (developer) and TerraForm Power (YieldCo). Terraform bought solar and wind projects from SunEdison but half the board members of Terraform were also on SunEdison's board. Terraform expected a high rate of growth with which it could fund the purchases, but that turned out to be unrealistic. SunEdison built more projects than Terraform could buy and needed cash to repay its debt. SunEdison went bankrupt and Terraform was purchased by Brookfield Renewables, thus enabling Brookfield to diversify from its portfolio of hydro to include solar and wind as well.

There are other examples that show just how successful a close developer/YieldCo relationship can be. NextEra Energy Partners (a YieldCo) is a very successful publicly traded subsidiary of NextEra Energy and purchases projects from NextEra Energy Resources (a developer). Its share price grew by 25–30% per year from 2017 to 2021, paralleling that of its parent company.

The key to success in relationships between developers and YieldCos is independence. A YieldCo should be able to buy projects from any developer. A developer should be able to sell projects to the highest-bidding YieldCo.

Summary

In this chapter, we have described four sources of finance for solar projects including bank loans, issuing tradable securities and private and public equity. Developers use the first two to finance the construction of solar projects. They sell projects to YieldCos who use private and public equity to finance the purchases. The YieldCos operate the projects, obtaining income from PPAs and interest payments on loans. The relationship between developers and YieldCos needs to include an element of independence to reduce risk. We have seen how to assure the investment community about the low level of risk in the solar industry by bundling a diverse range of projects into a tradable security and getting it rated by a ratings agency.

Takeaways

- Developing a solar project is high risk, operating one is low risk.
- Debt financing is suitable for the developer; equity financing is suitable for the operating company, which is known as a YieldCo.
- Developers sell projects to YieldCos, enabling them to pay off their debt and develop their next project.
- Loans and PPAs from several projects can be combined together into tradable securities and rated by agencies such as Moody's and Standard and Poor's.

- A diverse mix of projects (e.g. wind, solar and hydro in different parts of the world) is key to reducing risk and hence the cost of capital.
- To further reduce risk, developers and YieldCos should be independent of each other and YieldCos should buy projects from multiple developers.

Probe Deeper: The Why?

Why would an institutional investor buy a bundle of solar projects from a developer? They want to acquire the stream of income from the PPAs and the loan repayments. Why would an investor buy shares in a YieldCo on the stock market? They want the liquidity of being able to sell the shares at any time plus the dividend payments they expect from the YieldCo.

Process

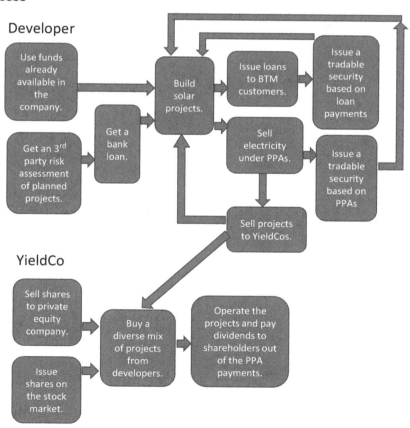

Note

1 Donovan, Charles, UK Green Companies Generate Greater Returns for Clean Energy Investing, Centre for Climate Finance and Investment at Imperial College, London, https://www.imperial.ac.uk/news/186375/uk-green-companies-generate-greater-returns/

8
Managing Risk

Introduction

The U.S. National Renewable Energy Lab says,[1] "The main stumbling block for solar financing is assessing the risk of the investment". In this chapter, we will identify what those risks are and how to mitigate them by good management practices. Sometimes we can transfer the risk to someone else, for instance, a subcontractor, a manufacturer (using their warranty) or an insurance company.

As you read this chapter, you might want to have at the back of your mind the question of who is taking the risk. During construction, the developer is taking the risk, but so is the investor who has given a loan to that developer. During project operation by a YieldCo, they are certainly taking the risk and also their equity investors have their money on the line. The financing arrangements described in the previous chapter are related to the risks identified in this chapter since investors need to be confident the risk in their investment is being managed as well as possible.

Many risks cannot be measured; the best we can do is to reduce them by some of the management methods described here. We will start with international standards, compliance with which is important for risk mitigation. Then we will deal with risks that apply during a specific stage of a solar project: planning, project development and project operation. The last section of this chapter analyses those risks that can be measured quantitatively and shows how to calculate their impact on internal rate of return (IRR) and levelized cost of electricity (LCOE).

International Standards

Compliance with international standards is used to reduce risk during design and manufacture of solar modules and at all stages of developing and

DOI: 10.4324/9781003262435-10

operating a solar project. The International Electrotechnical Commission (IEC) has provided standards specific to the solar industry and companies such as IECRE (IEC Renewable Energy) provide inspections and issue certificates to confirm that the standard is being met. Investors regard such certifications as important in reducing the risk involved in investing in solar projects. Some of the standards available at the time of writing, in 2021, are described briefly in Table 8.1. Standards are always a work in progress and are continuously being updated, particularly for emerging technologies. For instance, at the time of writing, IEC 61853 on solar module testing applies only to one-sided, flat modules and is currently being extended to include bifacial modules and curved, building-integrated modules, which are commercially available today.[*] Investors are nervous about funding projects involving technology that is not covered by international standards and it is important that standards keep pace with industry needs, despite the fact that this requires consensus and/or majority votes by standards committees in all countries interested in contributing to the process.

Table 8.1 IEC standards related to solar projects

IEC standard	Applies to...	Covers...
61215	Solar module	Testing of solar modules suitable for long-term operation in open-air climates up to 70°C
61724-1	Solar system	Performance metrics and monitoring equipment
61724-2 and 3	Solar system	Electricity production: actual vs expected
61730-1	Solar module	Safety for electric shock and fire due to mechanical and environmental stress
61853	Solar module	Performance testing and energy rating
62548	Solar power plant	Design safety for solar modules, wiring and electrical protection devices, excluding batteries and inverters
62446-1	Solar power plant	Commissioning tests, inspection criteria and documentation for safe installation and correct operation
62446-2 and 3	Solar power plant	Maintenance of roof-top and ground-mounted solar projects for reliability, safety, fire prevention and performance
62738	Solar power plant	Design and installation of ground-mounted, grid-connected solar power plants
62817	Solar tracker	Test procedures for solar trackers including both key components and the complete tracker system
62941	Solar module	Product design, manufacturing processes, and selection and control of materials used in the manufacture of solar modules
63049	Solar power plant	Activities necessary to implement an effective quality assurance program for installation, operation and maintenance of a solar power plant
63126	Solar module	Testing requirements for solar modules operating above 70°C

[*] These technologies are discussed in Chapter 13.

Planning

Planning a solar project is extremely important. It is at this stage that we estimate its IRR and LCOE and decide whether the project is economically attractive enough to go ahead. Simply comparing the IRR with a hurdle rate is not enough, even if the hurdle rate is adjusted for risk, see sidebar.[2] Instead we need to explicitly address each source of risk.

When we come up with a value for IRR or LCOE, it is important to recognize that it is only an "estimate". We are projecting 30 years into the

How NOT to Do Risk Assessment

"Models for investment in the power sector rarely provide an explicit treatment of risk. Often it is assumed that, given a hurdle discount rate for the cost of capital, NPV positive investments will happen; sometimes the hurdle rates are increased for project risk, but these tend to be ad hoc suggestions".

future and can never be sure what the profitability of our project will be. One thing we can do is to identify which factor has the biggest impact on our estimated profitability and the answer turns out to be the capital cost. The costs given in Chapters 1–3 are estimates for the USA and can be used to get an initial estimate of profitability. But we should firm up this estimate as soon as possible by getting quotes from suppliers. If we are doing the installations ourselves, we will need quotes from competing suppliers of solar modules, inverters, wiring, racking, trackers, etc. If we are outsourcing the installation to another company, we need quotes on the price of a fully installed and operational system from two or three alternative installers.

Other important steps to take at the planning stage include:

- *Firming up the Operations and Maintenance (O&M) costs.* If we are doing the O&M ourselves, we need to modify the estimates in Chapters 1–3 according to our past experience of O&M costs on similar projects, taking into account the travel time to the project site.
- *Ensuring it is sunny enough.* There are many databases of solar irradiance measurements, and some days are sunnier than others. These short-term fluctuations average out over a 30-year project and have very little effect on IRR and LCOE estimates. However, year-to-year variations are more troublesome and a long history of measurements is needed to even out these fluctuations. Satellite estimates go back longer but are less accurate than ground-based measurements, which are more recent in many parts of the world. Another source of risk is the way in which the data was compiled. Some databases provide many years of hourly data from

which we can calculate the mean, median or a percentile as we wish. Use of, say, the 10th percentile of irradiance gives a 0.9 probability that the irradiance is above this value, which is often referred to as P90 (more on this in Chapter 10). Other irradiance databases provide a "typical meteorological year" in which the January measurements may come from 2005, and the February measurements may come from 1999, etc. The database provider has analyzed past years and months and decided 2005 was most representative of January and 1999 was most representative of February. Providers of solar modeling software may have built their own database that they use to estimate electricity production from any given site. The bottom line here is to check out the profitability of a project based on multiple datasets and using different software packages.

- *Ensuring that we can obtain the necessary land.* This is particularly important for utility-scale projects that require a lot of land. Before bidding in a power purchase agreement (PPA) auction, we do not need to actually purchase or lease the land, but we should be sure to negotiate the *option* to purchase or lease it if our PPA bid is accepted.
- *Obtaining planning permission.* Again, before negotiating a PPA, we must apply to the local authorities for planning permission to construct the project. Planning permission needs to be obtained for roof-top projects as well as for ground-mount projects.
- *Obtaining grid connection.* If we are planning to sell power to the grid, we must obtain permission for the connection. This is not just a matter of paperwork. The issue is whether the local distribution line or transmission line has sufficient capacity to accept the power we are generating. There are sad tales of farmers who built solar projects on their fields only to find that the distribution line to their farm was designed to supply the few tens of kW that a typical farm needs. It simply was not engineered to carry the hundreds of kW generated by the solar project. Who would pay to upgrade the line? not the distribution company, not the farmer. Even if the line has the capacity, the distribution or transmission company may not actually need any more electric power at that particular location.
- *Obtaining insurance.* There are basically two types of insurance relevant to solar projects: loss of physical assets and business interruption. The physical assets, i.e. the solar modules and racking, may be damaged by a storm, flood, theft, vandalism, etc. Asset insurance should provide the cost of replacement, i.e. the new equipment plus its installation. However, it takes time to replace damaged equipment and all the while that equipment is not generating electricity. Business interruption insurance covers the cost of that lost electricity in addition to the cost of replacing

the equipment. It also gives the insurance company an incentive to replace the equipment fast.

- *Obtaining political instability guarantees.* War, terrorism, civil disturbance, etc. are not covered by insurance companies. However, many countries with high solar irradiance are politically unstable and developers are risking valuable assets by installing solar projects there. Protection can be obtained from the Multilateral Investment Guarantee Agency (MIGA) of the World Bank, which covers both physical asset loss and business interruption; see the sidebar example from Chad in the Sahara.

> **Solar in the Sahara**
>
> Chad, a country including part of the Sahara desert has very high solar irradiance and seems to be a natural place for large solar projects. But it was tough to get insurance in a country bordering Libya, Niger and Sudan from which conflicts can spill over the border.
>
> Then, in 2020, MIGA approved a €15m guarantee for a 32 MW project just outside the capital city, providing 20 years of coverage against risk of expropriation, transfer restriction, breach of contract, war and civil disturbance.

Development

When a developer is building a behind-the-meter solar project for a commercial, industrial or residential customer to own or lease, the first step is to secure a contract with project details and price. The continued profitability of these projects over their lifetimes may depend on existing regulations and electricity tariffs remaining unchanged. For instance, a multi-site project using virtual net-metering can end up losing money if a future government removes the virtual net-metering option. To deal with this situation the developer may be able to negotiate an agreement with the current government to protect it from future regulatory changes.

In the case where the project will remain under the control of the developer and will supply power to the grid, the first step is to obtain a PPA specifying how much electricity is to be supplied and at what price. Many utility-scale projects have PPAs, ideally for 20–30 years, including price escalation clauses over that period. A risk-mitigation strategy for PPAs is for the developer to get a rating on the company purchasing the power, sometimes called the "offtaker" (e.g. from Moody's or Standard and Poor's). A high rating could indicate a low risk that the offtaker will default on its payments or go bankrupt over the lifetime of the project.

There is a trend for shorter-term PPAs (e.g. only ten years). These pose a problem for solar developers, since ten years of revenues may not be enough to offset the capital cost of the project, let alone produce a reasonable IRR. In ten years, the owner of a solar installation will be in a weak position to negotiate another PPA. They could sell electricity on the wholesale market, but what will the price be at that time? We could extrapolate past trends in wholesale market prices or hire a consultant to forecast the price. Either way, a ten-year PPA puts a solar developer in a difficult position, and is unattractive to investors too. They are not interested in solar projects per se; they are interested in continuing streams of revenues from PPAs.

During the actual construction, a solar project is subject to much the same risks as any other construction project and they are managed in much the same way.

- *Managing cost overruns and delivery delays in the supply chain.* Clearly contracts with suppliers include penalty clauses for not supplying items at the contracted price and delivery schedule. Nevertheless, things can go wrong and developers need to monitor suppliers' performance carefully to proactively anticipate problems and have alternative suppliers available as a backup.
- *Managing the quality of sub-contractors work.* Again, regular inspection of contractors' work can ensure that quality is maintained. In addition, developers sometimes obtain surety bonds from contractors, which cover risks that are not included in insurance coverage or contractual obligations. A surety bond is a contract between three parties, an insurance company and two parties to a construction contract, for instance, the developer and an electrical contractor. If the electrical contractor does not fulfill the obligations of their contract, the insurance company will make a payment to the developer.

Operations and Maintenance

One way of monitoring the operations of a solar project, through the lens of the YieldCo or their investors, is to track whether costs and income are in line with the estimates used during project planning. This provides an assessment of whether the project is on track to deliver the IRR or LCOE originally planned. A second approach is to ask the question: "Could we do better than those planning estimates?" For instance, are we doing as well as other YieldCos in our geographical area? These questions can be answered using databases of solar project performance data that have been accumulated over the years from many operating solar projects. YieldCos released this data on condition that it will be anonymized and aggregated with data from other projects before being made available to other YieldCos as shown in Figure 8.1. The bigger the database, the better each individual project, and each YieldCo can be benchmarked against industry averages. Investors use these databases to track how well the YieldCo they have invested in is doing compared with their competitors and whether there are any trends indicating that their YieldCo may become riskier in the future.

YieldCos often outsource the O&M of their projects to companies that specialize in that area, resulting in the need to exchange information among O&M contractor, YieldCo and investors. One way to reduce the cost of such data exchange is to use an industry standard from National Renewable Energy Lab (NREL) called "Orange Button."[3] This defines thousands of terms used in the solar industry and assigns each of them a standardized data format. It also uses this terminology to define a standard applications programming interface (API), which can be used by third parties to access a company's database; see Figure 8.2. For instance, an O&M contractor could authorize a YieldCo to use its API to monitor its performance database. The YieldCo's software then accesses the contractor's database without the need for manual intervention.

We will now describe how to deal with risks during the operation of a solar project according to what is impacted by the risk: costs, revenues or the relationship with trading partners, known as "counterparty risk".

Risk of Increased Costs

O&M costs include cleaning the solar modules and replacing failed parts, which depend on the geographical area where the project is located and whether it is roof-top or ground-mount. Cleaning modules sounds simple,

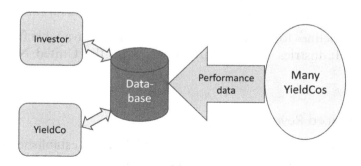

Figure 8.1 Collection of anonymized data for benchmarking purposes.

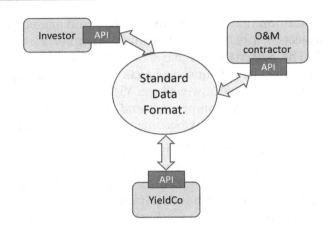

Figure 8.2 Use of standardized data format and applications programming interface (API) to facilitate data exchange among solar industry players.

but the cost depends on what you have to clean: near the coast, it is the sticky droppings of sea birds; in a desert, it is dust; in a field, it is vegetation growing up around the modules; in a city, it is particulate pollution from gasoline vehicles. Rainy places have lower O&M costs since the rain washes away the dust and dirt. The cost of replacing failed parts, similarly, depends on what has caused the failure – regular aging, theft, hail and sandstorms affect the modules themselves. Floods, hurricanes, lightning and earthquakes damage the supports and racking as well. When benchmarking our project against a database of other projects, it is important to use projects in similar locations with similar needs for maintenance. We also need to take into account the cost of travel to the site to perform the maintenance.

When a component fails, some of the cost of replacing it may come from the manufacturer's warranty or from insurance coverage. Across the industry, about half of insurance claims are weather-related so that locating a project in an area without extreme weather can reduce insurance premiums.

Detailed guidelines for effective risk management are available from the Solar Energy Industries Association (SEIA),[4] and the United Nations risk matrix.[5]

Risk of Reduced Revenues

When a solar project is operating under a PPA which establishes a price at which electricity is sold, a major source of risk is underperformance of the solar modules in generating electricity. If less electricity is generated than in the initial estimate for the project, revenue is affected in two ways, first from the simple fact that there is less electricity to sell and second from penalties that may apply under the PPA if less electricity is delivered than required under the PPA contract. The YieldCo needs to investigate whether such underperformance is an isolated event or evidence of a long-term trend. Two factors need to be considered in that investigation:

Volcanos

When a volcano erupts, it spews out ash into the upper atmosphere partially blocking the sun and reducing the electricity generation of solar modules. The ash spreads around the Earth affecting solar output globally. During the past 35 years, there have been four volcanos sufficiently powerful to reduce solar output by at least 20% for an entire year.

1. When comparing the electricity generated with the industry average in the local area, we need to use "weather-adjusted" figures. Clearly cloud cover impacts electricity generation and data for a particularly cloudy February should not be compared with the industry average for all Februarys over many years. What is less well known is that module temperature affects electricity production. It is an inverse effect: higher temperatures reduce electricity generation by 0.45% for each degree Celsius. The term "weather" should be interpreted broadly, including the need to adjust for volcanos, see sidebar.
2. Solar modules naturally degrade with age, producing 0.75% less electricity each year,[6] and this is built into the initial estimates of electricity generation. If the degradation rate is significantly higher, a warranty claim may be possible with the module supplier. Weather-adjusted year-on-year comparisons can be used to estimate degradation. Degradation must also be taken into account in comparisons with industry average electricity production data, by adjusting the production of modules according to their age.

PPA penalties for undersupply at certain times of day may be reduced by short-term forecasting of local weather. This allows a YieldCo to fully charge their batteries in advance of cloudy periods. Commercial weather forecasts are clearly useful for this and "sky imaging" is also used to predict clouds passing overhead. There is a blossoming consulting industry providing forecasts of solar generation a few hours ahead (sometimes called nowcasts) and also optimizing battery scheduling. Such approaches are low cost compared with the cost of PPA penalties, but if they are insufficient, it may be necessary to install additional solar modules and/or additional batteries.

Counterparty Risk

The main counterparty for a YieldCo is the offtaker who purchases the electricity generated. For a utility-scale project, this is the transmission company or the distribution company. For behind-the-meter projects, it is either a commercial building operator or a residence. Combining these together, the offtaker is either a company or a residence. The main risk here is default, i.e. non-payment over an extended period of time. Experience has shown that if a company fails to pay for 90–120 days, they are in default, i.e. the chance of them resuming payment is small. Legal action becomes necessary to enforce the PPA contract.

For residences, we need to be more flexible, and look at the reason for non-payment. The probability of resuming payment is high in the case of house sale, decease and divorce; intermediate in the case of foreclosure, and lower in the case of bankruptcy. The default rate on residential solar loans is also related to the same demographic factors (income, age, employment status) as the default rate on residential car loans.

Community solar power generation can be particularly susceptible to counterparty risk. A developer builds a solar project near a residential community and offers to supply electricity over the public electricity grid to residences at a discount to the regulated price from the distribution company. Some businesses may also purchase electricity from the community solar project under long-term contracts, which can be enforced in court, but residential customers have the right to switch suppliers and the maximum contract length is one or two years. Customer "churn" is therefore a potential problem with customers frequently switching from one supplier to another, particularly if several community solar projects are competing with each other. The key to reducing churn is a smooth transition from the distribution company to the community solar provider, with minimal paperwork, billing glitches and long hold times at the call center. When customers are happy with the community solar service, the churn rate is low.

Impact on Internal Rate of Return and Levelized Cost of Electricity

The risks described so far in this chapter are qualitative, as are the approaches to managing them. The *degree* of risk and the *extent* to which it has been reduced by our efforts is not measured quantitatively. However, at the end of the day, investors need to know how much profit they can expect and to what extent it might be reduced by risk. Insurance companies underwriting solar projects that are being bundled into a tradable security need as much of the risk as possible to be quantified. In Chapters 5 and 6 we showed how to calculate quantitatively the benefit of a solar project in terms of IRR (profitability) and LCOE (cost of electricity generated). Those calculations assume knowledge of several data items such as the capital costs, the O&M costs and the module degradation rate. P90 values are sometimes used to give estimates of IRR that we have a probability of 0.9 of exceeding, or estimates of LCOE that we have a probability of 0.9 of being below. This approach is described in Chapter 10. In the final section of this chapter, we investigate how much our estimates of IRR and LCOE are affected if our input data values are off by a given amount.

On the face of it, the approach is straightforward. If you estimate your annual O&M costs as $16/kW giving IRR = 17.6%, and you want to know what would happen if O&M costs were 10% higher, then you simply recalculate the IRR and get a new value, say IRR = 16.1%. This is known as scenario analysis and computers are very good at churning out the results of hundreds of different scenarios for multiple values of multiple data items. But which scenarios are interesting or useful or likely to happen in practice?

The simplest type of scenario analysis is sensitivity analysis in which we investigate what would happen if each of our data items was changed by a certain percentage, say ±10%. We are not saying that our data items *are* likely to be off by 10%, but we are investigating what would happen if they were. In the example in the previous paragraph, suppose that IRR becomes 14.9% if the capital costs increased by 10%. Then we conclude that it is more important to get an accurate estimate of capital costs than of O&M costs since capital costs have more impact on IRR that O&M costs do. This is useful but it does not give us an estimate of how much risk remains in a project after we have done our best at estimating data values.

Risk analysis is a second type of scenario analysis that involves estimating the range of data values that are *likely to happen in practice* and seeing what happens to IRR or LCOE for that range. For instance, suppose we estimate our annual O&M costs at $16/kW and we know from published reports of other similar projects, or from anonymized data in industry databases, that O&M costs range from $14.5/kW to $20.5/kW, then that is the range to use in calculating the impact on IRR or LCOE. These realistic ranges for data values are easier to get for some data items than for others. In one published study, degradation rate was measured for a large number of solar installations that had been operating for approximately ten years. Will they degrade more when they have been sitting out in the weather for 20 years? No one knows, and that is true of many data items. Will solar modules need more O&M expenditures 20 years after installation, and what will have happened to electricity prices? The good news is that it probably doesn't matter much, since cash flows far into the future are discounted a lot. A project giving an IRR of 17.6%, is discounting a cash flow 20 years in the future by multiplying it by $\frac{1}{1.176^{20}} = 0.039$. Whatever cost and revenue uncertainties there are in 20 years, only 3.9% of them will impact today's net present value.

The data item having the most impact on IRR and LCOE is the initial capital cost of installing the system, since solar projects, like any electricity generating projects, are very capital-intensive. However, this does not constitute a risk to an investor or to a developer, since contracts will be signed with suppliers and installers, firming up this capital cost, so that it does not contribute to the risk involved in the project itself. The only time that capital cost contributes to uncertainty is during the planning stage, before we have firm prices from contractors. At that stage we may be investigating whether to build the project this year or one or two years down the road. Estimates of capital costs for future years contribute to uncertainty in the planning process, but once we have decided when we want to build the project, we will obtain firm prices when we go out to tender with suppliers during the construction year.

The data item contributing the least risk to IRR and LCOE is the hour-by-hour variation in solar irradiance. At first sight, this may seem counter-intuitive. There is considerable variability in irradiance from one hour to another and electricity generation is directly affected. However, over the life of a solar project, these fluctuations cancel each other out, so that the effect on IRR and LCOE is very small.

I will illustrate the approaches described here with example results from projects I have been involved with. For IRR, I will use a behind-the-meter project in a medium irradiance city, Ottawa, Canada,[7] and for LCOE, I will use an off-grid project in the high irradiance area of Yanbu, Saudi Arabia.[8] We investigate the extent to which uncertainty in some data items contributes to the risk, either making IRR too low for an acceptable level of profitability or making LCOE too high compared with alternative ways of generating electricity. The numerical results will, of course, be different for projects in other locations, but they should give an idea of which data items have the greatest effect on IRR and LCOE and which have less effect.

The behind-the-meter project is on an office building and Table 8.2 gives the uncertainty in some of the data items and the corresponding proportional variability in IRR (i.e. a percentage of a percentage). For instance, suppose

Table 8.2 Example of the effect of uncertainty in input data items on IRR for a behind-the-meter solar project

Data item	Uncertainty in data item	Proportional variability in IRR
Capital cost	15%	45%
Annual O&M cost	15%	6%
Degradation rate, per year	25%	8.5%
Irradiance, hourly	14%	0.7%
Hourly electricity price, hourly	40%	0.5%

the IRR is 20% and its proportional variability is 5%, then the IRR varies between 20% ± 5% * 20%, i.e. 20% ± 1%, i.e. between 19% and 21%. This gives us a quantitative measure of risk: instead of the IRR being 20%, it could turn out to be 19%.

For both capital cost and O&M cost, the uncertainty is 15%; however, the effect on IRR is far greater in the case of capital cost, 45%, compared with 6%. Once contracts are signed and the developer is ready to start the project, the uncertainty in capital cost is removed. If we outsource O&M at a contracted price for several years, then the risk associated with uncertainty in that cost is transferred to the contractor. The risk associated with uncertainty in the degradation rate is only 8.5% of IRR. In this project, the savings on the electricity bill are based on the hourly electricity price on the wholesale market for electricity, which varies by ±40%[†] and the hourly electricity generation, which varies by ±14%[‡]. However, these variabilities almost cancel out over the life of the project and the impact on IRR is <1%.

We performed a similar analysis for an off-grid project to supply solar electricity to villages near Yanbu, Saudi Arabia, and the proportional variability in LCOE is given in Table 8.3. The same comments apply to capital cost, O&M cost and degradation rate as for IRR in Table 8.2. For this project, we separated out the costs of inverter and battery replacement half-way through the lifetime of the project and also the recycling cost at the end of the project. The latter is a small cost that is heavily discounted and uncertainty in the cost contributes only a tiny amount of risk. A major difference between LCOE and IRR is that LCOE requires an estimate of the discount rate. It can be seen from Table 8.3 that uncertainty in this estimate contributes significantly to the risk of the LCOE being too high. This is one reason

---

[†] Based on one standard deviation in the price data.
[‡] The same as the variability in the irradiance.

Table 8.3 Example of the effect of uncertainty in input data items on LCOE for an off-grid solar project

Data item	Uncertainty in data item	Proportional variability in LCOE
Capital cost	15%	13%
Annual O&M cost	15%	1.5%
Cost of inverter and battery replacement	15%	0.5%
Cost of recycling	15%	0.02%
Degradation rate, per year	25%	1.5%
Discount rate	20%	10%

why we prefer to use LCOE mainly for off-grid projects, for which there is no other measure of profitability available. Since LCOE is sensitive to the discount rate, we use IRR for other projects since IRR does not involve knowledge of the discount rate.

The above estimates of the variability in IRR and LCOE were obtained by re-running the IRR and LCOE calculation for different values of the input data items. This recalculation can be avoided by using an analytical formula for the change in IRR or LCOE as shown in the Optional Math Box. For some input data items, the analytical formula is 100% accurate, for others it was found to be off by <1%. Most software packages for the economic analysis of solar power provide sensitivity analysis in which the model is run repeatedly for different input data values. The advantages of the analytical approach are that it does not require re-running the model and therefore reduces computational requirements and improves response time to the user.

Optional Math Box

Analytical Approach to Risk Analysis

From Chapter 5, we know that IRR is the discount rate that gives a zero net present value (NPV):

$$\sum_{n=0}^{N} \frac{(I_n - O_n)}{(1+\text{IRR})^n} - C = 0 \qquad (1)$$

From Chapter 6, the definition of LCOE is:

$$\text{LCOE} = \frac{\sum_{n=0}^{N} \dfrac{O_n}{(1+d)^n} + C}{\sum_{n=0}^{N} \dfrac{E_n}{(1+d)^n}} \qquad (2)$$

where:

N is the length of the project in years;

C is the capital cost in year 0;

O_n is the operations cost in year n;

d is the discount rate;

I_n is the income in year n, i.e. the savings on the electricity bill:
$$I_n = I_0 (1+r)^n (1-D)^n$$

E_n is the electricity generated in year n:
$$E_n = E_0 (1-D)^n$$

where:

I_0 is the savings in year 0;

E_0 is the electricity generated in year 0;

r is the future escalation rate of electricity prices;

D is the degradation rate of the solar installation.

Let us take the situation where we have calculated IRR and/or LCOE for certain values of the input data and want to see the effect of varying one of those input data values slightly. For instance, for capital cost, C, changed by an amount δC, the change in IRR and LCOE are obtained using differential calculus[8] as:

$$\delta\text{IRR} = \frac{\partial\text{IRR}}{\partial C}\delta C = \frac{-\delta C}{\sum_{n=0}^{N} t(I_n - O_n)[1 + \text{IRR}]^{-n-1}} \qquad (3)$$

$$\delta\text{LCOE} = \frac{\partial\text{LCOE}}{\partial C}\delta C = \frac{1-k}{E_0\left(1-k^{N+1}\right)}\delta C \qquad (4)$$

where: $k = \dfrac{1 - D}{1 + r}$.

It can be seen that (3) involves less computation than (1), since (1) must be solved iteratively for IRR, involving summations for each iteration, whereas (3) involves just one summation. Also (4) requires no summation at all and therefore requires less computation than (2). Reduced computational requirements translates into faster response time to the user, which is noticeable when risk analysis is required for several input data items.

Summary

This chapter has described a range of risks involved in solar projects at the planning, development and operating stages, which affect the developer, the YieldCo and their investors. We have also given management approaches to mitigating the risks or transferring them to a contractor or insurance company. Some international standards have been referenced that ensure quality from manufacture of solar modules, through project development to project operation. Many of these risks are not quantifiable but we have also shown how to deal with uncertainty in the data that determines IRR and LCOE so as to quantify the risk of IRR becoming lower than acceptable or LCOE becoming higher.

Takeaways

Planning

- The main uncertainty at the planning stage is the capital cost. Once a contract is signed with an installer, that uncertainty is reduced. In the same way, O&M risk can be reduced by outsourcing to an O&M company.
- Areas with extreme weather should be avoided since that is the cause of much equipment failure.
- Estimates of profitability can be obtained comparing several different databases of solar irradiance, with an emphasis on those using ground-based measurements.
- It is important to obtain an option on land purchase, planning permission and a grid connection before signing a PPA.
- Risk can be reduced by insuring the physical solar assets and also obtaining insurance against business interruption. The World Bank can provide insurance against political instability.

Development

- Risk can be reduced by obtaining a credit rating on the offtaker and also on suppliers and contractors.
- Surety bonds can be obtained from contractors and the quality of their work should be closely monitored.
- The construction of the project should be monitored closely to avoid cost overruns.

Operations and Maintenance

- Performance data from other YieldCos in the same geographical area can be compared with the performance of our project.
- If there are not many projects in a similar geography, weather-adjusted data from other areas should be used.
- Short-term forecasts of solar irradiance can be used to schedule power in and out of a battery to avoid PPA penalties for undersupply of power.
- Data can be efficiently exchanged among YieldCo, investors and contractors using the "Orange Button" standard data exchange format.
- A community solar project can avoid customer churn by ensuring a smooth transition from the distribution company.

Quantifiable Risk

- Uncertainty in the data items feeding into the calculation of IRR and LCOE, contributes to the risk of IRR being below expected and of LCOE being higher than expected.
- Risk quantification involves estimating realistic ranges of possible values of these data items and recalculating IRR and LCOE for these ranges.
- P90 values are sometimes used and are described in Chapter 10.
- Recalculation can be avoided and response time to users can be improved by using analytical approaches based on differential calculus.

Probe Deeper: The Why?

I am a young engineer and I know how to build a solar project, why should I bother with risk analysis? If you need investors to finance your endeavor, they will need a risk analysis. If at some time in the future you wish to sell your project, the purchaser will need a risk analysis.

Process

Planning

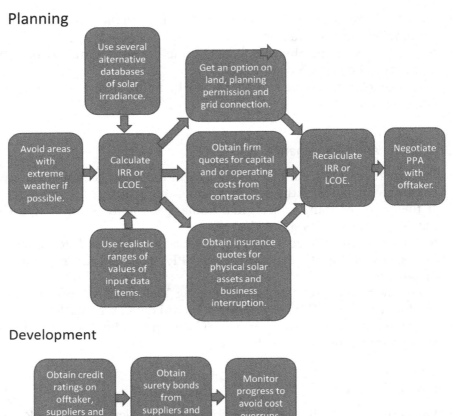

Development

Operations and Maintenance

Notes

1 Eber, K., 2015, NREL-Led Efforts Help Bring Financing to Solar Projects, Clean Energy Innovation at NREL. No 8.

2 Munoz, J.I., Bunn, D.W., 2013, "Investment Risk and Return Under Renewable Decarbonization of a Power Market", *Climate Policy*, 13 (S01) S87–S105, http://dx.doi.org/10.1080/14693062.2012.750473.

3 NREL, Orange Button Data Exchange, https://www.nrel.gov/analysis/orange-button-data.html

4 SEIA, Solar Energy Industries Association. Best Practices for Solar Risk Management, https://www.seia.org/research-resources/best-practices-solar-risk-management

5 UNECE, United Nations Economic Commission for Europe, Solar Risk Matrix, https://unece.org/fileadmin/DAM/energy/se/pp/eneff/6th_IFESD_Yerevan_Oct.15/d2_30.Sept/tc.bp/D.Vitchev/pps/3c_Solar.Risk.Matrix.pdf

6 Deceglie, Michael G., Jordan, Dirk C., Nag, Ambarish, Shinn, Adam, Deline, Chris, March 2019, Fleet-Scale Energy-Yield Degradation Analysis, Applied to Hundreds of Residential and Nonresidential Photovoltaic Systems, *IEEE Journal of Photovoltaics*, 9(2):476–483.

7 Tomosk, S., Haysom, J.E., Wright, D.J., August 2017, Quantifying Economic Risk in Photovoltaic Power Projects, *Renewable Energy*, 109(August 2017):422–433, DOI: 10.1016/j.renene.2017.03.031.

8 Guindon, A., Wright, D., 2020, Analytical Approach to Quantitative Risk Assessment for Solar Power Projects, *Renewable and Sustainable Energy Reviews*, 133:110262; doi.org/10.1016/j.rser.2020.110262.

Part 3
Getting the Biggest Bang for Your Solar Buck

Part 3 of this book shows how we can get *extra revenue* from our solar installation in addition to the value of the electricity we generate. But, before we start, let's face it, many people would say solar installations are actually worth *less* than the value of that electricity, since output is variable, known in the industry as intermittent. We are not using just the literal meaning of intermittent (going on and off) but we are also including general variability. People say that less electricity on cloudy days, at night and in winter means that solar needs to be combined with wind or hydro into a "hybrid" and/or a way of storing electricity for those times when our solar generators are not performing well. And they are right. The purpose of Part 3 of this book is to show that this is not bad news. For sure, storage is an additional cost, over and above the costs analyzed in Part 1 of this book. However, since we need storage to tide us over solar intermittency, the next three chapters will show how to use that storage to bring in additional revenue.

But, before we do that, let's just take a step back and look at the big picture of operating the electricity grid. Basically, it's a job of balancing demand and supply. If someone switches a microwave on or some industrial machinery off, the grid has to increase or decrease the amount of electricity generated within a matter of seconds. When a lot of people do that at about the same time, as when they go home from the factory and cook their dinners, coal and nuclear don't ramp up and down fast enough; they provide a stable level of baseload power. The current electricity grid increases and decreases its generating capacity by ramping up and down gas turbines, hydro-electric plants and electricity storage. In other words, we already know how to deal with intermittency, but it is intermittency of demand. Solar adds intermittency of supply, but it's not as though intermittency is some new problem that presents a hurdle to solar deployment. It's a problem we've been coping with ever since 1882 when Edison founded his "Illuminating Company" in New York City.

DOI: 10.4324/9781003262435-11

Solar is intermittent in three ways: fluctuating between sunny and cloudy periods, between day and night and between summer and winter. Electricity demand is intermittent on much the same timescales: consumers and businesses demand more electricity some days than others (e.g. workdays and weekends), over the course of a day, there are evening peaks and early morning troughs, plus there is enormous seasonal variation in demand for electric heating and air-conditioning. Electricity system operators balance conventional supply with intermittent demand. As intermittent solar and wind are introduced into the grid, they will use much the same techniques to balance supply and demand, and storage is a major contributor to addressing this issue.

Selecting the appropriate type of electricity storage, an evolving field, is described in Chapter 9. In Chapter 10, we will see how to use hybrids and storage to increase the profitability of solar installations. In Chapter 11, we will discuss how to use the same storage to provide grid stabilizing services to the grid operator and get paid for doing so.

9
Storage: Improving Solar Profitability

Introduction

When someone talks of storing electricity, a knee-jerk reaction is to think of a battery and, for sure, batteries are very important. There are, however, many other ways of storing electrical energy and the first purpose of this chapter to describe them and their different characteristics. Storage can be used to improve the profitability of a solar project and our second aim is to review how that can be done. We expand on this in the following two chapters. Adding storage to a solar project improves its profitability, as described in Chapter 10 and also enables the YieldCo to provide grid-balancing services, which give an extra stream of income, as described in Chapter 11.

The capacity of a storage device can be measured in two ways: how much electric energy (kWh) it can store and how much electric power (kW) it can accept/provide. Storage suppliers offer a range of different energy storage and power ratings. For example, a lithium-ion battery that can store 100 kWh of energy may be able to provide that energy at a rate of 50 kW, in which case it will last two hours. Another 100 kWh battery may provide 20 kW (in which case, it will last five hours).

The cost of a storage device is often given in dollars per kWh of storage capacity, but it also depends on the power in kW that it can accept and deliver. Our 100 kWh battery capable of 50 kW of power costs more than one capable of 10 kW. To complicate the issue further, some batteries charge slowly and discharge fast. For instance, excess solar energy generated during the day can be used to slowly charge the battery and it can be discharged over a shorter period in the evening when demand is high. However, this flexibility in storage design means that it is not possible to come up with a single dollar cost figure as we did in Chapters 1–3 for a solar project. This chapter will therefore describe the range of storage options available, leaving cost to be determined on a case-by-case basis.

DOI: 10.4324/9781003262435-12

Storage devices can be characterized in five ways:

1. How much electric energy they can store (S, measured in kWh).
2. How much electric power they can accept and deliver (P, measured in kW).
3. How fast we can switch them on and off (the response time, measured in seconds).
4. How efficient they are. For each kWh of electricity we put in, how much do we get back out (measured as a percentage, %, sometimes called the "round trip" efficiency).
5. How many charge/discharge cycles they can provide.

The amount of time for which a storage device can accept or deliver electricity is S / P hours.

In this chapter, we will discuss five types of electricity storage that are currently used in the electricity grid, together with how they can be developed in the future: pumped hydro, batteries, supercapacitors, flywheels and compressed air. A comparison among their capabilities is shown in Figure 9.1. Of course, there is a wide range of capabilities within each technology. We will then review a couple of storage options that may be useful in the future, concentrated solar power (CSP) and hydrogen. We conclude this chapter by describing a broad range of examples of how storage is used to improve the profitability of solar projects.

Storage Options

Pumped Hydro

Pumped hydro is by far the most widely deployed way of storing large amounts of electricity in today's public electricity grid: essentially it is a reversible hydro-electric project with two lakes (or reservoirs) at different altitudes. When water flows from the top lake to the lower one, it powers a turbine that generates electricity. When we want to store electricity, we reverse the operation of the turbine so that it becomes an electric pump, sending water from the lower lake to the upper one. The amount of electric energy that can be stored is limited only by the size of the lakes. The power that can be provided depends on the size of the turbines and the cost depends very much on the topography and geology of the site. The response time of pumped hydropower depends on the power of the turbine/pumps. A 250 MW turbine takes a couple of minutes to get up to full power whereas and smaller one would be faster.

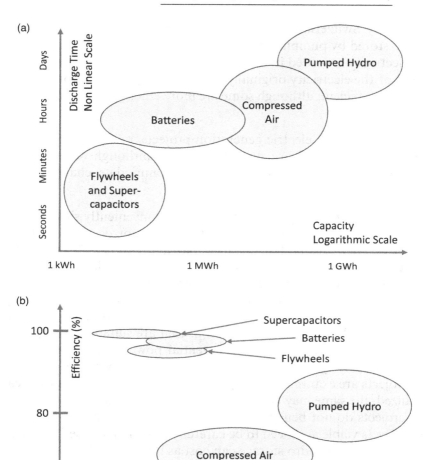

Figure 9.1 Overview of performance characteristics of major electricity storage technologies: (a) discharge time against capacity and (b) efficiency against response time.

Pumped hydro storage can be added to an existing hydro-electric generating plant. For instance, in Switzerland, a country that has a lot of experience with hydro generation, the Linth-Limmern plant was expanded from 500 MW of generating capacity by adding 1,000 MW of pumped storage. It links Lake Limmern with Lake Mutt, which is 600 meters higher up the valley and has a "round trip" efficiency of 80%. If excess electricity was produced by Switzerland's solar farms on a sunny summer afternoon, it could be stored by pumping water from Lake Zimmern to Lake Mutt, and when electricity is needed in the evening, it could flow back down, generating 80% of the electricity originally used for pumping. No storage technology is 100% efficient, although some are more efficient than pumped hydro; see Figure 9.1.

In contrast to hydro-electric generation projects, pumped hydro does not involve damming a river or flooding a valley, although walls may sometimes be built around the reservoirs to accommodate changes in water levels.

Conventional pumped hydro needs two lakes conveniently situated relative to each other, a geographical oddity that does not occur close to many utility-scale solar farms. For instance, Northern India, Eastern Pakistan and Western Australia, which have excellent solar irradiance, have few locations suitable for pumped hydro. Vast areas of the Earth's land area are too flat, and some mountainous areas are too costly for construction equipment to access. Professor Blakers of the Australian National University has produced a world map showing locations that are suitable.[1] Many of these locations are smaller (in terms of potential power, energy or both) than existing pumped hydro installations. In the same way that small/medium solar projects are examples of energy resources being distributed instead of centralized, the same may become true of pumped hydro storage. However, small projects do not benefit from the economies of scale that have made large projects viable and need to be carefully costed on a case-by-case basis. Very large pumped hydro storage can cost as little as $20/kWh.

Costing Pumped Hydro in a Mine

Professor Schubert of Indiana University and Purdue University has costed a project for a 200 MW/1,400 MWh pumped storage system in a 150-meter-deep mine. The capital cost comes to $210/kWh (slightly higher than the cost of a lithium-ion battery from Figure 9.2 plus installation cost).

An alternative innovative approach for flat geographical regions is to use abandoned underground mines with watertight voids (cavities). Water is pumped up to a surface reservoir and generates electricity when it flows back down again. The USA has 190,000 abandoned mines, and repurposing selected ones for pumped hydro storage could provide employment for laid-off workers, particularly as demand for coal subsides.

Pumped hydro storage uses the gravitational potential energy of water as a storage mechanism. Water is not very dense, but other materials are denser. Could we use electricity to lift something other than water and drop it back down again to regenerate the electric energy? Various schemes have been proposed, driving trains up disused mountain tracks and stacking massive blocks on top of each other. The former is not very efficient due to the rolling resistance of the train wheels. The latter presents an enormous engineering challenge (see sidebar), which a Swiss company, Energy Vault, is surmounting.[2] They have

> **Lifting Blocks**
>
> To get an idea of the scale of the engineering challenge, imagine a two-story house with 7 kW of solar on the roof and a Tesla Powerwall battery storing 14 kWh of electricity for evening use. You would need to raise 700 tons of weight the height of the house to get the same storage capacity. You might not want your kids to play underneath it!

implemented a prototype tower, looking like a crane, but with six arms. Each arm raises and lowers 35 tonne blocks, stacking them in concentric rings. When any block comes to rest, power output is zero from that arm, which is the reason for having six arms so as to smooth out this intermittency. The blocks are constructed locally from dirt bonded together with a polymer glue (cement manufacture, by contrast, causes a lot of carbon emissions). Meanwhile, in Scotland, Gravitricity is lifting and dropping even larger weights (500–5,000 tons) up and down disused mine shafts, but not to store electricity for long. Their time scale is to smooth out second-by-second fluctuations in the electricity grid.

Batteries

Batteries store electricity as chemical energy and there is a wide range of chemistries that can be used from the lead-acid batteries that start legacy gasoline cars to the lithium-ion batteries that power the electric vehicles of today. The differences among these technologies are constantly evolving and are beyond the scope of this book. We will focus on lithium-ion batteries that are currently the most widely used in both behind-the-meter (BTM) and front-of-the-meter (FTM) applications.

Batteries respond fast (within a second) to the need to charge or discharge (see Figure 9.1) and are highly efficient (90–95% round trip efficiency). They are modular, so that if we need more storage in the future, additional batteries can be added. They do not perform well at very low temperatures and need to be clad in insulating material, with some of their stored electricity used to maintain the necessary operating temperature, thus reducing efficiency. High temperatures reduce the number of charge/discharge cycles that a battery can provide and ideally many lithium-ion batteries require a temperature-controlled installation, 25°C ± 5°C, which is important to bear in mind for solar projects in areas with cold winters or hot summers.

Batteries for electric power applications come as a "battery pack", consisting of a case, electrical control equipment, a battery management system and the battery cells themselves, which actually store the electricity. The cells constitute about 70% of the total cost. In addition to the cost of the battery pack itself is the cost of installation, which depends on the scale of the project and on the type of installation (outdoor or indoor).

Batteries degrade, just as solar modules do, and their rate of degradation depends on the temperature, the length of time since manufacture and the number of charge/discharge cycles. Degradation happens gradually and batteries are often replaced when they are at about 70% of original capacity, which, in practice, is after about 4,000 charge/discharge cycles. When batteries are used in conjunction with solar power, they are often used to "move" electricity from the time of day when it is generated to the time when it is used, that is, one cycle per day. Such a battery would therefore last 4000/365 = 11 years, much shorter than the life of a solar installation, which is more like 30 years. It is the battery cells that degrade and since they constitute about 70% of the total cost, when the battery needs replacing, the cost is 30% less than the cost of an entire new battery pack.

To get as many charge/discharge cycles out of a battery as possible, the battery should be operated from 10% of its capacity to 90%, not over the full range. Thus, a 100 kWh battery should be operated between a state of charge (the amount of electricity stored in the battery) between 10 and 90 kWh, that is, the maximum amount of electricity we can put into a 100 kWh battery is 90 − 10 = 80 kWh. When purchasing a battery for a solar project, it is important to clarify whether the quoted capacity is before deducting this 20% or after.

A common criticism of lithium-ion batteries is that the supply of lithium is limited by geopolitical factors. In fact, current lithium-ion batteries also need nickel, copper, cobalt and manganese, which may also be limited in a geopolitical sense. In 2021, China processed 70% of cobalt and 60% of lithium globally. A detailed discussion is beyond the scope of this book, particularly since battery suppliers do not necessarily state the ingredients in their batteries, but it is important to bear in mind that many battery designs are available, and if one encounters resource constraints, other designs are waiting in the sidelines, probably at an increased price.

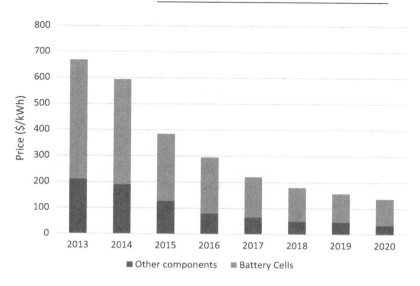

Figure 9.2 Lithium-ion battery pack prices split between cells and other components, excluding installation cost (source: Bloomberg New Energy Finance[3]).

Unlike the other storage options discussed in this chapter, the cost of lithium-ion batteries is well-defined and documented. For instance, Bloomberg New Energy Finance provides historical records of prices indicating that they are declining at about 13% per year as shown in Figure 9.2. The cost of installation needs to be added to these figures on a case-by-case basis.

Supercapacitors

Tiny capacitors have been used in all electronic devices since their inception and that is why we use the term "supercapacitors" to refer to the much larger capacitors that store enough electricity to be useful in electric power grids.

Supercapacitors are the only storage technology option that stores electricity as electricity. They do not convert it to potential, chemical or kinetic energy, as do pumped hydro, batteries and flywheels. As the capacitor is charged, electrons are accumulated on a surface and they are released during discharge. The advantage of this is that performance is much better than when energy is converted from one form to another. The response time is very rapid (less than a second), the efficiency is very high (approaching 100%), the discharge *power* is very high (five times that of a lithium-ion battery of the same weight) and the number of charge/discharge cycles is virtually unlimited.

The first downside to supercapacitors is that the amount of electric *energy* they can store is only about 5% of what a lithium-ion battery of the same weight can achieve. Weight is important in electric vehicles, but for stationary applications associated with solar power and the electricity grid, it matters less. However, such a heavy supercapacitor costs a lot just based on the weight of materials from which it is made.

The other downside is that supercapacitors discharge very fast, but this can also be an advantage. If you need a burst of power for less than a minute to smooth out short-term fluctuations in supply or demand in the electricity grid, a supercapacitor can be very useful, but when power is needed for a longer time, batteries are a better bet.

At the time of writing, research is underway to combine supercapacitors and lithium-ion batteries into a single device that provides the best of both worlds.

Flywheels

Flywheels have been used for decades to smooth out short-term fluctuations in demand in the electricity grid from customers switching appliances on and off. Now we also need to smooth out short-term fluctuations in the supply as the sun goes behind a cloud. Flywheels, supercapacitors and batteries can be used for this.

Flywheels use an electric motor to store energy by speeding up the rate of rotation of a wheel. Electric energy is thus converted to the kinetic energy of the flywheel. The motor doubles as a generator to recover the electricity while slowing down the flywheel. The operation of a flywheel is similar to the use of regenerative braking in electric vehicles.

The amount of energy stored is proportional to the mass of the flywheel and therefore steel has often been used because of its high density. However, the amount of energy stored is also proportional to the *square* of the rate of rotation of the flywheel, giving advantage to a very strong material, which can withstand fast rotation without ripping itself apart. Carbon fiber is less dense than steel but is much stronger and is therefore used in modern flywheels. To further improve the efficiency of flywheels, they usually operate in a vacuum to eliminate air drag.

The advantages of flywheels are that they can respond very fast (about 1 s), they can accommodate a very large number of charge/discharge cycles and they can deliver high power.

The main disadvantage is that they can store a limited amount of energy and are in that sense similar to supercapacitors. Flywheels are not as efficient as supercapacitors, however (around 90%), because of friction on their bearings. This is being improved (to about 95%) with the use of magnetic levitation to eliminate the friction.

Compressed Air

An electric compressor can store energy in compressed air. When the pressure is released, the air drives a turbine to generate electricity. On a small scale, compressed air can be stored in cylinders. On a large scale, it can be stored in underground caverns, for example, in salt formations that are (or can be made) airtight. Some innovative ideas are described in the sidebar.[4]

Compressed air stored in cylinders can provide high power for a short time when the pressure is released in the same way that flywheels and supercapacitors do and is used to stabilize the grid to fluctuations in demand and supply of power.

Storing Electricity Underwater

In Canada, Toronto Hydro stores off-peak electricity using compressed air in balloons 55 meters underneath Lake Ontario for use during peak periods. This is a pilot project with just 1.5 MWh of storage delivering power at 700 kW. The balloons expand against the pressure of the lake water.

An alternative design uses concrete spheres instead of balloons. During charging, air pumped into the top of the spheres displaces water out through the bottom and vice versa for discharging.

Compressed air storage in underground caverns is limited only by the size of the cavern just as pumped hydro is limited only by the size of the lakes or reservoirs. The problem, however, is finding a cavern, plus it has to be the right sort of cavern. It must not leak air and the rock surface should not oxidize when exposed to compressed oxygen.

But the unavoidable Achilles heel of compressed air storage is the heat generated when air is compressed. That heat contains some of the energy that we are trying to store and we cannot therefore let it go to waste. Heat is tough to store efficiently, so we may use it for district heating or for industrial purposes. When the pressure is released to generate electricity, the air cools down (acting like a refrigerator) and can freeze up the turbine. If we managed to store the heat generated during compression, we can use it to heat up the expanding air, but if we use the heat for other purposes, we need

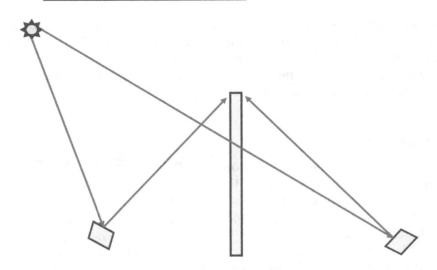

Figure 9.3 Concentrated solar power, with mirrors focusing the sun's rays on to a thermal collector at the top of the tower. The diagram shows just two, of what would, in practice, be thousands of mirrors surrounding the tower.

to heat the expanding air using another source, for example, natural gas. The net result is that compressed air storage is the least efficient of all our storage options (around 70%).

Concentrated Solar Power (CSP) also known as Solar Thermal Power

The solar modules discussed in Part 1 of this book are "photovoltaic" (PV) since they convert photons of light into volts of electricity. Figure 9.3 does *not* show PV modules; instead it shows mirrors focusing sunlight on the top of the tower. The mirrors, known as heliostats, rotate to maintain this focus as the sun moves across the sky. The tower absorbs the heat in the sun's rays and uses it to generate steam, which drives a turbine and generates electricity. CSP plants of this type constitute only about 2% of all solar installations worldwide; the remainder are PV, and that is why they were not included in Part 1 of this book.

The reason why I am including CSP in a chapter on storage is that it often has "inherent storage", that is, storage can be part and parcel of the design. Whereas PV modules generate *electricity* immediately, CSP plants generate *heat* immediately, and can store that heat, passing it on to the steam turbine at a later time. A CSP plant can therefore generate electricity during the night.

At the top of the tower, the heat in the concentrated sun's rays can be used to melt salt bringing it to temperatures over 500°C. The molten salt is stored in insulated tanks until it is required, and it is then used to boil water, producing steam that powers the turbine and generates electricity.

CSP plants have been successful in bidding on power purchase agreements (PPAs) that require electricity to be delivered on a daily schedule that does not match the output from a PV plant. To compete with CSP, a PV plant needs to incur the additional cost of a battery or one of the other forms of storage described in this chapter.

Internationally, there was a rapid growth in CSP deployment between 2008 and 2015, which has slackened off since then, due to competition from declining PV prices. Spain[5] has the most CSP plants, totaling 2.3 GW in capacity.

As solar and wind are deployed internationally and come to constitute an increasing percentage of total electricity generating capacity, their intermittency has an increasing impact on the grid. At some point in the future, we may see a renewed interest in CSP because its "inherent storage" can smooth over that intermittency and assist in balancing supply and demand for electricity.

Hydrogen

Some people regard hydrogen as a way of storing electricity, and this short section is intended to cast doubt on that notion, at least for most applications.

We electrolyze water, splitting it into hydrogen and oxygen, the latter of which is sold for medical or industrial purposes. When we want to recover the electricity, we burn the hydrogen, drive a turbine and generate electricity, or alternatively use the hydrogen in a fuel cell to generate electricity. Either way, the hydrogen is oxidized back to the water from which it originated. That is the theory. In practice, electrolysis is only around 75% efficient and fuel cells are about 80% efficient for a round trip efficiency of $0.75 * 0.8 = 0.60$. An efficiency of 60% is too low for commercial use as an electricity storage option today compared with other storage options. One way around this may be to develop fuel cells that have hydrogen peroxide (H_2O_2) as a by-product instead of water (H_2O). Hydrogen peroxide can be sold thus generating an additional revenue stream that may compensate for the lack of efficiency.

One application in which hydrogen is used as a store of electricity is to power electric motors in inter-city trucks using hydrogen fuel cells. Hydrogen from solar electrolysis is very important as a feedstock for industry and as an alternative to natural gas for heating, and in these uses, it is not converted back to electricity. These applications are discussed in detail in Chapter 14.

———

Having reviewed characteristics of the storage options available, let's look at electricity storage from the point of view of where and why it would be used in conjunction with a solar project. We will divide these applications into Behind- and Front-of- the Meter.

Benefits of Storage

Behind-the-Meter Applications

Energy storage is used in conjunction with solar in BTM projects to construct a microgrid, which is described in more detail in Chapter 10. In these applications, the most used form of storage is a lithium-ion battery. The applications are:

- *Self-consumption.* Most customers need electricity at night and can get it from the grid. However, if the grid price is higher than the cost of our solar electricity, then a battery allows us to install more solar than we need during the day, feed the excess power into a battery and discharge the battery to supply our needs at night.
- *Peak shaving.* For customers subject to demand charges on their peak consumption each month, flattening out the peaks in the consumption pattern can reduce those charges. We are not aiming to reduce total electricity consumption, instead we are shifting electricity purchases from the grid away from times of peak consumption to other times, for example, times earlier in the day when we can charge our battery and discharge it during peak consumption periods.
- *Time-of-use (ToU) bill management.* Customers subject to ToU billing can use batteries to shift grid purchases from times of high electricity charges to times when the charges are lower. Many jurisdictions do not allow this shifting in conjunction with net-metering, which means customers cannot buy electricity at one time, store it in a battery and sell it back to the grid later. However, it can be bought during a low price period and used to offset consumption at a later time.
- *Demand response.* The electricity system operator can sometimes anticipate that the supply of electricity is going to be insufficient for demand a day or two in advance. For instance, weather forecasts may indicate a

hot summer afternoon with a lot of air-conditioning demand. Another reason is that maintenance may be scheduled on a certain part of the grid, with electricity being re-routed from other parts, with a limit on how much can be re-routed. This mismatch between supply and demand is not necessarily a question of insufficient electricity being generated. It is also due to the limited capacity of equipment such as transformers and transmission and distribution lines. In situations when the grid is forecast to bump up against one or other of these limits at a certain time of day, the grid operator will offer customers a payment in return for reducing their demand during that period. This is known as "demand response" because customers are asked to adjust their demand in response to a limit on the supply. In many jurisdictions, demand response payments are higher than the price of electricity and commercial customers can receive hundreds of thousands of dollars over the course of a year by complying with demand response requests. Suppose a commercial customer has agreed to reduce demand by 1 MW between 2:00 and 4:00 p.m. tomorrow afternoon. They could shut off equipment using 1 MW of electricity or they could charge the battery on a solar microgrid prior to 2:00 p.m. and use electricity from the battery from 2:00 to 4:00 p.m.

- *Backup.* If the solar project or the grid fails, a battery can be used to provide backup, but the size of battery that is economically optimal for a solar microgrid will probably only last a few hours; see Chapter 10.

Front-of-the-Meter Applications

The electricity grid has used flywheels, compressed air and pumped hydro storage to balance supply and demand, long before the advent of solar or lithium-ion batteries. As more intermittent renewables such as solar and wind are added to the grid, the need for balancing becomes more acute. Solar power fluctuates at every timescale. There are variations in solar electricity generation on a timescale of seconds and minutes as clouds move across the sky and as the wind causes variations in air density and dust, thus absorbing more or less solar irradiance. Short-term fluctuations of this type can be dealt with using flywheels, supercapacitors and batteries that absorb and provide small amounts of electricity at short notice. Overcast skies can last for hours or days, requiring very large capacity storage such as pumped hydro.

The applications of these types of storage in the public electricity grid are as follows:

- *PPA compliance.* PPAs specify minimum amounts of electricity that are required at different times of day and year. If the weather forecast indicates there will not be enough solar irradiance, we can plan to have a battery charged enough to ensure that we meet the PPA requirement and avoid financial penalties that apply for undersupply.

- *Solar smoothing.* Short-term fluctuations in solar generation of the order of seconds or minutes can be smoothed out by using a battery, supercapacitor or a flywheel. This smoothing is often required before electricity can be fed into the grid under the terms of the grid connection contract.

- *Renewable ramping.* Prior to the introduction of renewables into the grid, gas turbines and hydro-electric plants were used to deal with changes in demand. Coal and nuclear, by contrast, are good at providing a constant stream of baseload power 24/7 but cannot be ramped up or down fast. As the sun sets, solar electricity output ramps down rapidly and this is also a time of day when residential demand ramps up. The required rate of increase in supply may exceed what can be obtained from gas plants and many jurisdictions[*] do not have much hydro generation. Pumped hydro storage comes to the rescue. Most pumped hydro is owned and operated by the grid, but some is controlled by renewable generating companies.

- *Decreasing curtailment.* If the grid has enough electricity so that wholesale prices are very low but solar is still generating well, it may be curtailed, that is, switched off by the electricity system operator. The marginal cost of generating solar electricity is almost zero, so curtailment means a loss of net income. The YieldCo can compensate for this by using storage to absorb the electricity generated during curtailment. Often curtailment can be predicted, for example, if a sunny afternoon is forecast so that all solar installations in a local region are generating at their maximums. If we can predict that curtailment will be necessary, we can plan to have the battery almost completely discharged at the start of the curtailment period so that it can absorb as much power as possible.

- *Arbitrage.* A utility-scale solar plant selling electricity on the wholesale market can forecast when prices will be low and when they will be high. Instead of supplying electricity at a low price, it can store it in a battery and supply it when the price is high.

- *Frequency regulation.* When supply and demand in the grid are not balanced, the frequency of the AC deviates from the required value, usually 50 or 60 cycles per second depending on the jurisdiction. When demand is higher than supply, the frequency drops and when supply exceeds demand, the frequency rises. Some equipment attached to the grid can be damaged or malfunction if the frequency deviates from its required

[*] For example, Europe.

value. Measurements of grid frequency have been used for decades to control grid-based flywheel storage, taking power from the flywheel to the grid when frequency drops and absorbing power into the flywheel when frequency rises. This helps balance supply and demand in the grid and maintains the frequency at the required value. Grid operators pay for frequency-regulation services. If we already have a battery at our solar installation, we can use it to provide frequency regulation to the electricity system operator and get paid for doing so; see Chapter 11. The amount of payment varies greatly from one jurisdiction to another. In Europe, the electricity grids of many countries are interconnected, resulting in a very large electricity system that absorbs mismatches between supply and demand in any single country. Frequency regulation is less necessary in a large system like this, and the payment is therefore small. By contrast, small electricity systems such as the one in Alberta benefit more from frequency-regulation services and pay more.

- *Spinning reserve.* A spinning reserve is an electricity generator that can be brought online within a few seconds of being needed, for example, to compensate for a failure in other grid equipment. Electricity system operators pay high prices for spinning reserves and a battery associated with a utility-scale solar farm could act as a spinning reserve, albeit for a limited amount of time until it becomes discharged.

Summary

The capabilities of the storage options described in this chapter are summarized in Table 9.1.

This chapter has also described a wide range of applications of storage that can improve the profitability of a solar project both in front of and behind the meter.

Table 9.1 Summary of the characteristics of storage options

	Pumped hydro	Li-ion battery	Supercapacitor	Flywheel	Compressed air: cylinder	Compressed air: cavern
Storage capacity	Very large	Small to large	Small	Small	Small	Very large
Power output	Very large	Small to large	Medium	Medium	Medium	Very large
Response time	Slow	Fast	Very fast	Fast	Fast	Slow
Efficiency	Medium	High	Very high	High	Low	Low
Cycle lifetime	High	High	Very high	Very high	High	High

Takeaways

Storage Options and Their Characteristics

Pumped Hydro

- Strength: capacity limited only by the size of the lakes or reservoirs
- Weaknesses: limited availability of locations for large-scale installations; possibly limited profitability of small-scale installations compared with batteries.

Lithium-ion Battery

- Strengths: modular design allows a range of sizes; declining prices.
- Weakness: lifetime less than that of solar modules, thus requiring replacement

Supercapacitor

- Strengths: very high efficiency and very fast response time
- Weakness: low storage capacity

Flywheel

- Strength: fast response time
- Weakness: low storage capacity

Compressed Air in a Cylinder

- Strength: fast response time
- Weakness: low efficiency

Compressed Air in a Cavern

- Strength: capacity limited only by the size of the cavern
- Weakness: low efficiency

Applications of Storage That Improve the Profitability of a Solar Project

Behind the Meter

- Self-consumption; peak shaving; ToU bill management; demand response; backup.

Front of the Meter

- Power purchase agreement compliance; solar smoothing; renewable ramping; decreasing curtailment; arbitrage; frequency regulation; spinning reserve.

Probe Deeper: The Why?

Why is there so much hype about lithium-ion batteries when there are so many other storage options available? Because lithium-ion batteries are dropping in price and have the features needed when we deploy intermittent renewables: high efficiency, rapid response time, and modular design for increasing capacity.

Process

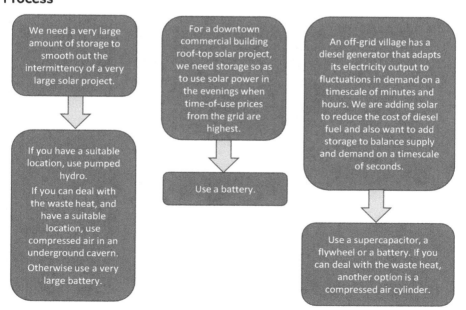

Notes

1 Blakers, Andrew, Australian National University, Global Pumped Hydro Atlas, http://re100.eng.anu.edu.au/global/
2 Moore, Samuel, Jan 5, 2021, Gravity Energy Storage Shows Its Potential, IEEE Spectrum.
3 Bloomberg New Energy Finance, 2020, *Battery Price Survey*.
4 Andrews, Roger, 2018, A Review of Underwater Compressed Air Storage, https://euanmearns.com/a-review-of-underwater-compressed-air-storage/
5 Sener, Gemasolar Solar Thermal Power Plant, https://www.energy.sener/project/gemasolar

10
Profitability of Solar Microgrids and Hybrids

Introduction

A solar microgrid is an electricity network consisting of solar modules plus something else, for instance, wind turbines, electricity storage, a legacy generator (e.g. gas or hydroelectric), a connection to the public electricity grid and/or a connection to a customer's electrical loads. When it includes other electricity generators in addition to solar it is sometimes called a "hybrid", but we will use the general term "microgrid" in this chapter. Microgrids can be large, utility-scale projects, mid-sized projects covering an office park, through to small-scale projects for an off-grid cabin in the woods. Originally the industry used different terminology for these: minigrids, microgrids and nanogrids, but there is no clear dividing line between them; so, this book uses one term for all three: a microgrid.

Microgrids are continuously evolving. This chapter focuses on profitability analysis and illustrates it with reference to solar, wind, batteries and natural gas generators. Chapters 12 and 14 give examples that include wave, tidal and biomass generation, fuel cells and hydrogen production. The general principles of economic analysis described in this chapter apply to a broad range of any technologies that can be connected to microgrids.

Microgrid profitability analysis is an entire career path. Very few modern installations are solar-only. Instead, solar microgrids are the name of the game today. Professionals use software that does most of the grunt work, but still need to spend months planning and optimizing the profitability of large-scale solar microgrids. In a single chapter, we cannot distill all the experience of such a professional, but what we will do is describe the tools of their trade, the factors they consider and the principles upon which they work.

DOI: 10.4324/9781003262435-13

There are two main reasons for building solar microgrids:

1. They are sometimes more reliable than the public electricity grid, particularly in extreme weather.
2. They smooth out the intermittency in the electricity generated by solar and wind alone.

We therefore start this chapter with sections on those two topics, followed by sections on the profitability of utility-scale, behind-the-meter (BTM) and off-grid solar microgrids.

Reliability

Often microgrids are portrayed as a way of improving reliability of electricity supply, particularly, in the wake of extreme weather causing blackouts. Closer analysis can identify situations in which microgrids might be just as susceptible to failure as the conventional grid and other situations in which microgrids are very beneficial. For instance, in February 2021, a severe winter storm with snow, ice and frigid temperatures knocked out 185 power plants in Texas causing a blackout. In this case, it is not clear that solar microgrids or hybrids would have fared any better. Snow may cover the solar modules and ice may build up on wind turbine blades. In this case, the storm affected the electricity infrastructure across the entire state. Tornados, by contrast, cause more localized damage. A tornado could knock out a transformer in a city distribution network affecting 100,000 customers. If that city instead had 100 microgrids servicing 1,000 customers each, the same tornado might take out a microgrid, impacting only 1,000 customers. However, there is 100 times more chance that a microgrid will be hit compared with the chance of the single transformer being hit. In this case, microgrids reduce the chance of a big blackout and increase the chance of a small one.

There are two situations in which microgrids clearly improve reliability. If the public electricity grid is unreliable because of problems on its long-distance transmission lines, then microgrids will help since they do not have transmission lines. If the entire public electricity grid is unreliable because of lack of maintenance, then microgrids can help so long as they are properly maintained.

Western Australia, a state over ten times the size of Texas, has an electricity grid consisting of transmission lines running north and south of Perth along the west coast with spurs going east to serve sheep and cattle ranches, wheat farms and mining communities. Electric utilities do not like running power lines hundreds of kilometers to serve small customers; they can be damaged by bush fires causing blackouts. Farmers do not like power lines running across their land; they can arc over to vegetation and cause bush fires. One utility, Western power, found that solar microgrids reduced blackouts by 90%, and reduced operations and maintenance costs. Microgrids are not just for the outback. The tourist destination of Kalbarri, 600 km north of Perth, with its beaches and national park is powered by a microgrid with wind, solar, a large battery and a connection to the grid. High winds causing salt spray along the coast sometimes damage the grid transmission line and the microgrid significantly improves reliability. Not all transmission line problems spawn microgrids. When Hurricane Maria damaged transmission lines in Puerto Rico in 2017, there was much talk of building microgrids instead of rebuilding the transmission lines, but no action. When an ice storm struck Quebec in 1998, the weight of the ice build-up on the transmission cables dragged the pylons over blacking out Montreal. However, the transmission lines were rebuilt because Quebec has too much electricity from its vast James Bay hydroelectric scheme and needs the transmission lines to export it to New York State.

Nigeria has an electricity grid serving about half the population, many of whom have backup diesel generators because of frequent power failures. Well-maintained microgrids could provide reliable power to customers who are currently on-grid as well as to those that are off-grid and the World Bank has financing available to support such deployment. Providing electricity to off-grid rural communities in Africa requires customer engagement to identify what applications of electricity are required (e.g. irrigation pumps, Internet cafes or refrigerators) and to ensure a supply chain for those products. Also microgrid maintenance is vital. Africa is littered with technology that broke down and wasn't fixed. Assuming solar modules, racking, supports, inverters and batteries can be supplied to construct the microgrid, we need to be sure that replacement modules are available to deal with breakages and replacement inverters and batteries can be delivered to the site in 10–15 years time. Competition from the public grid also poses a risk. A microgrid installed at an off-grid community today, will face competition if the public grid expands tomorrow. A microgrid in Uhuru Bay, Kenya to power ice-making equipment for the local fishing community was dismantled after three years when the grid expanded to serve the area at a lower price. There is also political risk associated with African microgrids. In Tanzania, the government mandated a single electricity tariff for the entire country, putting many rural microgrid operators out of business.

This section has identified situations in which microgrids can provide more reliability than the conventional grid; however, we have not attempted to quantify reliability or put a dollar value on it. The rest of this chapter addresses issues more related to quantifiable financial profits.

Intermittency

The International Energy Agency says that solar delivers "the cheapest electricity in history."[1] The main reason to combine it with anything else is intermittency. Let's distinguish three types of intermittency:

1. *Short term*: on a timescale of seconds to minutes as the sun goes behind a small cloud, or wind currents in the atmosphere create dust or variations in air density that absorb more or less of the suns irradiance before it reaches our solar modules.
2. *Medium term*: on a timescale of hours to days as the sun rises and sets and as some days are cloudier than others.
3. *Long term*: on a timescale of months to years as the daylight is longer in the summer than in the winter and as volcanos produce more sunlight-absorbing ash in the atmosphere some years than others.

Short Term

Short-term intermittency needs to be dealt with to maintain a constant voltage at the point of interconnection, where the microgrid delivers electricity. Voltage fluctuations in a utility-scale installation that delivers electricity to the public grid can destabilize the grid and adversely affect other customers' equipment. Voltage fluctuations in a BTM installation that delivers electricity to the electrical system on the customer site can similarly impact equipment there.

A supercapacitor, a flywheel, a compressed air cylinder or a battery can be used to smooth out these short-term fluctuations. If we are using a battery to handle medium-term intermittency, it can do double duty for short-term intermittency.

Medium Term

Medium-term intermittency needs to be dealt with if we are relying on electricity from the microgrid to power our equipment, for example, in an off-grid application, or if we need to fulfill the electricity delivery schedule of a power purchase agreement (PPA), for example, for a utility-scale project. In a BTM project, we can purchase electricity from the grid if solar is not generating well, in which case it is not essential to use a microgrid. However, solar microgrids with batteries can be used to shift purchases from the grid away from times when the purchase price is high or when customer peak consumption incurs demand charges. The way to deal with medium-term intermittency is with a battery, unless our site happens to have access to pumped hydro storage or an underground cavern, which can be used for compressed air storage.

Long Term

Long-term solar intermittency sometimes does not matter. For instance, if we are powering an aluminum smelter 24/7 from a combination of hydro-electric and solar, and there is more sun in the summer and more rain to fill the reservoir in the winter, we may be able to choose the relative capacities of solar and hydro so that they provide constant power throughout the year. The hydro is dispatchable and should therefore be able to handle any discrepancies and also cope with medium-term solar intermittency.

Similarly, with a utility-scale solar project in an area where there is a lot of air-conditioning demand when solar is generating well, the increased demand and increased supply may balance each other out. On the other hand, they might not; see Figure 10.1, which shows a sunny summer day in California. Solar generation peaks three hours before the peak in air-conditioning demand so that other generators need to ramp up output.

We need to deal with long-term solar intermittency for off-grid projects and also for projects that need to fulfill a PPA. The lowest cost pumped hydro storage at $20/kWh is too expensive to be used on a seasonal basis. Even if it has a lifetime of 100 years, that is $0.20 per kWh per year. If we can generate 1 kWh for $0.03, it is unreasonable to spend $0.20 to move it from summer to winter. It would be better to install overcapacity solar or wind and generate more electricity in the winter. But how much overcapacity should we install? We answer that question using a statistical approach based on a concept first introduced by the National Renewable Energy Laboratory,[2] known as P90, the 10th percentile. 10% of the data is below this value and 90% is above it. Similarly, P80 is the 20th percentile, that is, a value with 20% of the data below it and 80% of the data above it. The P90 idea was originally introduced to give investors confidence that there is a base level of revenues, which we will exceed 90% of the time. It is also now used for irradiance and energy yield.

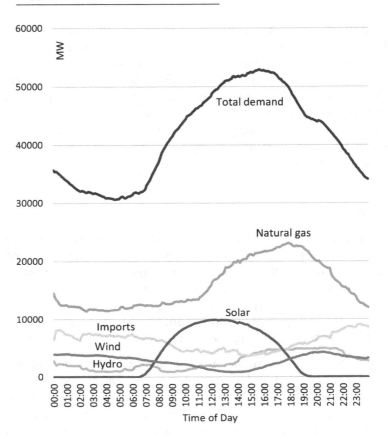

Figure 10.1 Generating mix for California on August 20, 2020, showing a classic pattern of solar with almost zero cloud. Since solar peaks at mid-day and the demand peak (due to air-conditioning) occurs mid-afternoon, additional power is needed from natural gas, hydro and imports from other states via the Western Electricity Coordinating Council. This graph also shows a negative correlation between solar and wind which drops during the sunniest time of day.

The more data we have, the more accurately we can calculate percentiles, and estimates of solar irradiance are available globally from satellite measurements of cloud cover dating back over 50 years. These *estimates* are not as accurate as ground-based *measurements* of irradiance, but the latter are available for shorter periods of time and only for the sites where the measuring equipment is installed. Life ain't perfect, and in this case, involves a choice between a long series of estimates or a shorter series of actual measurements.

Irradiance measurements come in two flavors: direct normal irradiance (DNI) (the direct beam of light from the sun) and global horizontal irradiance (GHI) (the total irradiance on a horizontal surface including the diffuse light from the whole sky plus the direct beam, taking into account the angle of incidence). Commercial software takes this information, together with air temperature measurements[*] and estimates the electricity output of our proposed solar installation on an hour-by-hour basis for each year in our data series. We can aggregate the results to obtain monthly[†] totals and use these to calculate percentiles. For example, from all the Januarys in or data set, we can get the P90[‡] value, that is, the value which is exceeded by 90% of those Januarys; see Figure 10.2. We can be 90% sure of having more electricity in future Januarys than this P90 value. We end up with 12 P90 values: for January, February, ..., December and can compare them with the monthly requirements of our PPA or off-grid application. This will enable us to calculate the capacity of our solar installation that will allow us to be 90% sure of having enough electricity in each individual month. Of course, if we want to be 95% sure of meeting requirements, we could calculate P95, that is, the 5th percentile. This is about as sure as we can get and for this, we would need at least 40 years of data. It is unrealistic to calculate P99 even from a 50-year data set.[§] As a rule of thumb, we need at least 20 years of data to estimate P90 and at least ten years of data to estimate P80.

Figure 10.2 illustrates a typical situation, showing modeled estimates of electric power output from a 1.7 MW proposed solar installation. We use these estimates to calculate the P80 and P90 values for just four months, representative of the four seasons of the year. It can be seen that the power output easily exceeds the PPA requirements for each month. Instead of using a 1.7 MW system, we can satisfy the PPA requirements with a smaller system. Based on the P90 values, we can reduce our system capacity to 1.51 MW and based on the P80 values, we can reduce our system capacity to 1.47 MW, thus reducing capital costs.

---

[*] Energy yield from silicon solar modules is reduced by 0.45% for each degree Celsius increase in temperature.

[†] We can ignore medium-term intermittency, i.e. hourly and daily variations, since it is being dealt with separately.

[‡] When the P90 idea was originally introduced by NREL in 2012,[2] it was for annual totals, since in those days the value of electricity did not vary from month to month as it does today in many PPAs. In this chapter, we are therefore using P90 for monthly data. If you have a flat rate PPA with the same electricity price throughout the year, an annual P90 would work fine.

[§] Some people fit a Normal distribution to the energy yields and use that to estimate any percentile they wish. However, this assumes that the energy yields are in fact Normally distributed and empirical results[2] indicate quite a discrepancy.

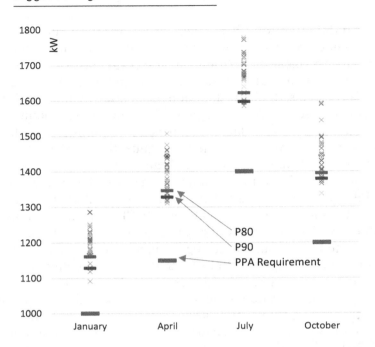

Figure 10.2 Comparison between PPA requirements and energy-yield estimates from 30 years of irradiance data. For simplicity, only four months are shown. Energy yield for each of the 30 years is indicated by *x*. Horizontal lines indicate P80, P90 and PPA requirements. This is an example of a PPA, which is designed for solar, since it varies with the seasons, mirroring the seasonal variation of solar at this particular geographical location.

Should we use P80, P90 or even P95? The answer depends on how serious a problem it would be, if we failed to have enough electricity for our PPA or for our off-grid project. PPAs have penalty clauses indicating what happens if the contracted amount of electricity is not delivered. If the penalty is severe, a high P number is indicated, for example, P95. Another consideration is whether we have another use of our electricity if we are generating too much. For instance, do we have access to the wholesale market to sell it there? If so, there is not much downside in using a high P number. If not, we can compare the cost saving from building a smaller system with the penalty. For instance, the data in Figure 10.2 shows that we have a choice between 1.51 MW P90 system and a 1.47 MW P80 system. At $1/W capital cost, we can save 1.51−1.47 = $0.04m = $40K by using the P80 system. We also save operating costs of $0.017/W/yr for a total over 30 years of 30*0.04*17 = $20.4K (ignoring discounting for simplicity). For these savings, we incur a 10% increased chance of paying a penalty. Suppose the penalty is $1,000 for dropping below the PPA on any individual month. Assuming each month is affected equally, over the 30-year life of the system, the increase in the expected number of months with a penalty by switching from P90 to P80 is 10%*30*12 = 36, for an increased penalty of $36K (before discounting).

To summarize, if we choose to build a 1.47 MW P80 system, instead of a 1.51 MW P90 system, we save $40K in capital costs and $20.4K in operating costs (before discounting) and incur an expected increase of $36K (before discounting) in penalty charges. In financial terms, the P80 system is preferable. We would also need to consider whether the increased number of months when we fail to meet our PPA would adversely affect our business relationship with the company purchasing our electricity from the viewpoint of securing future contracts.

This calculation takes into account the seasonal variation of solar irradiance by dealing with each month separately. It also deals with the year-by-year variation by using percentiles. Clearly solar irradiance varies randomly from one year to another. In addition, there are random major events that absorb up to 30% of sunlight in the upper atmosphere, for example, volcanos causing ash (El Chichon, Mexico in 1982 and Pinatubo, Philippines in 1991) and El Niños causing cloud (in 1997–1998 and 2015–2016). It is important to include such events in the dataset since similar events may occur during the life of our solar project.

The above analysis is for solar. If our project combines solar and wind, it is important to total the electricity generated by solar and wind before calculating P90 values or percentiles. We cannot take the P90 value for solar and add it to the P90 value for wind because wind and solar are negatively correlated. In many geographies, cloudy days tend to be windier than clear days and nights tend to be windier than days.

Wind power varies with small changes in location and depends very much on the topography. Wind speed in a valley is different from wind speed on the hills on either side. Also, wind speed depends on height above the ground. For these reasons, satellite estimates of wind speed must be adjusted by making local measurements at the proposed locations of wind turbines and at the height of those turbines. At least a year of measurements is necessary to give an estimate of wind power at different times of the day and months of the year. The locations of wind turbines need to be planned in conjunction with the layout of the solar modules. Large cranes need to be brought on site to maintain wind turbines and it is important to have access through the solar modules for these cranes.

Table 10.1 Chapter 10 focuses on approaches indicated by X. Other approaches are also used

	Utility-scale wholesale market	Utility-scale PPA	Behind-the-meter	Off-grid
P90 for energy yield	X			
P90 for prices	X			
Battery charging optimization ·			X	
Wind, gas, etc.		X		X
Case example				X

We now move on to how microgrid economics applies in three different situations: utility-scale, BTM and off-grid. Many of the tools of our trade apply to all three, so, instead of repeating ourselves, we will focus on one approach for each situation. Please bear in mind that, in practice, we use the other approaches as well. Table 10.1 summarizes which approach will be our focus.

Optimizing Internal Rate of Return for Utility-Scale Microgrids

Front-of-the-meter projects are typically large, utility-scale projects selling electricity to the grid or a large corporate customer, either on the wholesale market or under a PPA. Although PPAs are often awarded on the basis of an auction, which establishes a competitive price for long-term contracts, the winner of the auction then enters into a bi-lateral contract, which is not subsequently tradeable. By contrast, the wholesale market facilitates ongoing trading of short-term contracts.

Wholesale Market

	Utility-sc mkt	Utility-sc PPA	BTM	Off-grid
P90 energy	X			
P90 prices	X			
Battery schedule			X	
Wind, gas		X		X
Case				X

Wholesale electricity markets may encompass a single country, for example, Chile (one of the first countries to implement such a market), an interconnected group of countries, for example, European Power Exchange (in Western Europe) or part of a country, for example, New England within the USA. Not all countries have a wholesale market for electricity. Pakistan, a prime location for solar irradiance, started to implement one in 2021. Not all wholesale markets are the same. They generally include a real-time market and a day-ahead market, and may also include other terms, for example, intra-day and week-ahead.[¶] Some countries, like India, have a green market for trading renewably generated electricity. In this chapter, we will deal with the wholesale market for electric energy (MWh); Chapter 11 deals with ancillary services that are traded on the wholesale market for electric power (MW).

Many real-time markets are based on a five-minute interval, during which each generating company bids a price and the amount of electricity they can supply at that price. The market operator matches these bids with the demand for electricity, selects the lowest price bids to satisfy the demand and sends automated generator control signals to each generating unit selected. It is essential that the generators can respond immediately to the control signals, that is, the generators must be dispatchable. Solar installations need to be combined with a form of electricity storage to make them dispatchable so that they can participate in the market.

Market prices fluctuate, sometimes wildly, and can go negative if the demand is less than supply. Figure 10.3 shows the spot price[**] of electricity in South Australia together with the demand for four days in April 2021.[3] There was so much BTM solar power that mid-day demand for electricity from the public electricity grid dropped drastically causing negative prices on April 4 and 5. During the evening of April 7, the sun set at the same time as exceptional evening demand causing an enormous spike in prices.

A utility-scale solar installation combined with storage and with access to the real-time market would seek to sell electricity at times when the price is high, that is, not at mid-day in South Australia when demand from the grid is depressed because of BTM solar. Figure 10.3 and similar graphs for other jurisdictions show an underlying daily pattern in prices that is to some extent correlated with customer demand from the grid, but there is also a lot of variability around that pattern. Forecasting electricity prices is very important in all jurisdictions where there is an electricity market,

---

[¶] There are also futures and options markets, which are less relevant in a book on the profitability of solar projects.

[**] The spot price in Australia is the average of six consecutive real-time prices during a 30-minute interval. In some countries, a 60-minute interval is used instead.

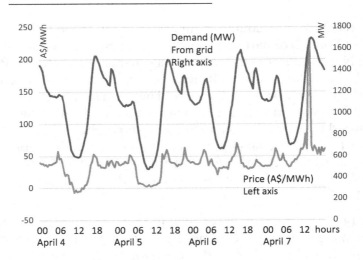

Figure 10.3 Spot price of electricity in South Australia together with the customer demand, for four days in April 2021.

and is assisted by the fact that the electricity system operator often publishes forecasts of demand, based on daily and seasonal patterns, modified by estimates of air-conditioning and heating requirements from weather forecasts and other factors. Solar alone needs to be sold whenever it is generated. Integrating solar with storage in a microgrid not only makes solar dispatchable but also facilitates playing the game of delaying those sales until a time when prices can be expected to be higher. A solar installation operator also needs to forecast how much electricity will be generated based on forecasts of temperature and cloudiness. Sky cameras monitor the whole sky for clouds and software estimates how much they will impact electricity generation. Forecasts from sky cameras are short term and are sometimes called "nowcasts".

At the planning stage for a solar installation, estimates of selling prices, P, are based on historical records of wholesale prices, as are estimates of electricity output, E, based on historical records of solar irradiance. We can simulate optimal scheduling of electricity into storage and selling it at a good price. The estimated revenue, R, is:

$$R = PE$$

Estimates of the economic viability of the project need to be based on revenues, and could, for instance, use the P90 value of R. It is important to note that this is *not* equal to the P90 value of P multiplied by the P90 value of E.

$$R_{P90} \neq P_{P90} E_{P90}$$

Nor is the average value of R equal to the average value of P multiplied by the average value of E.

$$R_{avg} \neq P_{avg} E_{avg}$$

We need software that takes into account the statistical distribution of prices, the statistical distribution of electricity outputs and how the two are correlated to come up with a P90 or average estimate of revenue. Unfortunately, some energy-yield software estimates P90 values of E and some market analysts estimate P90 values of P separately from each other.

Once a revenue estimate is available, it can be used to calculate the internal rate of return as described in Chapter 5.

There is a big difference between planning a solar installation that sells on the wholesale market and operating one. At the operating stage, each day is planned individually, based on the weather forecast, the sky cameras and the demand forecasts from the electricity system operator. The schedule of charging and discharging the storage is optimized each day individually. More information is available at the operating stage than at the planning stage and, used well, can contribute to a revenue stream and corresponding internal rate of return higher than the estimation at the planning stage.

Power Purchase Agreement

	Utility-sc mkt	Utility-sc PPA	BTM	Off-grid
P90 energy	X			
P90 prices	X			
Battery schedule			X	
Wind, gas		X		X
Case				X

Under a PPA, there is a schedule of how much electricity must be provided at different hours of the day and months of the year. Since solar is intermittent and may not generate enough electricity at all times, it needs to be combined with another form of generation and/or a form of electricity storage. If it is combined with wind, which is also intermittent, a storage device is also needed. If it is combined with a dispatchable form of generation, such as a gas turbine, which can be switched on and off whenever necessary, then storage is not necessary. However, if the PPA requires zero carbon emissions from electricity generation, the gas generator needs to have carbon capture and storage (CCS). Our choice is therefore between two options:

- Solar (plus optionally wind) plus storage
- Solar (plus optionally wind) plus a gas generator with CCS

We therefore need to cost out storage compared with a gas generator with CCS. If we have the good fortune of a site suited to pumped hydro or underground compressed air storage, then it probably costs less than a gas generator plus CCS. Otherwise, the only major commercial large-scale storage option of this type is a lithium-ion battery with an installed price of, say, $150/kWh. The capital cost of a gas generator plus CCS is about $2000/kW. Note that the battery cost is a dollar figure per kWh of energy stored, whereas the gas generator + CCS is a cost per kW of power generated. To illustrate the trade-offs involved, we now present a highly simplified comparison between these options.

Let us first deal with the situation without wind. To compare our two options, let us take a simplified example of a solar installation with a PPA requiring 2 MW of electricity to be provided to the grid for 12 day-time hours and 1 MW for 12 night-time hours. To simplify this example further, we assume that days and nights are 12 hours long throughout the year and that solar generates a constant amount of power between sunrise and sunset, that is, we are ignoring the fact that less power is generated early morning and late evening. Without the gas generator, we need to generate 3 MW during the day and store 1 MW of it to use during the 12 hours of night, that is, we need a 12 MWh battery. The cost of our two options now becomes:

1. 3 MW of solar ($3m) plus a 12 MWh battery (12*150*1000 = $1.8m): Total = $4.8m
2. 2 MW of solar ($2m) plus 1 MW gas generator + CCS (2000*1000 = $2m) plus the cost of gas for fuel. Total = $4m plus fuel.

The lower cost option depends on the cost of fuel over the lifetime of the equipment.

This simplified calculation illustrates the important point that a storage device is essentially equivalent to a fossil fuel generator plus CCS. Each option fulfills the PPA with carbon-free electricity. It also illustrates the point that the trade-off between these two options depends on how long we need

1 MW of electricity during the night. If we need it for 4 hours instead of 12, option 1 would involve 2.33 MW of solar generating for 12 hours with a 4 MWh battery delivering 1 MW for 4 hours. The cost would therefore be:

3. 2.33 MW of solar ($2.33m) plus a 4 MWh battery (4*150*1000 = $0.6m): Total = $2.93m,

whereas the cost of option 2 remains $4m + fuel. Option 3 now has the lower cost. In option 2, we are purchasing costly capital equipment but only using it for 4 hours out of 24.

Let's now include wind and go back to the original example of a PPA requiring 2 MW during the day and 1 MW during the night. The cost of solar plus wind is:

4. 1 MW wind turbine ($2m) plus 1 MW of solar ($1m). Total = $3m.

Option 4 is now lower cost than options 1 or 2, but I think all of us have at the back of our minds the question of what will happen if the wind fails to blow, or, for that matter, if the sun fails to shine.

It is unrealistic to expect a PPA to require electricity for only four of the night-time hours, but this scenario becomes realistic if we combine solar with wind, which blows intermittently. For the original example of a PPA requiring 2 MW during the day and 1 MW during the night, suppose the wind fails to blow during 4 of the

Carbon Capture and Storage Potential in Canada

Carbon dioxide is captured from waste gases from a gas generator or other equipment. It can be stored by reacting it with mine tailings to precipitate solid calcium and magnesium carbonates. Alternative storage is in porous rock formations, sealed by non-porous rock above. For instance, the Western Canada Sedimentary Basin could store 1,000 times Canada's 2022 carbon emissions. Carbon dioxide can be transported by pipeline to appropriate locations for storage. Costs vary with local situation:

*   Capture: $30–80/tn
*   Pipeline transport: $1–10/tn
*   Storage: $2–5/tn

Capturing carbon dioxide directly from the air is more costly: $135–345/tn, but avoids the need for transport. Companies could set up direct-from-air capture systems in the Western Canada Sedimentary Basin and offer CCS services to the world, if the cost was substantially reduced to below the price on emissions trading markets. The southern part of this basin coincides with Canada's highest irradiance area so that solar electricity could be used to power the CCS operations.

Carbon Capture and Storage in Iceland

Iceland can store a century of carbon emissions in its basalt rock formations and has built the largest Direct from Air facility in the world at Hellisheiði. It also has experience of capturing carbon emissions from geothermal power plants, dissolving them in water. The solution is pumped into the basalt, where the carbon dioxide solidifies as calcite. This is also done at Hellisheiði, and carbon dioxide captured at industrial facilities in Europe is shipped there for storage.

12 night-time hours, then we have the option:

5. 1 MW wind turbine ($2m) plus 1.33 MW of solar ($1.33m) plus a 4 MWh battery (4*150*1000 = $0.6m): Total = $3.93m.

Other options are also possible. For instance, looking at option 5, we have a wind turbine generating for 20 of the 24 hours, that is, with a capacity factor of 20/24 = 0.833. Solar generates half the time, that is, its capacity factor is 0.5; however, it costs half the cost of wind per megawatt. Half the cost and less than half the capacity factor looks like solar has an advantage over wind. Maybe we should decrease the wind capacity and increase the solar. The elephant in the room is the cost of the battery. Now the battery has to move solar electricity from day to night to cover the reduced wind capacity plus the night-time wind intermittency. With a 0.5 MW wind turbine, the battery capacity needs to be 0.5*12 + 0.5*4 = 8 MWh to fulfill the night-time part of the PPA. Now we need 8/12 = 0.667 MW of solar capacity to charge the battery, plus 1.5 MW of solar to fulfill the day-time part of the PPA. Let's see how the battery will influence the total cost:

6. 0.5 MW wind turbine ($1m) plus 2.167 MW of solar ($2.167m) plus an 8 MWh battery (8*150*1000 = $1.2m): Total = $4.367m

A smaller wind turbine implies more solar, and the cost of wind plus solar goes down as we expect from the capacity factor considerations. Unfortunately, the increased battery cost kills off that advantage and option 6 ends up costing more than option 5.

The above calculations provide a simplified analysis of the options and trade-offs to consider when planning a utility-scale project to satisfy a PPA. In practice, we need to model the daily solar electricity generation profile using the P90 concept described above. We use commercial software to perform the analysis of how much electricity to store in a battery for night-time use. The value of reviewing the options above is that we clarify in our own minds what options need to be considered and we can then ensure that our software is doing a complete job. Offloading the whole job onto a software package sometimes results in sub-optimal solutions, since some software may not consider all possible options. Informed use of software at the planning stage should come up with capacities of solar, wind and storage that are optimal in meeting the PPA requirements at a P90 level (or another specified percentile).

Once the system is designed and the capacities of solar, wind, battery etc. are determined, it can be costed and the revenues and penalties from the PPA can be estimated. The internal rate of return can then be obtained using the method in Chapter 5.

Once the project is completed and is operating, the use of sky cameras and weather forecasts on each individual day of operation can result in improved estimates of solar and wind generation during the course of that day. Careful use of that information to schedule charging and discharging of the electricity storage can result in less use of the gas generator and CCS, resulting in a reduced fuel cost.

Optimizing Internal Rate of Return for Behind-the-Meter Microgrids

	Utility-sc mkt	Utility-sc PPA	BTM	Off-grid
P90 energy	X			
P90 prices	X			
Battery schedule			X	
Wind, gas		X		X
Case				X

Before we get into a comprehensive analysis of the economics of combining solar with a battery in a BTM situation, let's review a quick way of assessing the value of a battery in that type of application.

When we buy a battery, what we are paying for is the functionality that the battery provides, basically charge/discharge cycles. If an installed battery costs $160/kWh and has a lifetime of 4000 cycles, then we are paying $160/ 4000 = 4 cents per cycle to move 1 kWh of electricity from one time of day to another time. If the difference in the cost of purchasing electricity between those two times of day is less than four cents, the battery does not make economic sense. This very simple calculation can be useful in the case of

Ace Natural, Organic Food Warehouse

Cold storage in food distribution is very important. With many fridges and freezers, electricity bills are high and reliability is of paramount concern. Ace Natural installed a microgrid consisting of 250 kW of rooftop solar with a 550 kWh battery and a biodiesel generator. It reduces demand charges, and the generator automatically kicks in if the grid power fails.

time-of-use (ToU) electricity pricing. Suppose we can buy electricity from the grid for $0.10/kWh during the day, when solar is generating well, but the grid price is $0.16 after sunset, then it makes economic sense to pay $0.04 for one battery cycle so that we can use 1 kWh of solar electricity in the evening (thus saving $0.16), whereas we would only have saved $0.10 if we had used it when it was generated.

ToU and Demand Charges

The above calculation works for a ToU tariff and can be used for residential installations to give an initial estimate as to whether a battery will make economic sense. But larger commercial buildings are subject to demand charges that apply to the hour during which our electricity purchases from the grid are at a maximum for each individual month. E.g. if our August grid purchases peak on August 10 at 4:00–5:00 p.m., then we pay a demand charge for purchases during that hour. Demand charges can be very high, for example, $10.00/kWh, compared with an electricity charge of, say, $0.05/kWh at all other times. Clearly, there is an incentive to flatten the curve of grid purchases and this can be done with a battery to move solar electricity from the time it is generated to other times.

Some jurisdictions combine demand charges with ToU electricity pricing; others combine them with spot pricing from the wholesale market. In either case, prices are probably low overnight, which is usually therefore the time to charge the battery from the grid, ready for use the next day. ToU prices are fixed, but spot prices need to be forecast as in the case of front-of-the-meter, utility-scale projects selling on the wholesale market as described above.

BTM solar reduces the total daily amount of electricity we need to purchase from the grid and therefore reduces electricity charges. A battery has a very small effect on that total. The advantage of a battery is to reduce demand charges and some electricity charges by allowing us to buy when the price is low and use when the price is higher (subject to the calculation at the start of this section of the cost of a battery cycle). To summarize: solar power reduces electricity charges; batteries reduce demand charges and also maybe electricity charges.

Figure 10.4 shows a microgrid for an office building in Lancaster, California. The battery and the solar modules use DC electricity and the building and the public electricity grid use AC. The two sections are connected by a bidirectional inverter that converts between DC and AC. Figure 10.5 shows optimized electricity flows in June, with an idealized demand profile of 410 kW from 8 a.m. to 6 p.m. and 140 kW at other times. Rooftop solar modules with a capacity of 250kW is combined with a 200 kWh battery to

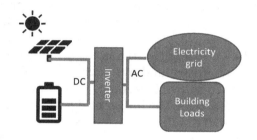

Figure 10.4 BTM microgrid with a bidirectional inverter used to interconnect the DC and AC sections.

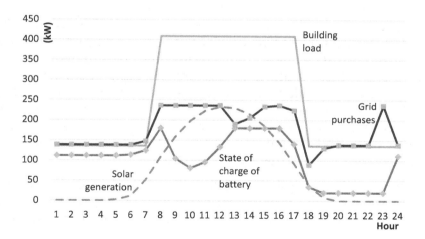

Figure 10.5 Daily schedule of electricity flows for an office building in Lancaster, California in June, showing building load, rooftop solar generation, state of charge of the battery[††] and grid purchases.

[††] The state of charge is the amount of electricity (kWh) stored in the battery at any given time.

reduce peak grid purchases from 410 kW to 240kW. Demand charges are therefore based on peak grid purchases of 240 kW.

We used an optimization algorithm to schedule charging and discharging of the battery to maximize the savings achieved from reduced grid purchases. The battery is charged at three times:

1. the middle of the night, when the price of electricity from the grid is low;
2. early morning, when the sun has risen but people have not yet arrived for work;
3. mid-day, when solar is generating well enough to provide some of the day-time demand from the building plus some spare for the battery.

The load profile shown in Figure 10.5 is for an office building with daytime use. Other commercial buildings such as shopping malls and recreation centers are used into the evening, with a fairly flat consumption profile from 8 a.m. to 10 p.m. The longer and flatter the consumption profile, the larger the battery we need to reduce demand charges, since the battery has to hold enough electricity to provide electricity from sunset to 10 p.m.

Figure 10.5 shows that optimal use of the battery has reduced peak grid purchases from 410 kW to 240 kW, but the battery is at full capacity[‡‡] during some of the hours when grid purchases are 240 kW. This makes us think that a larger battery might have enabled us to save more. And that is generally true for many BTM microgrids, but larger batteries cost more and there comes a point where the benefit of a larger battery is less than the increased cost. The savings are calculated annually, whereas the battery constitutes a capital cost. The two are combined together in the internal rate of return[§§] (IRR), and Figure 10.6 gives an example, from a project in Las Vegas, of how IRR depends on battery capacity. From this graph, we can see immediately that the optimal battery size is 200 kWh.

This approach is appropriate both for commercial installations with demand charges and also for residential installations subject only to a ToU tariff. In either case, it is important to optimize the battery charge/discharge

---

[‡‡] Although this is a 200 kWh battery, we do not charge it more than 90% of this capacity and we do not discharge it below 10%. This operating range puts less stress on the battery and allows an extended lifetime of battery cycles.

[§§] See Chapter 5.

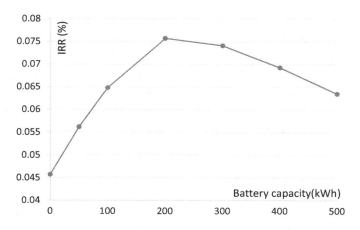

Figure 10.6 Impact of battery capacity on IRR for a BTM project in Las Vegas.

schedule to match the load pattern of the customer to choose the economically optimal battery capacity.

To summarize, we have now done two optimizations:

1. For each month of the year, we optimize the daily schedule of charge/discharge cycles of the battery to minimize the cost of purchasing electricity from the grid as in Figure 10.5. This gives us the annual savings that can be achieved from a given battery size. We repeat this calculation for a range of battery sizes.
2. We estimate the savings during each year of the life of a solar project as described in Chapter 5 and calculate the IRR for each battery size. We choose the battery size that maximizes IRR by eyeballing a graph similar to that in Figure 10.6 to identify its maximum.

Commercial software often combines these two optimizations into one. We have separated them here to give an understanding of what is going on.

The first of these optimizations takes into account the efficiency of the various electronic components involved in the microgrid, the battery capacity (kWh) constraints (it cannot be charged to above 90% of its capacity, and it cannot be discharged below 10% of its capacity[¶]), the battery power (kW) constraints (the rate of charging and discharging are limited by the battery

---

[¶] These constraints extend the battery lifetime in terms of number of cycles; see Chapter 9.

Solar Shopping Malls

A Greenpeace poll of Australians found that over 70% wanted retailers to use 100% renewable electricity.

In 2021, the largest privately owned Narellan shopping center installed a solar microgrid with 10 MW of solar and a 20 MWh battery, reducing retailers' electricity bills by 20%.

Vicinity, which operates shopping centers across Australia had also invested A$73m in solar microgrids for 21 sites by 2021.

design) and maximizes the savings from reduced electricity charges and demand charges.

If everything is modeled linearly, the optimization software always gives the optimal solution. If the model is nonlinear, the optimization software gives an approximation to the optimal solution. When using commercial software, which does not necessarily disclose the approach it uses, it is always important to do a sanity check on the solution to make sure that it is realistic. For instance, I have described above the times of charging the battery in Figure 10.5 and showed that there are intuitive reasons for charging at those particular times. It is also a good exercise to ask why it is discharged at the times shown in Figure 10.5.***

It is also important to ensure that your software adjusts for daylight savings time for the geographical location of your solar microgrid. Sometime in March, many people put their clocks forward, but the sun does not. Relative to the position of the sun in the sky, they are arriving at work one hour earlier. The software should also take weekends and statutory holidays (which are different in different jurisdictions) into consideration since the extent of electricity consumption is different on those days.

Figure 10.5 shows an idealized electricity consumption profile for a commercial building. In practice, the actual load from past electricity bills would be used. However, this may need to be modified. The building manager was already managing electricity consumption to reduce demand charges, before considering a solar microgrid. For instance, air-conditioning on hot summer afternoons may cause peak consumption and high demand charges. The building manager may pre-cool the building in the morning so that it is already a couple of degrees below normal in early afternoon, thus reducing the afternoon air-conditioning peak. If solar can adequately supply the

---

*** The battery is discharged twice. In the morning, people arrive for work before the sun is at its brightest. In the evening, people are still at work as the sun is getting low in the sky.

afternoon air-conditioning demand, pre-cooling may not be necessary and may in fact cause an artificial morning peak in grid purchases. In this case, the building consumption pattern that should be used for microgrid optimization is the one without pre-cooling.

System Peak Charges

In some jurisdictions, a system peak charge is applied to large electricity customers during the top few hours of the year when total grid purchases across the entire electricity system are at their highest, see Chapter 2. One option is to orient the solar modules to the position of the sun at the times of these system-wide peaks. However, the peak times change from year to year, and it is therefore necessary to use a solar microgrid, with solar modules facing south, in the Northern Hemisphere, or north, in the Southern Hemisphere, to generate the maximum electricity and a battery to move some of that electricity to the expected time of the system peaks.

Forecasting those peaks is a major consulting business, and if done accurately could form the basis of a business case for a solar microgrid. However, the long lifetime of a solar installation means that it is important that things do not change too much over the ensuing decades. For instance, peaks that are today due to air-conditioning in the summer, may flip to the winter if there is a move toward electric heating. If the peaks move to a time when solar is not generating well, the business case for a solar microgrid could fall apart.

Minimizing Levelized Cost of Electricity for Off-Grid Microgrids

	Utility-sc mkt	Utility-sc PPA	BTM	Off-grid
P90 energy	X			
P90 prices	X			
Battery schedule			X	
Wind, gas		X		X
Case				X

In the utility-scale situation described above, we need to satisfy the requirements of a PPA. A battery can smooth over the intermittency in solar generation to deliver what the PPA requires. Some off-grid projects also have a PPA, for example, when a solar YieldCo is contracted to provide electricity to a remote mining site, and are therefore analyzed in the same way as for a

Cleaner Cleaning

In Western Australia, Tellus is cleaning up hazardous waste and carbon emissions at the same time. Their remotely located processing facility is powered 100% by 1.2 MW of solar during the day. The microgrid also has a 350 kWh battery and a 2 MW diesel generator for night-time operations.

utility-scale project. In other off-grid situations, for example, those in the sidebars[4,5] for Western Australia and Colorado or a microgrid providing electricity to an off-grid village, there is no PPA and instead we seek to provide electricity at the lowest possible cost. This section deals with that situation.

In an off-grid situation, the battery has to cope with variable demand from our loads in addition to the intermittency in the solar output. The tools of our trade are the same as those described above: P90 values for solar generation and for the load profile, optimized scheduling of charge/discharge of battery and sky cameras to fine-tune the schedule after the microgrid is up and running. One difference is that instead of designing the system for maximum IRR, we design it for the lowest lifetime cost of electricity (LCOE),[†††] but the principle is very similar. Instead of repeating approaches that we have used earlier in this chapter, we will describe here the results of a project we did for off-grid installations in Saudi Arabia, using commercial software, to illustrate the type of results one can expect.

Wilderness Getaway

Bringing grid power to a remote location in Colorado, USA, would have cost $5m. Instead the owners installed a microgrid consisting of 84 kW of ground and roof mounted solar modules, batteries and two 125 kW propane generators for reliability, particularly when the solar modules are covered in snow in the winter.

Electric power consumption in villages in Saudi Arabia has peaks at 2–3 pm in the summer due to air-conditioning and at 6–8 p.m. in the winter due to evening residential use. Average monthly electricity consumption in June–September is almost double that in November–March. Thus any off-grid solar microgrid needs to have sufficient capacity for hot afternoons in the peak summer month of August. We can expect a considerable amount of excess generation at other times of the year, which, in an off-grid system, cannot be used. The LCOE

---

††† See Chapter 6.

Table 10.2 Optimal configuration of microgrids for a village near Riyadh in Saudi Arabia

	Solar/battery microgrid	Solar/wind/battery microgrid
Solar capacity (MW)	17.7	16.3
Battery capacity (MWh)	59.3	14.0
Inverter (MW)	6.5	5.2
Electricity generated (GWh/year)	31.7	29.2
Excess electricity (GWh/year)	10.5	16.7
Capacity shortage (GWh/year)	0.0176	0.0176
Solar capacity factor	20.4%	20.4%
Battery cost per cycle ($/kWh)	0.0188	0.0188
Battery lifetime (years)	14.7	15.0
LCOE ($/kWh)	0.124	0.135

reflects the cost of electricity that *is used*, and is therefore higher than in a BTM system where excess electricity can be used by being fed into the grid.

We will now describe the output from commercial software for a village near the capital city of Riyadh, using consumption data for a typical Saudi Arabian village. Table 10.2 summarizes the results. For a solar microgrid with a battery, the optimal capacities are 17.7 MW of solar and 59.3 MWh of battery. Figure 10.7 shows how these are linked together using DC and are connected to the AC loads via an inverter,[‡‡‡] which has a capacity of 6.5 MW. It therefore takes 59.3/17.7 = 3.35 hours for the solar electricity to completely charge the battery.

We first note that the ratio of battery capacity to solar capacity is totally different from the BTM project we analyzed above, which had 250 KW of solar and 200 kWh of battery. Solar electricity could charge the battery in 200/250 = 0.8 hours. In the BTM project, the battery is

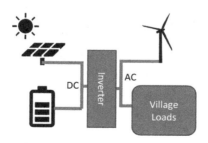

Figure 10.7 Off-grid microgrid showing DC and AC parts connected by an inverter.

‡‡‡ An inverter converts DC electricity to AC electricity.

used primarily to flatten the profile of grid purchases to reduce demand charges, whereas in the off-grid project, the main function of the battery is to store electricity during the day to meet the night-time load. In general, off-grid projects need larger batteries (in relation to the solar capacity) than BTM projects.

We also note that the capacity of the inverter is much less than the solar power-generating capacity. This is because most of the solar electricity generated during the day is used to charge the battery for night-time use. The capacity of the inverter is dictated by the peak load in the village.

The amount of electricity that is generated but not used (excess electricity) is 10.5 GWh per year, about one-third of the total. The system is sized to meet peak demand, but nevertheless there are exceptional times when demand cannot be met and there is a capacity shortage. Even with significant overcapacity, off-grid solar microgrids can sometimes fail to provide enough electricity.

Commercial software produces numerous other results, some of which are summarized in Table 10.2, the solar capacity factor, the charge/discharge cycle cost of the battery and the battery lifetime. Last, but not least, is the LCOE of $0.124/kWh.

For comparison, Table 10.2 includes a solar microgrid that also incorporates a 1.5 MW wind turbine, which generates AC electricity, which is therefore fed directly to the village without going through the inverter. The capacity of the inverter is therefore reduced compared with the previous situation. Another major difference is that when we have wind power available, a much smaller battery is necessary since wind is available at night. The final result is that the addition of wind to a solar microgrid does not improve the LCOE. Riyadh is not a windy city; however, our analysis of Yanbu, a coastal city with more wind, using 2019 capital costs showed that wind reduces the LCOE from $0.12/kWh to $0.11/kWh. Since then, capital costs have declined faster for solar than for wind so that, by 2022, there was no advantage in adding wind to a solar microgrid at any of our study locations, distributed around the country.

Summary

Solar microgrids and hybrids can improve reliability of electricity supply so long as they are well maintained. Their first advantage comes when compared with unreliable transmission lines in the conventional grid. The other advantage of microgrids is that they deal with the intermittency of solar and wind. We have described how to maximize the profitability of micro-grids using P90, optimal battery charging and combining solar with wind, gas, etc. for utility-scale, BTM and off-grid projects according to the following table:

	Utility-scale wholesale market	Utility-scale PPA	Behind-the-meter	Off-grid
P90 for energy yield	X			
P90 for prices	X			
Battery charging optimization			X	
Wind, gas, etc.		X		X
Case example				X

Takeaways

- Reliability
  - If the public electricity grid is subject to extreme weather, microgrids may not improve reliability if they are also susceptible to the same extreme weather.
  - If the public electricity grid is unreliable due to poor maintenance, microgrids can improve reliability so long as they are better maintained.
  - If the public electricity grid is unreliable due to transmission line failures, microgrids should improve reliability.
- Intermittency
  - Short-term intermittency on a timescale of seconds to minutes can be dealt with using supercapacitors, flywheels, compressed air cylinders or batteries.
  - Medium-term intermittency on a timescale of hours to days can be dealt with using a battery, pumped hydro or underground caverns of compressed air.
  - Long-term intermittency on a timescale of months to years can be dealt with by designing the system to provide P90 power, that is, to provide enough power 90% of the time. The analysis is based on data series of solar irradiance and customer requirements going back as many years as possible to capture the full extent of variability.
- Utility-scale
  - When selling electricity on the wholesale market, we have two sources of variability: the wholesale market price and the amount of electricity we will have available to sell. It is important to combine these together into an estimate of revenue, before calculating a P90 value.

- For PPAs, it is important to consider all options to combine with solar power in a microgrid, including wind, storage and gas generator.
- For zero carbon emissions, storage is often equivalent to a gas generator plus CCS and the costs of these options need to be compared.
- Behind-the-meter
  - The daily schedule of battery charging and discharging can be optimized to minimize the cost of grid purchases including electricity charges and demand charges. This calculation is performed for a range of battery sizes.
  - The IRR is based on these optimal schedules and the battery capacity that maximizes IRR is selected.
- Off-grid
  - For a case study in Saudi Arabian villages, we compared a solar/battery microgrid with a solar/wind/battery microgrid. In the latter case, the battery size was very significantly reduced but the excess (unused) electricity was increased, resulting in a higher levelized cost of electricity.

Probe Deeper: The Why?

Why are the methods described in this chapter (P90, battery scheduling, combining with wind, etc.) so different from each other? Because they are handling different situations: P90 deals with annual variability, battery scheduling deals with daily variability, combining with other electricity generation options may reduce the need for a large battery with solar.

Process

Short-term (seconds & minutes) Intermittency

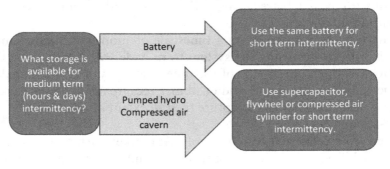

Utility-scale using the wholesale market

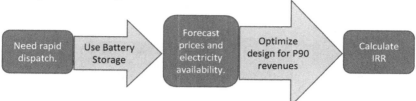

Utility-scale using PPA

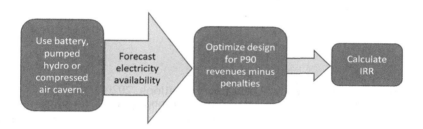

BTM

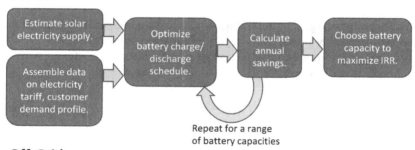

Off-Grid

Operating a Solar Microgrid

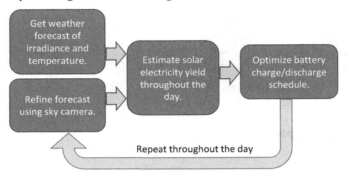

Notes

1 International Energy Agency, World Energy Outlook, 2020.
2 Dobos, A., Gilman, P., Kasberg, M., 2012, P50/P90 Analysis for Solar Energy Systems Using the System Advisor Model, NREL NREL/CP-6A20-54488, World Renewable Energy Forum Denver, Colorado.
3 Australian Energy Market Operator, Aggregated price and demand data, https://aemo.com.au/
4 https://www.pv-magazine-australia.com/2020/12/03/hazardous-waste-facility-now-100-renewably-powered-in-daytime-thanks-to-solar-microgrid/
5 https://microgridnews.com/alternative-power-enterprises-designs-off-grid-ranch-system-with-homer-pro/

11
Extra Revenue from Grid-Balancing Services

Introduction

Up to now in this book, we have discussed how to bring in revenue from selling the electricity generated by our solar modules and use it to offset the capital and operating costs of a solar project, thus making a profit. Is there anything else coming out of a solar project that we can sell, other than electricity? On the face of it, the clear answer to that question is "no!"; solar modules do not generate anything other than electricity. But if we can use that electricity to help grid operators balance out any mismatches between supply and demand, they may pay us more for providing that "grid-balancing service" than the value of the electricity itself. I am *not* referring here to selling electricity at times when the wholesale price is high. We are doing that anyway, and it does help balance supply and demand, but sometimes this wholesale electricity price mechanism is not sufficient to cope with all eventualities and additional "grid-balancing services" are required. Grid services, like electricity, can be sold on markets, and in this chapter, we will see how those markets work and how solar projects can participate in them.

First let's clarify what we mean by "balancing" supply and demand. The electricity grid uses alternating current (AC), which cycles 50 or 60 times per second (50 or 60 Hz), depending on which part of the world we are in.* Coal fired and nuclear steam turbines and gas turbines have a shaft that rotates in sync with the required frequency. If there is an increase in the demand for electricity, the turbine is stressed to increase the amount it is generating, resulting in the speed of rotation slowing down and hence the frequency of the AC power it generates dropping below 50 or 60 Hz. This variation in

---

* Most countries use 50 Hz. North America, South Korea, some parts of Latin America and some Caribbean and Pacific Islands use 60 Hz, Chapter 11.

DOI: 10.4324/9781003262435-14

Setting Clocks

A dispute between Serbia and Kosovo resulted in an average European grid alternating current (AC) frequency of 49.996 Hz instead of 50 Hz. It doesn't look like a big deal but after several weeks, clocks throughout Europe were running six minutes slow. The grid operator decided to run the grid at 50.01 Hz for a while, which allowed the clocks to catch up, ... except of course for those that had been manually corrected and they had to be corrected again.

the AC frequency can damage equipment in the grid and in customer premises, which is synchronized to the nominal frequency. It can also cause clocks that take their time from the grid to record the wrong time. When we talk of "balancing" supply and demand, we mean balancing *without* the frequency changing from the nominal value. In the example above, we would need to increase the steam pressure or burn more gas, so that the turbine does not slow down but produces more electricity at the required AC frequency, 50 or 60 Hz.

It is important to appreciate this aspect of "balancing" since it has two profound implications:

1. If the grid operator requests power from a generating device that is sitting idle, the generator cannot simply start generating electricity and feed it into the grid right away. It must first synchronize both the frequency and also the phase of the AC it is generating with the grid (Figure 11.1). This can take a few minutes for a gas turbine or hydro-electric generator, since the shaft of the generator has to be brought to a speed that synchronizes with the grid. For a device without moving parts, such as the inverter on a solar project or a battery, synchronization is much faster. This means that a solar project, particularly a microgrid (with a battery) is well placed to provide "balancing" grid services, particularly if required at short notice. This is a major topic in this chapter.
2. A device attached to the electricity grid, whether a generator, storage device or customer load does not need to be told by the grid operator that the grid is out of balance. The device can measure the frequency of the grid AC and determine for itself whether more or less electric power is needed. This is called frequency sensing and regulation and will also be discussed in this chapter.

Suppose we were in charge of designing how the electricity grid works. How would we do it? One option might be to set up a single vertically integrated

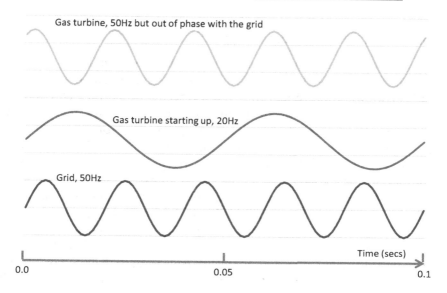

Figure 11.1 Synchronizing frequency (Hz) and phase with the grid.

company that does generation (nuclear, coal, gas, hydro), transmission (from generators to cities) and distribution (within cities to customers). Since this company is by definition a monopoly, we would also need a government regulator to ensure that prices to customers are reasonable. This is how the electricity industry used to operate, and in some jurisdictions it still does. But monopolies and government regulators aren't known for entrepreneurial spirit and many jurisdictions have set up a more competitive structure.

Electricity Market (also known as Wholesale Electricity Market)

A second option is to break up the industry with several different competing companies in each of its three parts: generation, transmission and distribution, and to set up a market on which electricity is traded. The government regulator determines the rules under which the market operates. Throughout each day as more electricity is demanded by customers, the market price goes up providing an incentive for generators to increase production. That sounds too simple to be true, and it is.[1]

For a start, bulk coal and nuclear generators cannot increase and decrease their output fast enough to meet changes in demand. They are good at providing a constant amount of "baseload electricity" 24/7, which lends itself more to long-term contracts than dynamic market trading. The wholesale electricity market is still open to them but they only trade small amounts compared with their contracted output.

Another reason why a simple market mechanism to incentivize electricity generation will not work, is that no one wants to switch their generator on and off all the time. When they bid a price at which they can generate electricity, it needs to be for a certain amount of time, say one hour, and they also need to know whether their bid is accepted long enough in advance to get their generator up and running, say another 15 minutes. Each jurisdiction is different,[2] but for illustrative purposes, let us take the case of a grid operator who forecasts that they need an extra 50MW between 2:00 p.m. and 3:00 p.m. They need to make the forecast by 1:00 p.m., advertise their "ask" by 1:15 p.m., receive "bids" until 1:30 p.m., choose the accepted bids in an auction process by 1:45 p.m., and the generators will be ready to supply electricity between 2:00 p.m. and 3:00 p.m. This is all so fast that it needs to be automated, and the generator needs to be dispatched by the grid operator, not by the generating company, requiring remote control of the generator. The generator also needs to be monitored to be sure it is delivering the required number of MW, requiring some Internet of Things[†] (IoT) sensors sending measurements to the grid operator.

Generators that bid on the electricity market are coal and nuclear, who may marginally increase supply compared with their contracted baseload amount, natural gas and hydro-electric, who switch on and off to match increasing and decreasing demand and who can also adjust their output if necessary and wind and solar microgrids who may adjust their output using their batteries. Each electricity market has a minimum amount of electricity that it deals with and some smaller wind and solar microgrids may use the services of an aggregator to bring them up to the required minimum (see Figure 11.2).

This "real-time" market is supplemented by a "day-ahead" market in which the grid operator forecasts how many MW it will need tomorrow and receives bids from generators. There may also be a "week-ahead" market. Forecasts of tomorrow's demand for electricity depend on such things as the weather forecast for estimating air-conditioning and heating requirements. However, as we all know, weather forecasts are not perfect and when tomorrow dawns, we receive an updated weather forecast, which we use to fine-tune the number of MW required in an "intra-day" market. The

---

[†] Some people refer to this as the "smart grid". However, we will not use that term in this book since it means different things to different people. It can refer to the internal operations of the public grid, the operations of a customer microgrid and the interactions between them.

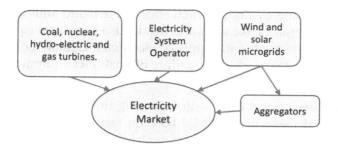

Figure 11.2 Players in the electricity market.

real-time market is used to resolve deviations from these estimates of demand on a timescale of an hour or two.

Each jurisdiction is different as to how many markets it has and what timescale they deal with, but they have one point in common: the closer we get to the time at which electricity needs to be delivered, the higher the price. Providing electricity at short notice is more valuable than planning it in advance.

The electricity market is used to control heavy equipment like gas turbines. This makes it very different from the stock market on which we can trade shares almost instantaneously. Planning a day ahead is useful for gas turbine operators who can bid to keep their turbines running for several hours to fulfill a forecast of air-conditioning demand tomorrow afternoon. When tomorrow afternoon comes around, they can bid on the real-time market for one-hour blocks of electricity, ramping up their generators if necessary. A day-ahead electricity market is used to plan the allocation of physical generating equipment. A futures market on a stock exchange is used for quite different purposes: speculative and hedging investments.

In this section, we have described the operation of the wholesale electricity market, not because it is the main subject of this chapter (which is grid-balancing services), but because much of how it works is similar to the grid-services market.

Grid-Services Market (also known as Ancillary Services Market, Balancing Services Market and Operating Reserve Market)

In the electricity market described above, a lot has to be done in the time between a demand forecast being made and the electricity being generated and fed into the grid. However, even that fast timescale is not fast enough to cope with minute-by-minute fluctuations in demand and in output from intermittent generators like solar and wind. Also some grid equipment may fail causing a sudden drop in supply of electricity. Equally problematic is a sudden drop in demand, due to a failure of customer equipment (e.g. at an industrial plant).

The grid-services market deals with balancing these short-term fluctuations in supply and demand and is based both on methods of supplying electricity and also on customer demands for electricity that are dispatchable, within very short periods of time (e.g. a few seconds or minutes). For decades, gas turbines and hydro-electric plants have been the workhorses of the *electricity* market, ramping up and down electricity production to meet demand as it varies throughout the day. For *grid services*, the generators required are "spinning" reserves, that is, they are already synchronized in frequency and phase to the grid. In the case of a gas or steam turbine, the shaft of the generator is physically spinning, hence the origin of the term, but solar microgrids also count as a spinning reserve even though they have no moving parts. Their inverters synchronize them to the grid electronically and therefore fast enough to contribute to the grid-services market. The same is true of batteries like the one in the sidebar for South Australia. Many other organizations that play in this market providing grid services can be bundled into two groups:

> **Big Battery**
>
> Tesla's big battery in South Australia was 150 MW/194 MWh when originally installed and resulted in the price of grid-balancing services dropping by more than half.

1. *Downward balancing services:* for when supply exceeds demand. A source of electricity needs to be reduced or a demand for electricity needs to be increased. For instance, part of a solar generator could be switched off, or a customer's hot water heater could be switched on.
2. *Upward-balancing services:* for when demand exceeds supply. A source of electricity needs to be increased or a demand for electricity needs to be decreased. For instance, a battery in a solar microgrid could discharge electricity, or a cold storage warehouse could switch some of its cooling equipment off.

Three points stand out in these services.

1. The grid-services market is not trying to sell as much electricity as customers need. That is what the electricity market is for. Our aim in the grid-services market is to balance supply and demand so that the AC

frequency does not deviate from its nominal value, potentially causing equipment attached to the grid to malfunction. Balancing can be achieved by adjusting demand, just the same as it can be achieved by adjusting supply.

2. Solar modules can only be switched off, not on; we are assuming they are already on. Since there is no fuel cost for solar, we leave it on all the time, by default. However, if the grid operator will pay us more to switch it off than the value of the electricity it generates, then we will switch it off. Grid balancing is an important service and in many jurisdictions, it can be worth several times the value of the electricity involved.

3. A solar microgrid can obtain revenue from providing both upward and downward balancing services since it contains a battery. In Chapter 10, we saw that the capacity of a battery in a microgrid is optimized when the developer plans the project and it is therefore already being used to optimize the profit from generating electricity. For that purpose, the battery goes through only one or two charge/discharge cycles per day; see Figure 10.5 for an example. There are plenty of other times when it could be used to obtain extra revenue from providing grid-balancing services. Even at times when we had already planned to use the battery to optimize profits from selling electricity, we may be able to increase our profit by providing a higher-paying grid-balancing service.

High paying grid services that we can provide using equipment that is already making a profit from selling electricity, may sound too good to be true. We should bear in mind that we are offering these services in a market with plenty of competition. For sure, our solar microgrid already has a battery that we can use to provide upward and downward balancing services, but so do electric vehicles. How much does it cost to switch off refrigeration equipment in a cold storage warehouse? Nothing, ... until the food starts to warm up too much. How much would it cost to store the food at a lower temperature than necessary so as to offer balancing services over a longer period of time? The point here is that, as a solar generator, when we offer balancing services, we are competing against companies very different from our own, and an increasing number and diversity of companies are participating in the grid-services market.

Another point is that some public electricity grids are already well balanced and are resilient to equipment failures and other unexpected disturbances. The Continental Europe (CE) grid spans many countries and is one of the largest integrated electricity systems in the world. If a major 1.5 GW generator fails, the AC frequency decreases by only 0.1 Hz, and CE already has another 1.5 GW generator on standby waiting to be called into action. The failure of such a large generator in a smaller grid, e.g. Ireland or Texas, would be much more serious. Payments for grid-balancing services in the USA, with multiple smaller electricity systems, are higher than in CE where the size of the grid absorbs variability in demand and supply with less impact on AC frequency. In a nutshell, revenue from grid services depends on where you offer them.

Above, we referred to hot water tanks and cold storage facilities, which are examples of "flexible" loads on the grid that the customer needs, but does not need right now. They are controlled by a thermostat that maintains the hot water and the food within an acceptable range of temperatures. When the temperature goes outside these limits, the equipment switches itself off or on to keep within the operating range. The flexibility comes from the fact that even within the operating range, the equipment could switch itself off or on to provide grid services. Other residential equipment of this type are swimming pool pumps, ventilation system fans, air conditioners, and battery rechargers. Commercial and industrial equipment includes heating ventilation and air-conditioning (HVAC) systems, electric furnaces, pumps, dimmable lighting, electrolyzers and a range of more specialized equipment, even an aluminum smelter in Scotland; see sidebar. Allowing the electricity system operator to control this equipment is called "demand response" (DR). Customer demand is responding to the needs of the grid. When DR is used to control customer equipment, it automatically counts as a spinning reserve, since no synchronization with grid frequency is required. DR is sometimes called a virtual power plant (VPP). From the viewpoint of balancing demand and supply, shutting off customer loads is virtually equivalent to generating electricity in a power plant.

System operators often impose a lower limit on the number of MW they will accept for DR (e.g. 1MW). They do not want to deal with every individual residential air conditioner or hot water tank. Recent decades have seen a flourishing industry of "aggregators" that control many small customer loads and present the grid

Aluminum Smelter DR

The Simec aluminum smelter in Lochaber in Scotland is powered by its own 80MW hydro-electric plant using water from two lochs, and also acts as a large DR facility. At times, when the North Sea offshore wind generates excess power, Simec switches from its hydro plant to the grid and is paid £40–£50/MWh to absorb up to 80MW of power. The alternative of curtailing the wind power would negatively impact the amount of renewable power in the UK electricity grid.

operator with an aggregated DR capability, e.g. 2MW, above the lower limit. The aggregator bids on the grid-services market, receiving revenue for providing DR. The business relationship between the aggregator and the small customers could include paying the customer a fixed or variable amount per month and giving the customer a free remotely controllable thermostat or pool pump controller, allowing the customer to opt out of individual events.

There is also a second and larger type of aggregator that combines together a diverse range of organizations that are large enough to provide DR individually, but which prefer to outsource that function to a third party. Such organizations include office buildings, shopping malls, electric vehicle charging point operators, pipeline operators, industrial plants, campuses, business parks and the DR aggregators we described in the previous paragraph. These large aggregators are interested in providing a full range of upward and downward balancing services to the grid, not just DR, and therefore also include solar farms, wind farms, microgrids and companies operating many of the storage technologies described in Chapter 9. The full range of organizations competing on the grid-services market is shown in Figure 11.3 and is much larger and more diverse than those competing on the electricity market as shown in Figure 11.2.

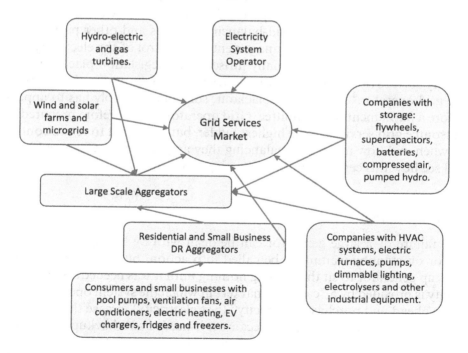

Figure 11.3 Players in the grid-services market.

This diverse range of companies contributing to grid balancing includes large organizations connected to the transmission network and smaller ones on the distribution network.[3] Before accepting bids from these companies, the system operator needs to check where they are connected to the grid and whether the transmission and distribution lines and equipment have sufficient capacity to accept an injection of additional electricity at that point. This is clearly important for extra electricity provided by a solar microgrid battery. It is also important in the case of DR. If an office building with solar on its roof shuts off its HVAC system, there may be extra electricity flowing into the grid from the rooftop solar.

There are two ways in which all these organizations can contribute to balancing the electricity grid. One is by participating in the grid-services market as described in this section and the other is via frequency sensing as described below.

The grid-services market is similar to the electricity market described in the previous section, except for one key point: the timescale is much shorter. For instance, auctions could happen every five minutes instead of every hour, although the exact timescale varies from one grid operator to another. The use of auctions also distinguishes between this market and the stock market in which anyone can buy or sell. In the grid-services market, it is the grid operator that buys grid-balancing services and other participants compete to sell. This retains management and control of the electricity grid with the system operator. In many jurisdictions, legislation places responsibility for providing citizens with electricity squarely on the shoulders of the grid operator.[4] If there is a blackout, someone probably has to appear before a parliamentary committee. Grid operators are therefore prepared to outsource grid services to the highest bidder, but they want to retain control of when and how much grid balancing they are buying. In Chapter 12, we will see how this central control is starting to be eroded.

Capacity Market

The failure of a large generator can be dealt with by having another generator on standby waiting to be called into action, but who paid for that backup generator to sit there doing nothing until it was needed? Backup capacity is provided by a "capacity market" in which the system operator plans years ahead and purchases "capacity" (not electricity) in case that capacity is needed to generate electricity, because it is needed as a backup (to replace a failed generator or to replace one that is out of action for planned maintenance) or to provide for peaks in electricity demand. It is unlikely that solar operators would bid on the capacity market since the marginal cost of generating solar electricity is zero, and therefore, we will not go into detail here on how capacity markets work. They are mentioned just for completeness.

Trends in Markets

The way the electricity industry works is not static. Above we have seen the general principles of the market mechanisms and a major difference between the electricity market and the grid-services market is the timescale within which they operate. This timescale is itself changing in the direction of finer granularity, as Internet of Things sensors and remote control capabilities allow increasingly fast and efficient operation. Electricity markets that used to auction electricity over one-hour periods are moving to 30 minutes and 15 minutes. Grid-services markets that used a five-minute time period are moving to one-minute time periods. Also there is a trend to allowing bids closer to the time of delivery.

A second major trend is the increasing amount of storage being attached to the grid (including solar microgrids) and offering grid-balancing services. This has been leading to a decline in the price of grid services. However, as increasing amounts of intermittent wind and solar provide electricity to the grid, the need for grid balancing is expected to increase, leading to a potential recovery in grid-service prices.

Another trend is toward finer spatial granularity. Up to now, we have talked of the market determining a price for grid services, implying a single price throughout the entire electricity grid controlled by a system operator. In large grids, some electricity is lost if it has to travel from a point where it is injected into the grid to a different geographical area that needs balancing. For this reason, some markets operate on a zonal basis, dividing the system into zones with a separate market for each zone. For instance, Italy has six zones with a separate price for each zone. Some jurisdictions are moving to an even finer granularity based on the nodes on transmission lines at which electricity can be injected or withdrawn, with a market mechanism determining the price of grid services at each node separately. Chapter 12 takes this one step further, describing local markets in which solar microgrids can compete.

Frequency Sensing and Regulation

The AC frequency of the grid gives an indication of whether balancing services are required. If the frequency is too low, the grid needs upward-balancing services and vice versa. A solar microgrid could therefore sense the grid frequency

Big Battery

Three months after Tesla's big battery was installed in South Australia, a 560 MW generator failed and grid frequency fell from 50 Hz to 49.8 Hz within 20 seconds, triggering the big battery to inject 70 MW into the grid. Even a big battery is small compared with a major generator, but the battery stabilized the grid, until a backup generator kicked in 15 seconds later.

and increase or decrease the output from its battery accordingly, similar to the big battery in South Australia described in the sidebar. It does not need to go through a market to do this. The same is true of customer loads. The residential fridge illustrated in Figure 11.4 maintains the temperature around 4°C by switching itself on when the temperature rises to 5°C and switching itself off when the temperature drops to 3°C. If the grid frequency drops too low while the fridge is running, it switches itself off early and if it senses a grid frequency higher than nominal while the fridge is idle, it switches itself on.

Frequency regulation could therefore take place at the edge of the electricity grid without any action on the part of the system operator and without any market mechanism. Although this is technically feasible, no one is

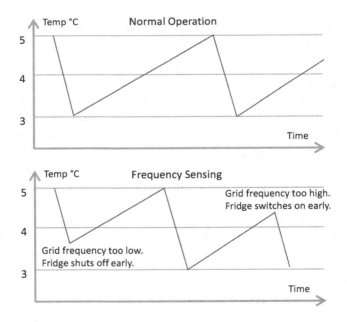

Figure 11.4 The upper graph shows a fridge switching itself on when the temperature reaches 5°C and off at 3°C. In the lower graph, the fridge senses the grid frequency and switches itself on or off early if the frequency deviates from its nominal range.

getting paid for providing this service and the grid operator has no way of controlling whether too much grid balancing is taking place. It is all very well for the fridge illustrated in Figure 11.4 to switch itself off at a certain grid frequency. The grid frequency should bounce up a little. But if all the fridges have the same algorithm in their thermostats, and they all switch off at the same moment, the grid frequency may bounce back too much so that it is now too high. The fridges then switch themselves on again and off and on … Instead of helping to stabilize the grid, too many fridges doing the same thing could destabilize it.

The system operator can control the amount of frequency sensing in the grid by contracting with some companies to provide a certain amount of frequency regulation and paying for this service. Solar microgrids are in a good position to provide such a service as are any batteries connected to the grid. Manufacturers of fridges, pool pumps, hot water heaters, etc. could also contribute up to a certain number of their products sold within a system operator's territory. Some companies provide flywheels, supercapacitors and compressed air devices specifically for this purpose.

Summary

This chapter has shown how solar projects, particularly solar microgrids, can provide grid-balancing services and get paid for doing so. This can be done, either in response to requests from the grid operator on the grid-services market or by contracting to provide frequency sensing and regulation services. The amount of payment depends on whether the grid is already well balanced and on how many competitors are also offering grid-balancing services. Grid-services markets operate on short timescales so that we need to automate our bids. Also we need to give remote control of our solar microgrid to the market operator and install sensors to confirm whether we are complying with their requests.

Takeaways

- Grid balancing involves matching electricity supply and demand while maintaining the grid AC frequency at its nominal value of 50 or 60 Hz.
- Additional generating capacity with moving parts such as gas and hydro-electric turbines takes a few minutes to synchronize with the required frequency whereas electronic equipment such as an inverter on a solar project synchronizes within a fraction of a second.

- Generating companies (including solar) bid on the wholesale electricity market to sell electricity for time periods of about an hour.
- On the grid-services market, a much shorter timescale is used, of the order of minutes, and customers can bid as well as generators.
  - A customer bidding to reduce demand by shutting off a load is equivalent to a generator bidding to increase supply and their payment for providing grid balancing is the same.
  - Downward balancing reduces supply or increases demand. A solar project does not need a battery to provide this service.
  - Upward balancing increases supply or reduces demand. A solar microgrid with a battery can provide this service.
  - The grid-services market requires a minimum of about 1 MW in bids. Aggregators bid on behalf of several small organizations (e.g. residential solar rooftop microgrids) to bring the total bid above the required minimum.
  - Large aggregators may combine generators and customer loads into a VPP for bidding on the grid-services market.
  - There is a trend for markets to operate with finer granularity.
    - Finer time granularity implies operating at shorter notice and for shorter periods of time. Solar project inverters can provide this service.
    - Finer spatial granularity implies different pricing at different geographical locations.
- Frequency sensing provides similar balancing services to the grid-services market.
  - It operates on a timescale of seconds. Solar project inverters can provide this service.
  - The grid operator does not have to request balancing services, the service provider senses the grid AC frequency and determines when balancing is required.
- Grid balancing is important for solar projects in two ways:
  - It allows more solar power to be used on the electricity grid by compensating for its intermittency.
  - It provides an additional source of revenue for solar project operators who wish to participate.

Probe Deeper: The Why?

Why are grid-balancing services important to the solar industry? First, because they help smooth out the intermittency in solar electricity generation, allowing the solar industry to expand the proportion of grid electricity coming from solar power. Second, they are a source of additional revenue to solar projects, particularly microgrids.

Process

Grid-Services Market

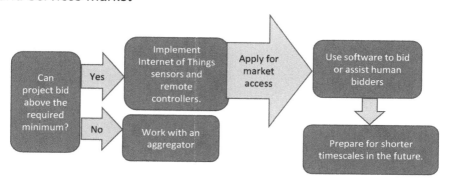

Frequency Sensing and Regulation

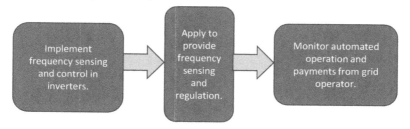

Notes

1 IRENA, 2019, Innovation Landscape for Renewables, Chapter 2.
2 IRENA, 2017, Adapting Market Design to High Shares of Variable Renewable Energy, Chapter 2.
3 IESO, Independent Electricity System Operator, Exploring Expanded DER Participation in the IESO-Administered Markets.
4 Meeus, L. with Schittekatte, T., Reif, V., 2020, The Evolution of Electricity Markets in Europe, Chapter 5.

Part 4
Preparing for Future Solar Opportunities

Anyone working in a high-tech industry such as solar power needs to have an eye on the future. The future might bring competition from new solar technologies or new ways of doing things. Alternatively, we can regard these developments as opportunities for ourselves to exploit. Either way, we need to be aware of them. In Part 4 of this book, we alternate between new ways of doing things and new technologies.

First, we describe an emerging way of trading electricity and grid services, which is more local than that described in Part 3. Smaller companies and even consumers can play a more active role in trading. Second, we describe emerging solar technologies that may impact silicon cells and modules that have been the workhorse of the solar industry for many years. Third are new applications for electricity, particularly in industry and transport that promise to expand the market for electricity at the same time that we are negotiating a transition to renewables. Solar developers and YieldCos can see these as opportunities to sell more electricity to the grid and also as opportunities to sell electricity directly to the industrial and transport sectors of the economy. Last, we provide two case examples showing how to do a cost comparison between emerging technologies and current ones.

Clearly, a non-fiction book cannot describe the future. Part 4 of this book describes things that are already starting to happen commercially today and which can be expected to develop into exciting opportunities for the solar industry in the future.

DOI: 10.4324/9781003262435-15

12

Participative/Transactive Electricity Markets

Introduction

There is nothing new about having a market for electric power. Most electricity system operators have a wholesale market, but access is limited to large companies and the minimum amount traded is about 1 MWh. What is new with "participative" markets is that they are local and allow much smaller participants, thus bringing many more resources to contribute to managing the electricity grid and getting paid for their contribution. Some people prefer the terms "transactive energy" or "transactive market" to emphasize that there are many small transactions among participants. These are early days and many implementations are pilot projects to learn what works and what needs tweaking. Differences will perhaps emerge between participative and transactive markets, but in this chapter, we will treat them as equivalent.

Another buzzword is "Distributed Energy Resource Management System (DERMS)". However, the use of the word "management" implies that the distribution company is managing its suppliers and consumers of electricity. We will not use that term in this chapter to focus on the more customer-centric concept of the participatory market in which a broad range of organizations contribute to managing the grid.

Opening up the electricity grid in this way provides a financial incentive to consumers and businesses to make assets that they already have, such as generators and electric vehicle (EV) batteries, available to the grid as and when needed to balance demand with intermittent supply from solar and wind. Providing 100 kWh at just the right time to help balance the grid is worth much more than selling 100 kWh of electricity. The purpose of this chapter is to describe three examples of such markets and how they operate in practice, to illustrate their potential for more widespread future deployment.

DOI: 10.4324/9781003262435-16

ReFLEX (Renewable Energy Flexibility), in the Orkney Islands

The Orkney Islands, off the northeast coast of Scotland are battered, not only by the North Atlantic winds, but also by the waves they blow onto those rocky shores. The islanders pay high prices for electricity since they have to cover the cost of a transmission line from the mainland of Scotland. There is no natural gas network, so the islanders rely on electricity for heating and hot water. But sheep and cattle farmers have a canny and entrepreneurial bent and decided to turn their geographical situation to their advantage with wind turbines, wave and tidal power generators and even some solar, basking in the summer sunshine hours. Now they produce 30% more electricity than they consume and all of it is renewable. What to do with this excess? The no-brainer answer is curtailment, switch the generators off, and throw the generating capacity away. Could they do better? Orkney has a high percentage of EVs that consume some of the excess power, but the more innovative option is electrolyzing water to generate hydrogen; see Chapter 14 for details. They then use hydrogen for heating and to reduce the use of diesel fuel on the ferries that interconnect the islands. Beyond these local uses, electricity is also sent back down that transmission line to Scotland for sale on the UK wholesale market. Figure 12.1 provides an overview.[1]

Shapinsay, one of the Orkneys, with a population of 300, has a 900 kW wind turbine supplying the island's electricity needs and also powering an electrolyzer that generates hydrogen for the boilers that heat the local school using zero-flame catalytic combustion.

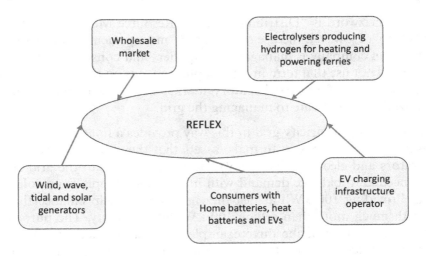

Figure 12.1 The ReFLEX market in Orkney, showing participants.

Electrolyzers on other islands produce hydrogen that is compressed into 250 kg cylinders and loaded onto ferries, to power the engines instead of fossil fuel. Initially only the auxiliary engines were converted but as more electrolyzers are installed, the main engines will also use hydrogen.

Residential hot water heating uses gels similar to those some people put inside their winter gloves. The gel releases heat and turns to a solid. Electricity is used to reverse that reaction so that the gel can be used again. Whenever hot water is needed, the gel is activated and heats the water as it is used. Energy is stored in the gel and is not released until activated, eliminating the heat loss from hot water tanks. Electricity is stored and released as heat when required, so that this device is called a "heat battery".

ReFLEX (Renewable Energy Flexibility), as this Orkney project is known, has £28m of UK government funding for electrolyzers, hydrogen compressors, EV charging points, lithium-ion batteries and heat batteries. If successful, it will be rolled out to other parts of the UK and a key to that success is software development. All the devices communicate their status (state of charge of batteries, amount of hydrogen generated, etc.) using an Internet-of-Things application, and the software schedules electric power flows to hydrogen generation, EV charging, the wholesale market, etc. Suppose you were in charge of software development for ReFLEX, how would you schedule those power flows? Here are a couple of extreme alternatives:

1. *Central Control.* Take the point of view of the distribution company. Agree tariffs with the government regulator for the price at which you will sell electricity for regular use, EV, hydrogen generation, etc. Determine prices at which you will purchase electricity from wind, wave, tidal and solar generators. Develop software that controls when hydrogen will be generated and when EVs will be charged in a way that optimizes your profits.

2. *Participative Negotiation.* This option is also sometimes called "Transactive Energy". In each electricity generator, battery and electricity-consuming device, we implement software agents, which are aware of the status of that device. The distribution company also has a software agent that communicates with these other software agents to negotiate deals that balance supply and demand. Deals could be negotiated every 15 minutes, say. For instance, if an EV wants to purchase electricity, it states a price that it is prepared to pay. If the distribution company is currently purchasing electricity sufficiently below that price so that it can make a profit, it can agree for the EV charging point to switch itself on. If the EV offers a price that is too low, it will have to

wait before charging. The software agent in the EV knows the driver's schedule and the state of charge of the battery and can decide whether it needs to offer a higher price during the next 15-minute time slot. Software agents in renewable generators have less flexibility in that they do not want to curtail electricity that is currently being generated, because the marginal cost of generation is essentially zero. However, they need to bid prices for selling electricity that is high enough to cover their capital costs, and they can judge, from past experience how much they should ask, taking into account the time of day. The distribution company software agent negotiates these deals and also keeps its eye on the price on the wholesale market[*] in the UK. At times when the wholesale price is high, it can reject lower prices offered by electrolyzers and heat batteries. All these software agents are also forecasting, using weather forecasts for supply and past consumption patterns for demand, to negotiate current prices based on anticipated future trends.

Participative negotiation is a far cry from the traditional business model of distribution companies that has sometimes been described somewhat disparagingly as "negotiate a tariff with the regulator, roll trucks with maintenance crews and keep the lights on". Software for intermediate options between #1 and #2 above may also be developed.

Trading Flexibility in Cornwall

At the diagonally opposite corner of the UK from Orkney is Cornwall, a sunny and windy county in the southwest. The growth of intermittent solar and wind power in Cornwall created a problem for the distribution company managing the local grid and also for the transmission company supplying that local grid. They needed more flexibility in managing their operation and so a local electricity market[2] (LEM) was created on which "flexibility" is bought and sold; see Figure 12.2. Market participants for a trial in 2019–2020 included:

- 100 residences with 185 kW of solar and 617 kWh of battery storage, managed through an aggregator since the LEM deals with a minimum of 50 kW of power.
- 113 businesses including 2.5 MW of solar, 2.3 MW of wind and 2.8 MW (3.6 MWh) of storage, together with diesel and natural gas generators.

[*] Real-time, hour-ahead and day-ahead markets.

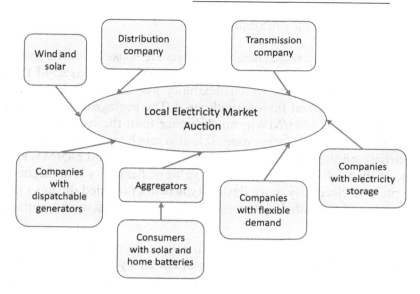

Figure 12.2 Local electricity market for flexibility, showing participants.

The LEM addresses not only medium-term intermittency on a timescale of hours and days, but also long-term intermittency since demand peaks in the winter and generation from wind and solar peaks in the summer.

Distribution and transmission companies can purchase "up" or "down" flexibility. Up-flexibility refers to increased supply of electricity or reduced demand. Down-flexibility refers to decreased supply or increased demand. Companies purchase flexibility for specific dates and times in the future, for example, 2 MW of up-flexibility from 2 p.m. to 5 p.m. on January 15. They also specify the location at which flexibility is required, for example, distribution line identifier, in which case, any participant on that distribution line can offer to provide flexibility. Participants (customers, storage providers and generators) respond by placing bids on the market indicating how much they will charge and how much of the requested flexibility they can provide.

The market is cleared as an auction, by selecting the lowest bidders, subject to the constraints of the physical electricity distribution network. For instance, each distribution line has limited capacity, both in the forward direction for sending electricity to the customers and also in the reverse direction for electricity generated by customers to be fed back to the network.

There are two markets for flexibility:

- a reserve market on which flexibility assets are *booked* months and weeks in advance. The average cleared price during the trial was £54/MWh.
- a utilization market on which flexibility assets are booked days and hours in advance and then actually *used*. The average cleared price during the trial was £281/MWh, much higher than the reserve price, since the assets are actually being used. It is also much higher than the price of electricity on the wholesale market, which was around £45/MWh at the time of the trial. This shows that the value of flexibility is far higher than the price of electricity, since flexibility is being provided during a precise time interval requested by the distribution or transmission company.

Storing Electricity in Ice

Cornwall has a long coastline with fishing fleets requiring ice to preserve the fish, and a large part of the cost of ice is the cost of electricity.

A company with over 500 kW of ice making equipment participated in the LEM by switching some of the equipment off at times when up-flexibility was required and switching additional equipment on when down-flexibility was required. They saved 30–35% of their electricity bill during the trial.

They purchase extra electricity at some times, essentially storing that electricity by making extra ice. At other times they use ice out of storage and reduce their electricity purchases. Storing ice costs less than storing electricity and the equipment to do it is already in place.

To encourage participation, the LEM is operated by an independent company, not by the distribution or transmission company, thus ensuring transparency. It is not intended to replace the national market for flexibility but rather to complement it. The software is written in a generic fashion so that it can be rolled out in other local markets by changing configuration parameters without having to rewrite a lot of code.

The Port of Amsterdam, Shared Energy Platform

The Port of Amsterdam is modernizing its operations and increased digitization and automation requires more electricity. Current supply from the electricity grid needs to be upgraded but the necessary engineering work takes time. Instead, the port decided to access local renewable generation of electricity including wind, solar and a waste-to-energy biomass plant. Many companies operate in the port and the distribution company, Alliander, developed the shared energy platform (SEP),[3] which allows those companies to trade electricity among themselves. Some companies have flexible demand, for example, cold-storage facilities, and others have intermittent demand, for example, supplying electricity to ships while they are docked. Some companies have solar modules on their roofs with batteries forming microgrids. An overview is shown in Figure 12.3.

Intermittency in wind and solar is dealt with in two ways:

- Customers switch loads such as refrigeration and heating on or off as solar and wind output increases or decreases. Price signals on SEP incentivize customers to adjust their loads in this way.
- SEP aggregates some wind, solar and biomass generation providing reliable renewable energy since biomass generation can be ramped up and down to compensate for intermittency in wind and solar.

SEP focuses on renewable electricity and transfers renewable energy certificates to customers who purchase from renewable generators.

The market balances supply and demand by clearing offers of electricity and bids to purchase electricity every 15 minutes. A cleared transaction establishes a contract between the purchaser and the seller for electricity to be delivered during the next 15-minute interval or at a time further into the future. Alliander does not act as an intermediary and does not receive a percentage of the transaction, thus enabling renewable generators to get a higher price for their electricity and purchasers to get a lower price for what they consume.

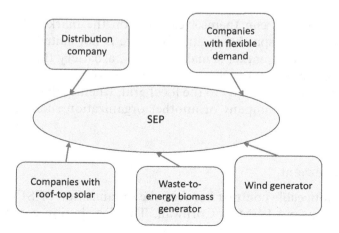

Figure 12.3 The SEP market in the Port of Amsterdam, showing participants.

Trends in Participative Markets

Generic Software

The three examples that have been described, ReFLEX, LEM and SEP, are very different from each other. A major motivation behind ReFLEX was to find a use for excess local renewable generation. LEM was set up to involve local customers in balancing supply and demand in the distribution network. SEP aims to efficiently trade electricity among companies in a port. Other reasons no doubt motivate other local electricity markets, but the general principle of trading and the financial benefits to participating companies are similar. Figures 12.1–12.3 have different market participants, but there is a lot of overlap among the types of participants, implying some commonality in the software functionality for ReFLEX, LEM and SEP. Generic software that can be configured for each situation is therefore a promising way forward.

Solar Industry Involvement

We can expect to see the solar industry becoming involved in participative markets for three reasons:

1. The market involves many organizations in compensating for solar intermittency, thus removing a major barrier to having a high percentage of solar energy in the generating mix.
2. The market allows customers with flexible demand to use more electricity at times when solar would otherwise have to be curtailed or stored.
3. Solar microgrids can themselves trade on the market. Solar without storage is not dispatchable and therefore is not suited to ramping up in response to a market signal. However, a battery that is installed to optimize the performance of a solar microgrid can also be used to increase or decrease supply to the local grid, whether that grid is the public distribution company or another organization such as the Port of Amsterdam.

Grid Management

There is a noticeable contrast between the organization of SEP in the Port of Amsterdam and LEM in Cornwall. The distribution company set up SEP for the Port of Amsterdam, whereas an independent organization set up LEM. One advantage of an independent organization is transparency, which creates confidence, attracting users to participate in the market. SEP also claims these advantages and does not charge a "brokerage fee" for facilitating transactions, so one might ask why Alliander went to the expense of developing SEP. Distribution companies are concerned about losing business to behind-the-meter distributed generation of electricity, particularly in the case of a large operation like the Port of Amsterdam. Providing a platform on which companies trade electricity locally, gives a distribution company access to a wealth of data on how successful such a market is. To what extent do different types of company trade electricity? How much financial benefit do they need to participate? How long does it take for a critical mass of companies to join such a market? How much of the intermittency in solar and wind can be smoothed out by trading electricity among customers with flexible demand or dispatchable electricity generation? The answers to these questions are very important to distribution companies and can be obtained by being involved in participative local markets and monitoring their progress.

Participative markets bring about a change in the way the electricity grid is managed, as summarized in Figure 12.4. The traditional approach by distribution and transmission companies is to monitor trends in electricity flows through each part of their networks and to formulate long-term plans for upgrading equipment to meet demand. We can call this a network-facing approach, whereas the participative local markets described in this chapter are customer-facing. Participative markets also operate on a much shorter timescale. Long-term planning will always be necessary, but with

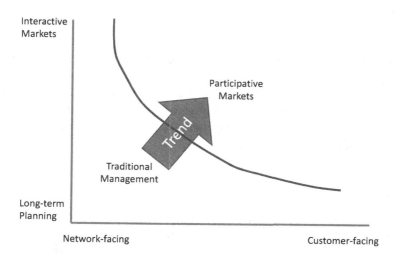

Figure 12.4 The trend toward participative markets in electricity grid management.

participative markets, the need for equipment upgrades will be reduced, thus efficiently reducing electricity prices for everyone.

Summary

Participative markets provide similar functionality to the wholesale market and the grid services market, but on a local scale allowing smaller companies and consumers to participate. This chapter has provided three case examples of participatory markets:

- ReFLEX: a market designed to find a use for excess local renewable generation including solar, wind, wave and tidal power. Power in excess of current requirements can be sold to heat batteries, electrolyzers and EV charging.
- LEM: a market designed to involve local customers in balancing supply and demand in the distribution network, including using ice manufacturing as a way of storing electricity.
- SEP: a market designed to trade electricity among companies in a port, some of which have rooftop solar and wind generation.

These markets represent a change in the way the electricity grid is managed, from grid-centric long-term planning to customer-centric participative markets.

Takeaways

Overall

- Wholesale electricity markets allow a few large companies to contribute to balancing supply and demand in the electricity grid.
- Participative/transactive markets open it up for more and smaller organizations to contribute on a local basis and get paid for doing so.
- There is a general trend from network-facing management of the grid to customer-facing participation.

Market Participants

- Participative/transactive markets include:
  - Dispatchable generators (e.g. natural gas, diesel).
  - Intermittent renewable generators (e.g. solar, wind, wave, tides, biomass).

- Electricity storage, (e.g. microgrid batteries, EVs).
- Customers with flexible demand (e.g. refrigeration, heating, electrolysis).
- Aggregators, bringing residential customers to the minimum trading amount.
- Distribution companies.
- Transmission companies.

Market Organization

- Ownership
  - Distribution company or independent.
- Business drivers
  - Avoiding curtailment of renewables.
  - Managing intermittency of renewables.
  - Efficient provision of low cost electricity.
  - Paying customers for use of their existing resources (e.g. batteries and dispatchable generators).
  - Paying customers for providing flexibility in demand (e.g. refrigeration, heating, electrolysis).
  - Enabling a higher percentage of intermittent renewables in the electricity generating mix, thus reducing carbon emissions.

Benefits to Solar Industry

- Compensates for solar intermittency, thus increasing the market for solar electricity.
- Avoids solar curtailment.
- Solar microgrids can increase their revenues by contributing their batteries to the market.

Probe Deeper: The Why?

Since small businesses and consumers can participate in traditional electricity and grid services markets via aggregators, why build smaller, local markets in which they can participate? Because, in the electricity industry as in others, it is important to "know your customer". The aggregator acts as a middle person, isolating the distribution company from their customers and amassing information about customer behavior for themselves. Operators of local, participative markets get to know how flexible each customer's demand and supply of electricity is, and the amount they will charge to provide that flexibility: new data, valuable in an industry that is trending toward more flexible supply and demand.

Process

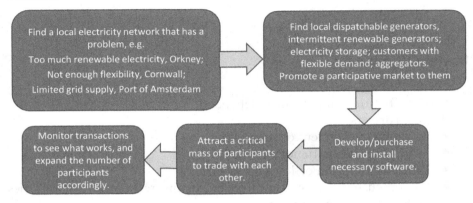

Notes

1 Step Forward for ReFLEX Orkney Project, 2020, Orkney.com/news/reflex.
2 European Union and Centrica, 2021, The Future of Flexibility, www.centrica.com
3 Entrnce, 2020, Port of Amsterdam Creates Energy Platform Allowing Companies to Share Electricity, https://entrnce.com/in/media/port-of-amsterdam-creates-energy-platform-allowing-companies-to-share-electricity

13
Emerging Solar Technologies

Introduction

Silicon semiconductors have been a very successful workhorse for the solar industry for the first two decades of this century. In this chapter, we take a look at what is coming next. First, we are already starting to tweak silicon by using it in new ways: capturing light on the back of our modules as well as the front and floating conventional solar modules on bodies of water. Second, we are developing alternative semiconductors some of which compete with silicon but are made of exotic materials and others that are less costly and can be used alone or as a layer on top of silicon. These emerging solar technologies have features that make them particularly suited to some of the applications discussed in Chapter 14. We present them in sequence from already commercialized to being at the development stage.

Bifacial Solar

Regular solar modules consist of silicon cells encased in weatherproof polymers and mounted in a frame. Sunlight landing on the front of the module goes through the polymers but not all of it is absorbed by the silicon cell. For this reason, the back of the module has a reflective coating on the inside to reflect back this stray light so that it gets another chance at being absorbed by the cell. Silicon has an efficiency of 24% for converting light energy into electrical energy and the more light it captures, the more electricity it generates. However, with this conventional design, there is no way it can capture more light than lands on the front of the module.

Bifacial solar modules allow light to enter from the back as well as from the front. To make the back transparent, we have to remove the reflective coating, which is an advantage if we can get enough light on the back on the module.

DOI: 10.4324/9781003262435-17

A common misapprehension is to say that bifacial cells are more efficient than regular cells. In fact, the cell has not changed and quantum mechanics keeps its efficiency at 24%. But we have gained more light on which the cell can work its magic. We therefore talk of a "bifacial gain" of, say, 15% if we have gained 15% more light striking the cell and hence 15% more electricity being generated.

When the module is not tilted very much, for instance, near the equator or to avoid wind load on the roof of a building, not much light can get to the back. When rows of solar modules are tilted at, say, 45°, we leave a gap between the rows so that one row does not cause too much shade on the next row. This gap together with the tilt makes for an ideal situation in which to deploy bifacial modules as shown in Figure 13.1. The bifacial gain depends very much on the reflectivity (technically called the albedo) of the ground. The reflectivity of grass is around 10–20%, and of desert sand is about 40% but the reflectivity of snow is much higher: between 50% and 90%, resulting in a bifacial gain of 30–70% for snow.

The higher we mount our modules off the ground, the better the bifacial gain; however, this benefit tapers off after about two meters. Higher mounting increases the cost of the supports. It also increases the cost of cleaning and maintenance, and an economic analysis weighs the advantage of increased electricity generation against the increased capital and operating costs, taking into account the reflectivity of the ground. For solar awnings over cars in parking lots, we need to pay for the increased height anyway, but unfortunately the albedo of black tarmac is one of the lowest at around 10%, and parking lots are not therefore ideal for bifacial modules.

Bifacial modules also open up a whole new world of possible solar installations, for instance, we can mount them vertically facing East–West. As

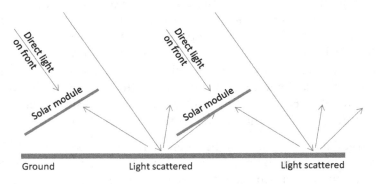

Figure 13.1 Direct sunlight scattered from the ground on to the back of bifacial modules.

the sun moves across the sky from East to West, it shines first on one face and then on the other, with scattered light from the ground also contributing to the total light available for converting to electricity. In this configuration, the solar modules look like a fence. If we need to build a fence (running approximately North–South), we could build it out of bifacial solar modules. We can subtract the cost of building a conventional fence (since we would have built it anyway) when we estimate the economic viability of the bifacials.

In 2021, at the time of writing, bifacial modules cost more than monofacials. Selection of installation sites with high albedos resulted in about 25% of solar modules installed being bifacial. As prices of bifacials are expected to drop faster than those of monofacials, the proportion of bifacials is forecast to increase to about 70% by 2030.[1]

Floating Solar (Float-o-Voltaics)

Deploying distributed energy resources brings electricity generation closer to the customer with two main advantages. First, power is not lost as it is transported long distances over transmission networks. Second, there is improved resiliency to extreme weather. A storm may knock out some solar installations in a city but not all of them. However, cities need a lot of electricity. Putting solar on the roof of a single-family home should generate enough for that home, but many buildings in cities are high rises with tiny roofs compared with their electricity consumption. There simply is not enough space in many cities to generate enough electricity from solar, and space nearby is expensive or is used for agriculture or is protected for environmental reasons.

But many cities have rivers, reservoirs and lakes nearby, which can be used for deploying floating solar generators. Regular solar modules are mounted on flotation devices and moored to the shore or anchored to the bottom. The electricity generated is transported in cables as DC* until it reaches land where it can be converted to AC, if necessary, using an inverter. Installing solar modules on water is in some ways similar to installing them on the roof of a high rise building: it can be windy, and therefore the modules are given a low tilt to withstand the wind load during storms. A low tilt reduces energy yield at higher latitudes but has the advantage that modules do not shade each other and can therefore be mounted without much spacing between rows.

* Underwater DC cables lose less power than AC.

There are various advantages of floating solar installations compared with ground-mount:

- There is no shading from nearby trees and buildings;
- The modules accumulate less dust and dirt;
- If they do get dirty, for instance, from bird droppings, there is a good source of cleaning water readily available;
- The temperature is lower on water than on land, thus improving the efficiency[†] of the solar modules;
- The solar modules reduce evaporation of water. This can be important when installed on a reservoir used to supply water to a city or on a lake used for hydro-electric generation.

All these advantages translate into improved profitability, but it is not all plain sailing for float-o-voltaics. In ground mounted installations, some light is reflected from the ground on to the modules. Water reflects less light, except when the sun is low in the sky and at those times irradiance is low. This limits the usefulness of bifacial modules that rely on reflected light to generate electricity from the back of the modules. Also, the gain from using bifacial modules is greater if they are raised 1–2 meters above the ground, which is tough to do on water as it increases the wind load during storms. The bottom line is that bifacial modules are not suited to floating installations.

Some critics complain about floating solar interfering with watersports. Others complain about sunlight being blocked from marine ecosystems. On the other hand, blocked sunlight also reduces the growth of algae, which can be a problem in reservoirs and hydro-electric schemes, and the jury is out as to whether there is a net benefit or dis-benefit.

Japan was the first country to install floating solar in 2014 and has since installed many systems, both large and small, for instance, an 18 hectare, 13.7 MW installation on Yakamura Dam at Ichihara. This plant also illustrates the susceptibility of floating solar modules to high winds, since part of it was damaged and caught fire in 190 km/h winds during Typhoon Faxai in 2019.

A survey[2] of human-made bodies of water in the USA assessed their suitability for float-o-voltaics. It found that 12% of their area was particularly suitable because it is in water-stressed areas with high electricity prices and high land prices for ground mounted solar modules. This area has the potential to generate 2,100 GW, which represents 10% of U.S. electricity

---

[†] Energy yield from silicon solar modules is increased by 0.45% for each °C decrease in temperature.

generation. This enormous generating opportunity from such a small proportion of the total water area (not including natural lakes and rivers) illustrates the potential of floating solar. However, it must also be said that it is a new technology with installation costs that vary considerably with the flotation devices used and for which multi-year data series on operating costs are few and far between.

Concentrating Photovoltaics

In this section, we discuss how to improve the efficiency of solar cells. Silicon has its limits; what about other semiconductors?

The sun emits light at a range of wavelengths and silicon can convert some of those wavelengths into electricity but not others. This imposes an upper limit on the efficiency of a silicon solar cell of about 32% and current cells are around 24% efficient. If we want a significant increase in efficiency, we need to look at other semiconductors, but each of them has its own range of wavelengths and upper limit on its efficiency, all around 30–34%. What we can do, though, is to make a solar cell with multiple layers of different semiconductors, each one working on its own range of wavelengths and passing the other wavelengths on to the layer below it. Figure 13.2 shows

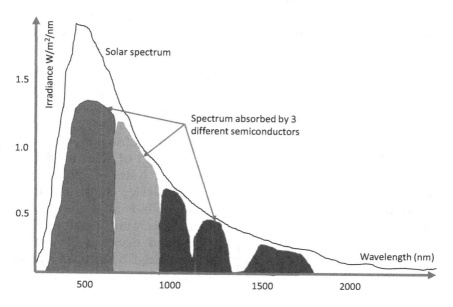

Figure 13.2 The sun's spectrum of wavelengths and the ranges absorbed by three semiconductors.

different parts of the solar spectrum being absorbed by three different semiconductors in a three-layer cell.

The top layers need to be transparent to the wavelengths needed by the layers beneath them. The electricity generated passes through each of the layers and we therefore need electrical junctions between them. They are therefore called multi-junction cells. To make this work, we need to search for semiconductors with a demanding set of characteristics and researchers have succeeded in that task, obtaining 47% efficiency out of a multi-junction cell.

The downside to this approach is that the semiconductors required are all based on exotic and expensive materials: germanium, gallium, indium, etc. To compete with silicon, we need to make the cell very small and concentrate the sun's rays onto that tiny cell. If, as a child, you ever played with focusing the sun's rays using a magnifying glass, you will know that you need to orient the glass at right angles to the direction of the light. This means that the concentrating device needs to change orientation to follow the sun across the sky, that is, we need a tracking mechanism. The operative word here is "need". With silicon PV, a tracking device is an optional extra, but with concentrating PV (or CPV), it is essential. Moreover, it needs to be a two-axis tracker so that our concentrating optics follows the sun as it moves from East to West and also as it moves higher and lower in the sky. Many CPV installations took place from 2010 to 2016 and used pedestal-based tracking, in which an array of several CPV modules is mounted on a central pedestal about which it rotates east–west and from high to low tilt.

Exotic semiconductors, multi-layer fabrication plus two-axis tracking all add to the cost of CPV, and what it gives us in exchange is increased efficiency. Let us look more closely at that word "efficiency". It measures how much electric power in watts we get for 1 watt of solar irradiance. If we get 0.2 watts of electric power, then our device is 20% efficient. Or we could look at it the other way round. If we want, 1 watt of electricity and our device is 20% efficient, then we need 5 watts of sunshine. The more efficient our device is, the less sunshine we need. This may all sound very obvious, but here is the

Free Lunch

"There ain't no such thing as a free lunch. That's the same as saying: nothing drops out of the sky for free".

"Sunshine does. So where's my free lunch?"

"You have to pay to *catch* the sunshine."

punchline. Isn't sunshine free? If so why are we trying to make a more efficient solar cell?

Sunshine is free but the surface area of our solar module is not. In a location with 1 kW/m^2 of solar irradiance, at 20% efficiency, we need 5 m^2 of area to capture 5 kW of irradiance. That is 5 m^2 of land, plus 5 m^2 of solar modules, plus 5 m^2 of racking and support structure, plus 5 m^2 of installation labor. If our solar cell is 40% efficient, we only need 2.5 m^2 of each of those costly items. This is where CPV saves us money, but it incurs an extra cost of the tracker and the fabrication process involves layering of exotic materials.

An idea of how these capital costs in $/W compare is given in Table 13.1. The CPV costs are estimates since companies have not been manufacturing CPV cells commercially, but the table shows how a cost comparison could be made if they were. The cost of module, racking and installation for CPV is based on the PV cost adjusted for the different area required for CPV, that is,

$$\text{CPV cost} = \text{PV cost} * \text{PV efficiency/CPV efficiency} = 0.9 * 0.24 / 0.47 = 0.46 (\$/W).$$

Annual operating costs are not included and will be higher for CPV because of the maintenance needs of the moving parts in the two-axis tracker.

The bottom line is that CPV is a sophisticated technology that was installed in subsidized projects up to 2016,[3] but has not been used since then because silicon PV is of lower cost. CPV is used to generate electricity for satellites and space vehicles where its advantages of small size and hence low weight outweigh its cost. Also in medical applications, where efficiency is more important than cost, it is used to provide power to retinal implants to treat macular degeneration. For mainstream terrestrial electric power generation, it is waiting on the sidelines to find its niche; see Chapter 15.

Table 13.1 Estimated cost comparison for utility-scale installation of PV and CPV

	Silicon PV	Multi-junction CPV
Efficiency	24%	47%
Cell ($/W)	$0.20	$0.50
Concentrating optics ($/W)		$0.10
Two-axis tracker ($/W)		$0.10
Module, racking and installation ($/W)	$0.90	$0.46
Total ($/W)	$1.10	$1.16

Thin-Film Photovoltaics

Continuing our search in the previous section for other semiconductors than silicon, here we investigate a whole range of possibilities that are not as costly as those needed for CPV.

Silicon solar cells are based on extremely pure silicon and are made using temperatures over 1000°C. The crystallized silicon is sliced into wafers 100–200 μm thick, which are rigid and supported with polymers or glass on either side to prevent them from breaking.

Thin-film solar cells, by contrast, are made of a range of materials using temperatures less than 100°C and do not require the same high standards of clean rooms that are necessary for silicon. They are made by depositing the PV material in very thin layers from a few nanometers to 10 μm on to a substrate by spraying, printing or vapor deposition. This is a simpler and less energy-intensive fabrication process than for silicon. If the substrate is flexible, then so is the resulting solar cell. Rolls of PV cells can be made. When flexibility is not required, thin-film PV is encased in polymers and glass in a similar manner to silicon PV.

Cadmium Telluride

About 4% of the world market for PV is cadmium telluride, a thin-film semiconductor that has been used for over a decade. Cadmium is toxic, and combined with tellurium, it is carcinogenic, but encased in polymers and glass, it has passed safety tests, even during a fire. However, the *perception* of toxicity together with a slightly higher degradation rate, a slightly lower efficiency and a slightly higher price per watt compared with silicon[4] has resulted in a declining market share.

Perovskites

An emerging thin-film option is perovskites, which encompass a vast number of chemical compounds with the same crystalline structure. They do not require exotic materials (as is the case for CPV) and, as with other thin films, are simpler to manufacture than silicon PV. A promising option at the time of writing is made from methane, ammonia, lead and iodine, all abundantly available low cost materials, although lead echoes the toxicity issues we saw for cadmium telluride. Low cost materials mean that we can use them in much the same way as for silicon PV, in modules without two-axis

Table 13.2 Cost comparison of silicon PV with a hypothetical perovskite for utility-scale installation

	Silicon PV	Perovskite
Efficiency	24%	19.2%
Cell ($/W)	$0.20	$0.16
Module, racking and installation ($/W)	$0.90	$1.13
Total ($/W)	$1.10	$1.29

trackers and without concentrating optics. Bifacial perovskites are also a possibility.

Various perovskites are available with efficiencies that match those of silicon PV, with manufacturing costs that match those of silicon PV and with degradation rates not much worse than silicon PV. The trick is to find a single perovskite that does well on all three counts. Manufacturing costs in 2020 were $0.5–2.9/W. Efficiency and cost are compared with silicon PV in Table 13.2, similar to Table 13.1 that we used for CPV. In this example, we have hypothesized a future perovskite, which is 20% less efficient than the silicon and 20% less costly per cell. Notice how the lower efficiency of the perovskite implies a 20% larger area of installation and hence 20% increased module, racking and installation costs, which swamps the lower cell cost.

A straight cost comparison between silicon and perovskite is by no means the end of the story. Perovskites absorb different wavelengths than silicon, so we can use the same layering trick we used for CPV to coat a silicon cell with perovskite and get a tandem cell that is more efficient than either the perovskite or the silicon alone; see Chapter 15. Bifacial tandem cells of this type are a research area at the time of writing.[5]

Extensive experience with silicon PV over decades has resulted in very stable cells and modules with a degradation rate of 0.75% per year[6] and 30-year warranties. Suppose a silicon PV project with an 8% discount rate has a levelized cost of electricity (LCOE) of $0.10/kWh. The impact of a degradation rate of, say, 1%, for a perovskite over 30 years would be to increase this LCOE to $0.107/kWh. If, in addition, the lifetime of the perovskite is 20 years instead of 30, the LCOE becomes $0.119/kWh.

Once low cell cost and high efficiency are combined with low degradation and long lifetimes, the future seems bright for perovskites, either as a layer in combination with silicon or maybe even going it alone, in competition with silicon.

Organics

Organic solar cells can be made of a range of polymers. Choice of polymer allows us to tune the organic to absorb in a given range of frequencies and to be transparent in other frequencies. At 10%, they are not as efficient as silicon or perovskites, but they have the advantage of being lightweight, with a power to mass ratio of about 10 W/gm. They can be manufactured using a roll-to-roll printing technique that ensures uniform quality in the resulting cells. Their main disadvantage is low stability and, outdoors, they degrade more rapidly than silicon cells.

The manufacturing cost of organics is currently much higher per watt than silicon cells, resulting in limited deployment. Estimates of the cost of volume manufacturing are $0.23–0.34/W, but there is a chicken and egg situation here in that we will not get volume manufacturing until there is volume deployment.

Profitability analysis of organic solar cells follows the principles illustrated in Table 13.2 for perovskites, and they can also potentially be used in tandem as a layer on top of silicon or another thin film.

Dye-Sensitized Solar Cells

Although dye-sensitized solar cells are based on completely different photoelectric materials, their properties are very similar to those of organics. They are flexible, tunable, transparent to some frequencies and are manufactured using roll-to-roll printing methods. They are a more mature technology than organics with manufacturing costs in the range of $0.5–0.94/W. They are particularly well developed when mounted on glass in applications that do not require flexibility. Similar to organics, they suffer from low efficiency of around 11% and a high degradation rate.

Profitability analysis of dye-sensitized solar cells is also based on the calculation in Table 13.2 for perovskites and, similar to organics, they can also potentially be used in tandem with another solar cell.

In future, we can expect to see competition among perovskites, organics and dye-sensitized solar cells for flexibility, tunability, transparency, cost, efficiency and degradation. They compete for use on their own, in tandem with silicon and with each other and in bifacial and niche applications; see Chapter 14.

Summary

In this chapter, we have described solar developments in three areas. These are presented in sequence from being well developed and commercially available to being at the development stage with some niche applications and requiring further development for large-scale deployment.

- *Module design.* Bifacial solar modules absorb light from the back as well as the front increasing the amount of electricity generated without changing the cell efficiency.
- *Racking and support design.* Float-o-voltaics mounts solar modules with low tilt on floating supports with advantages of no shading, lower module temperatures and less water evaporation.
- *Cell design.* Exotic semiconductors stacked in multi-junction cells have higher efficiency than silicon but are more expensive. Thin-film technologies such as perovskites and organics have the advantages over silicon of flexibility and low temperature fabrication.

Takeaways

- Bifacials
  - Bifacial modules collect light on the back as well as the front, thus providing a "bifacial gain", an increased amount of light available for converting to electricity.
  - Bifacials are suited to situations in which the modules are tilted with gaps between rows and when mounted vertically facing east–west.
- Float-o-voltaics
  - Floating solar modules on bodies of water-like reservoirs reduces evaporation.
  - There is no shading and the temperature of the cells is reduced by the water thus increasing their efficiency.
  - Installing solar modules on a small percentage of the water area close to land can significantly contribute to total electricity supply.
- Concentrating photovoltaics
  - The efficiency of solar cells can be increased by layering different semiconductors that absorb light from different parts of the solar spectrum.
  - The semiconductors required are very expensive and therefore very small cells are used with sunlight concentrated on them at about 1000:1 concentration.
  - The concentrating optics required tracking the position of the sun, thus adding to cost.
  - CPV is not economic for general purpose electricity generation, but is useful for powering space vehicles because of its light weight.

- Thin-film solar modules
  - Cadmium telluride constitutes 4% of the world market for solar but is perceived as being toxic and less efficient than recent developments in silicon.
  - Perovskites, organics and dye-sensitized solar cells are flexible, transparent to a selectable range of wavelengths but have high cost, low efficiency and high degradation rates. They can be used in tandem with each other and with silicon and in some niche applications.

Probe Deeper: The Why?

Why develop emerging solar technologies?

- Because there is always a quest for higher efficiency. Increased efficiency implies that less land area, racking, supports and installation labor are required for a solar project.
- Because the more technologies we have, the more they can be customized to specific applications.
- Because the more technologies we have, the more they can be used in tandem with each other to further improve efficiency.

Process

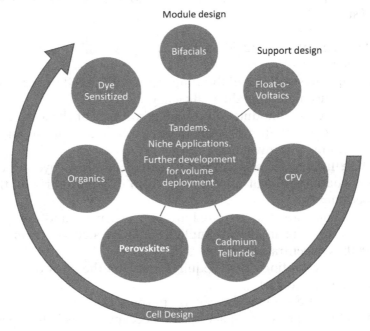

Notes

1 International Technology Roadmap for Photovoltaic (ITRPV) – 12th Ed., March 2021, VDMA. https://itrpv.vdma.org/en/ueber-uns

2 Spencer, Robert S., Macknick, Jordan, Aznar, Alexandra, Warren, Adam, Reese, Matthew O., 2019, "Floating Photovoltaic Systems: Assessing the Technical Potential of Photovoltaic Systems on Man-Made Water Bodies in the Continental United States", *Environmental Science & Technology*, 53:1680–1689, DOI: 10.1021/acs.est.8b04735.

3 Haysom, J.E., Jafarieh, O., Anis, H., Hinzer, K., Wright, D.J., 2015, "Learning Curve Analysis of Concentrated Photovoltaic Systems", *Progress in Photovoltaics: Research and Applications*, 23(11):1678–1686, http://dx.doi.org/10.1002/pip.2567

4 Rix, A.J., Steyl, J.D.T., Rudman, J., Terblanche, U., van Niekerk, J.L., 2015, First Solar's CdTe Module Technology – Performance, Life Cycle, Health and Safety Impact Assessment, Stellenbosch University Centre for Renewable and Sustainable Energy Studies.

5 De Bastiani, M., Mirabelli, A.J., Hou, Y., et al., 2021, "Efficient Bifacial Monolithic Perovskite/Silicon Tandem Solar Cells via Bandgap Gngineering", *Nature Energy*, 6:167–175. https://doi.org/10.1038/s41560-020-00756-8

6 Deceglie, M.G., Jordan, D.C., Nag, A., Shinn A., Deline, C., 2019. "Fleet-Scale Energy-Yield Degradation Analysis Applied to Hundreds of Residential and Nonresidential Photovoltaic Systems," *IEEE Journal of Photovoltaics*, 9(2), DOI: 10.1109/JPHOTOV.2018.2884948.

14
Emerging Solar Applications

Introduction

In this chapter we take a look at what to do with the electricity that solar generates. Can we use it in the tough-to-decarbonize sectors such as steel manufacturing, air transport and agriculture? We first describe how using solar electricity to produce hydrogen is the first step along this road. Then we move on to how we can integrate solar power into other infrastructure: buildings and agriculture and finally tie it all together with a look at the impact of these new applications on the electricity industry.

Hydrogen

Solar cells produce electricity, which is nice to have, but some sectors of the economy are tough to decarbonize using electricity alone. Can we really imagine flying 400 people from San Francisco to Brisbane in a battery-powered plane? How can we make steel or fertilizer out of electricity? These things and many others can be done if we use our electricity to generate hydrogen, which, as we will see in this section, is a many-splendored thing.

Making Hydrogen

Solar electricity can be used to produce hydrogen by electrolysis of water, which splits water into its component elements hydrogen and oxygen with an efficiency of about 75%. This is a low-temperature process at about 75°C. The capital cost of an electrolyzer is about $1/W and is declining. If solar electricity has a levelized cost of electricity (LCOE) of $30/MWh, this results in $2/kg of hydrogen. Hydrogen produced in this way is called "green" hydrogen because of its environmental benefits.

DOI: 10.4324/9781003262435-18

Conventional hydrogen manufacturing is based on a high temperature (~900°C) reaction between methane and steam that produces hydrogen and carbon dioxide.[*] Such hydrogen is dubbed "gray" hydrogen because of carbon emissions. If carbon capture and storage (CCS) is used on the waste gas, we refer to the product as "blue" hydrogen: not quite green because CCS is not 100% effective at removing carbon dioxide. Including the cost of CCS, blue hydrogen costs $1–3/kg.

> ## The Color of Colorless Gases
>
> People like giving colors to gases, and not just hydrogen. Carbon dioxide absorbed by mangroves, tidal marshes, and seagrass meadows is called "blue carbon" because it is beside the sea. "Blue hydrogen" is hydrogen obtained from steam processing of methane with the associated carbon dioxide captured and stored. Don't expect "blue" to mean the same thing for different gases!

Assuming we want renewable hydrogen, our choice is between green and blue, and the prices above look comparable so long as the LCOE of our solar electricity is low enough. Currently, solar electricity at $30/MWh is possible in high irradiance areas with the returns to scale of a utility-scale solar installation. This is reasonable in South Africa or Australia, but not today in the industrial heartland of Germany.

As the price of carbon increases (either in carbon markets or from carbon taxes), gray hydrogen becomes more expensive and green hydrogen becomes more competitive. But investment in green hydrogen is risky since it depends on the price of carbon. To finance green hydrogen, the German Government has Carbon Contracts for Difference (CCfD). They agree a price for carbon at which the green technology would be competitive. If the carbon price is lower, the government pays the difference. If the carbon price is higher, the government receives the difference. This discussion has focused on the *cost* of producing hydrogen, not on the *price* at which hydrogen is traded, because there is not much trade in hydrogen. Much hydrogen for industrial purposes is

> ## 10K Tons Green Hydrogen per Year
>
> One of the world's largest electrolyzers was built by the German firm Thyssenkrupp in Canada. With so much low-cost hydro-electric power that a lot is exported to New York State, Canada is well placed to manufacture green hydrogen.

---

[*] For the chemically minded: $CH_4 + 2H_2O = CO_2 + 4H_2$.

produced on site and is not bought or sold. In other cases, hydrogen is sold by a manufacturer to a customer, but this does not often involve international transport. Prices can therefore vary from one country to another.

Transporting Hydrogen

The National Hydrogen Strategy in Germany includes importing green hydrogen from the Middle East and North Africa. Siemens is implementing green hydrogen projects in Egypt and Saudi Arabia. There are three alternative methods of transporting hydrogen:

- *Liquefaction.* Liquefied natural gas at $-160°C$ is an established way of transporting natural gas, but hydrogen needs a much lower temperature, $-253°C$, almost absolute zero, which is expensive to achieve.
- *Pipeline.* There is an extensive network of pipelines for transporting natural gas, but hydrogen is the smallest molecule there is, and it squeezes through cracks in the pipe junctions that are too small for natural gas to get through. Also, it reacts with the materials some pipes are made of. So new or upgraded pipelines are required for hydrogen. It is possible to add 10% hydrogen to some existing natural gas pipelines, but then hydrogen loses its green credentials since it is piggybacking on a fossil fuel.
- *Compression.* Again, cylinders must not leak or react with hydrogen.

We cannot therefore transition from natural gas to hydrogen and re-use the existing natural gas transport infrastructure. Pipelines and liquefaction facilities need upgrading before they can be used for hydrogen. For hydrogen used in industrial processes, we can electrolyze water and produce hydrogen on site, thus avoiding the need for transport.

Using Hydrogen in Industry

In Europe in 2021, about the same amount of green hydrogen was used in industry as in transport, but industrial uses are expected to grow faster than those in transport during the first half of the 2020s. We therefore start our review of uses of green hydrogen by focusing on industrial applications. Two industries have always used hydrogen and two more are emerging new users:

- *Oil refineries.* About 50% of hydrogen is currently used in oil refineries, which is a declining industry and therefore unlikely to implement a new production process.

- *Ammonia production.* Another 45% is used in the production of ammonia, which is formed by combining hydrogen with nitrogen from the air.[†] Ammonia is an important chemical feedstock, particularly for the production of nitrogen fertilizer. It is here that green hydrogen would be welcome. Nitrogen is an essential component of every protein molecule in our bodies, and the only other mechanism for pulling nitrogen out of the air to form proteins is nitrogen-fixing bacteria, which only occur in the roots of legumes and a few varieties of maize. Research is underway to make other crops such as rice and sorghum bacteria-friendly crops, but green hydrogen is already established as an industrial process and can be used in existing production facilities for methane and nitrogen fertilizer.

> **Welsh Steel**
>
> Welsh law requires a 63% reduction of carbon emissions by 2030, but a single steel plant at Port Talbot causes 20% of Welsh carbon emissions. As countries implement their commitments to mitigate climate change, we can anticipate a lot of hydrogen and CCS at steel plants internationally.

- *Steel production.* Steel is produced by removing the oxygen from iron ore using coke and coal, thus producing iron and carbon dioxide.[‡] Instead of using coke and coal, hydrogen can be used, producing only water[§] as a by-product. This is not as easy as it sounds and involves costly modifications to blast furnaces, but it is a major possibility for mitigating the 4% of global carbon emissions that are due to the steel industry.[¶] Examples include ArcelorMittal in France, SSAB in Sweden, Tata in the Netherlands and Voestalpine in Austria.

The alternative, CCS, is not 100% effective. Green steel could be a business opportunity for Australia, India and South Africa, which have ample reserves of iron ore, together with abundant solar irradiance.

Scrap steel is currently recycled using an electric arc furnace, which can be powered with solar electricity directly without involving hydrogen.

[†] $3H_2 + N_2 = 2NH_3$
[‡] $2Fe_2O_3 + 3C = 4Fe + 3CO_2$
[§] $Fe_2O_3 + 3H_2 = 2Fe + 3H_2O$
[¶] Gray hydrogen has been used in the extraction of other metals since the industrial revolution, for example, the Mond process for the extraction of nickel: $NiO + H_2 = Ni + H_2O$. What is new is green hydrogen and its use in the production of steel, a much more widely used metal.

- *Industrial process heating.* Many industrial processes operate at high temperatures, which can be reached by burning hydrogen, as an alternative to natural gas. Once steel has been produced, it needs to be heated and rolled into the thickness required in a steel mill. Ovako's steel mill in Sweden, preheats the steel using a hydrogen furnace instead of a natural gas furnace.

Using Hydrogen for Transport and Space Heating

There are two more sectors of the economy, transport and space heating, in which green hydrogen can be used as an alternative to fossil fuels. For transport, the amount of energy per unit weight and per unit volume is particularly important and a comparison of hydrogen with lithium-ion batteries, diesel and gasoline is given in Figure 14.1. It can be seen that for a given amount of energy (corresponding to driving range), a hydrogen tank is bulkier but lighter weight than a fossil fuel tank.

- *Road Transport.* Prototype hydrogen-powered trucks and cars have been around for a couple of decades. Hydrogen, compressed in cylinders, powers a fuel cell that generates electricity to drive electric motors. Fuel cells are about 80% efficient. For a given driving range, a battery occupies much more space and is heavier than a hydrogen cylinder plus fuel cell.

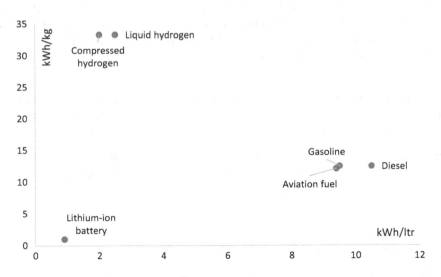

Figure 14.1 Comparison of energy density of transport options. The vertical axis shows the energy per unit weight and the horizontal axis shows the energy per unit volume.

Moreover, a battery takes longer to recharge than swapping out a hydrogen cylinder. These advantages of hydrogen are particularly important for commercial vehicles since money is essentially being lost during recharging, and freight capacity is reduced by the weight of a battery. Also, the lower weight of hydrogen implies a longer driving range so that it is suited to intercity trucking. By contrast, personal driving within a city is more suited to battery electric vehicles, since weight is less important, driving range is shorter and they can be recharged at home overnight.

- *Rail Transport.* In areas where rail tracks are not electrified, hydrogen fuel cells can be used to power trains, with the same advantages as for commercial vehicles described above.
- *Marine Transport.* Hydrogen is a natural replacement for natural gas to power ships, since weight, range and recharging time are important as with trucks. Ports, being adjacent to abundant water, can use electrolysis to generate their own hydrogen, thus obviating the need to pipe in hydrogen from elsewhere.
- *Air Transport.* Hydrogen can be used to power planes, either in a jet engine or to power a propellor using a fuel cell and electric motor. Clearly weight is of paramount importance for air transport and hydrogen packs about three times the energy per kilogram as aviation fuel. However, it is about four times as bulky. NASA's space shuttle could jettison its enormous hydrogen fuel tanks, but that is not a feasible option for commercial aircraft. Figure 14.1 shows that battery-powered electric planes are a non-starter from a weight perspective, except perhaps for small, short range flying cars. However, hybrid planes in which a jet engine generates electricity for batteries and electric motors have some advantages over regular jets. Jet engines are heavy and are only used at full power during take-off. A lighter electric motor used during take-off would reduce the size and weight of the other jet engines required. During take-off, jet engines are only about 30% efficient, whereas electric motors achieve 95% efficiency. While cruising, jet engines are 55% efficient and could be used to recharge the battery, or it could be recharged using a form of regenerative braking during landing. Such a hybrid plane would be quieter than a regular jet, would require less maintenance and would be suited to regional routes where take-off and landing constitute a large proportion of the operation.
- *Space heating.* Today many homes and commercial buildings are heated using natural gas, oil, electric heating or heat pumps.** Green hydrogen,

---

** Heat pumps use the same principle as refrigerators, taking heat out of something cold (the outside air or ground) and putting it into something warm (indoor air). The colder the outdoor air or ground, the less efficient is the heat pump.

piped to those buildings is another possibility, but needs to be weighed against the alternatives. It is inefficient and costly to implement carbon capture on small furnaces and boilers, so green hydrogen would be a less polluting fuel than natural gas or oil. The comparison with electric heating and heat pumps depends on the climate. In countries with very cold winters, such as northern Scandinavia and some parts of Canada and Russia, heat pumps are not economically viable but electric heating would be fine. Switzerland has a lot of heat pumps. France, which already has a lot of electric heating, is installing heat pumps because of their greater efficiency.

Electric heating and heat pumps use about the same amount of electric power as an air conditioner, more than the other electricity needs of the building. In countries with hot summers, where air conditioners are standard, the electric power supply to the building is probably sufficient for electric heating or a heat pump in the winter. In countries without the need for air-conditioning in the summer, such as the UK, the building electricity supply needs to be upgraded to power electric heating or a heat pump in the winter, giving an advantage to hydrogen heating. These options are summarized in Table 14.1. In each option, a means of transporting hydrogen to the building is required, which needs costing against the cost of upgrading the electricity supply in locations with a warm summer. In locations with hot summers where the electricity supply is already sufficient because of air-conditioning use, there is little advantage to hydrogen. Electricity is less costly to distribute over the existing grid and generating hydrogen from electricity is only 75% efficient.

A summary of the applications we have discussed is given in Figure 14.2.

Using Hydrogen as a Buffer

The applications described above show how green hydrogen can be used in many ways that reduce carbon emissions. Unlike electricity, hydrogen does

Table 14.1 Options for hydrogen space heating

	Cold winter	Very cold winter
Warm summer	Hydrogen or upgrade the electricity supply and use electric heating or a heat pump	Hydrogen or upgrade the electricity supply and use electric heating
Hot summer with air-conditioning	Electric heating or heat pump	Electric heating

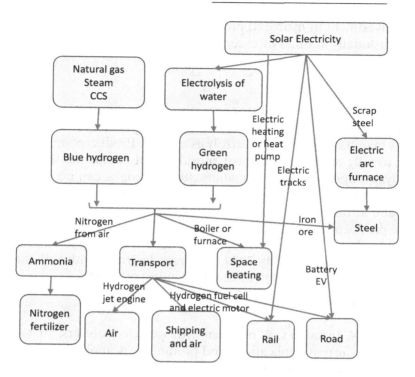

Figure 14.2 Applications of solar electricity. Direct applications are shown on the right of the diagram. Applications via the generation of green hydrogen are shown on the left together with the alternative of producing blue hydrogen from natural gas. CCS: Carbon capture and storage. EV: Electric vehicle.

not need to be used as soon as it is produced. Instead, it is compressed and stored or transported by pipeline until it is required. This is true even when hydrogen is produced on site for an industrial process.

Hydrogen can therefore be used as a buffer to absorb the variability in solar electricity generation both on a short timescale (seconds to minutes) and on a medium timescale (hours to days). We saw in Chapter 10 how the wholesale market price of electricity can go negative at times of high solar production. Those would be the times to electrolyze some water. However, hydrogen production is only economic if done at scale. It requires a source of water and a distribution channel to sell hydrogen and oxygen in bulk. If a solar project is designed from the start in conjunction with an electrolyzer that consumes some of the electricity generated, then ramping up and down hydrogen production is a way of dealing with solar intermittency. The capital investment in hydrogen production is currently too high to be used only occasionally at times of exceptional solar irradiance.

Trends in Green Hydrogen

Green hydrogen as a contributor to a sustainable economy is about where solar power was 10–15 years previously. Only 0.5% of the world's hydrogen was manufactured using electrolysis in 2020. Producers of electrolyzers do not usually receive government subsidies, but companies that purchase electrolyzers and use them to manufacture hydrogen can do. Electrolyzer manufacturers see an increasing number of orders exceeding 100 MW of capacity and as this market expands during the 2020s, the manufacturers can expand production and achieve cost savings from returns to scale. A commercial database[1] of green hydrogen production, distribution and applications tracks these trends. By 2030, the green hydrogen industry should be economic without incentives, as the solar industry is today.

The European Union Hydrogen Strategy has three phases:

- *2020–2024.* Install 6 GW of green hydrogen electrolyzers.[††] Use the hydrogen in current applications and promote new applications.
- *2024–2030.* Install 40 GW of green hydrogen electrolyzers, producing 10 million tons of hydrogen annually. Expand applications to include steel manufacturing, marine and road transport.
- *2030–2050.* Electrolyzer technology should reach maturity and green hydrogen should be used in hard-to-decarbonize sectors.

Green Hydrogen in Japan

In 2019 Japan launched the first ship designed to transport liquid hydrogen, the Suiso Frontier. It is a research and demonstration ship, promoting the development of international trade in hydrogen, in particular the import of hydrogen from Australia to Japan through its hydrogen terminal in Kobe.

The very rapid expansion between 2020 and 2030 envisages support from the EU ETS[‡‡] Innovation Fund and InvestEU. The focus is on green hydrogen from electrolyzers, with about 4% blue hydrogen.

JERA (the largest power generation company in Japan) is switching 30% of its gas turbines to hydrogen by 2025.

[††] Up from 1 GW in 2020.
[‡‡] ETS: Emissions Trading Scheme. The European carbon market.

Impact of Hydrogen on Solar Economics

Clearly solar has an impact on the economics of hydrogen. Solar electricity contributes more to the cost of hydrogen than the cost of an electrolyzer. More surprisingly perhaps, hydrogen can contribute to the economics of solar electricity. Deserts are great places for solar generation, but they tend to be far from centers of population, and the cost of a transmission line adds to the cost of the electricity. Hydrogen pipelines cost less than electricity transmission lines for the same amount of power,[2] and therefore can be seen as an enabler for constructing solar installations in remote high irradiance areas. Moreover, the hydrogen in the pipeline acts as a buffer, compensating for solar intermittency. Efficient hydrogen production and transport therefore contributes to the profitability of remote solar projects.

Building Integrated Photovoltaics

Solar modules generate electricity, which is useful, but some people regard them as ugly. Could solar modules be beautiful, enhancing the architecture of buildings? That is the question we address in this section.

When solar modules are installed on the roof of an existing building, they are "added" to the building, not "integrated" into the building materials. Examples of building integrated photovoltaics (BIPV) on residential rooftops include ceramic tiles with a thin-film PV coating and shingles incorporating thin-film PV. In the latter case, the use of thin film allows the shingles to retain their flexibility. In the former case, thin films match curved surfaces on the rigid ceramics.

Vertical facades of buildings can also have PV integrated into the building materials. Of particular interest are windows that can use glass with an integrated thin-film PV. The different types of thin films allow us to select one that absorbs light in a given range of wavelengths. For instance, a thin film absorbing ultraviolet and transparent to longer wavelengths acts as a sunscreen to the building occupants and does not reduce the amount of visible light passing through the window. Other thin films can transmit and reflect selected colors, contributing to the internal and external appearance of the building. Alternatively opaque PV squares can be alternated with plain glass to reduce the amount of heat getting into the building and enhance the architectural design.

These applications do not focus on cost-effective electricity generation. Apart from the low (but improving) efficiency of the thin films required, mounting PV vertically results in an oblique angle of incidence of the sun when it is at its highest and brightest in the sky. Curved surfaces are non-optimal for electricity generation.

Architects are interested in thin-film PV because it can contribute to the appearance of the building. The entrance hall to a large building with a curved glass roof can be made more interesting if some of the glass transmits selected colors. At night, architects use colored LEDs mounted around the ceiling to achieve similar effects. If the glass already includes wiring for the electricity generated by the PV during the day, the same wiring can be used for the LEDs at night. Thin-film solar also contributes to complying with energy efficiency regulations for buildings and BIPV is the fastest-growing segment of the market for thin-film PV.

Thin film PV can also be integrated into other outdoor surfaces, for instance on road vehicles, trains and aircraft.

Agriculture Integrated Photovoltaics – Agrivoltaics

Many farms and parts of farms are far from the electricity grid and solar is very useful in these areas, for example, to supply power to irrigation pumps. Also, we have seen above that green hydrogen from solar installations can be used to make nitrogenous fertilizer. However, these practical applications of solar are *not* what we mean by agriculture integrated photovoltaics (AIPV) or agrivoltaics. In the previous section on BIPV, we saw how solar cells are *integrated* into building materials. In AIPV, solar is *integrated* into agriculture to share sunlight and land between plants and solar cells, usually by installing solar modules above crops. Both agriculture and solar power are land-intensive industries, and agrivoltaics aims to share land between them.

The first time solar modules were mounted over agricultural land to combine food and electricity production was in 2004 in Japan. A retired agricultural engineer, Agira Nagashima, mounted solar modules on metal pipes above a plot of land with 2 m^2 of space for every 1 m^2 of modules to allow sufficient light through for the crops. With the high price of solar modules in 2004, the system was not profitable, but when Japan introduced a feed-in-tariff (FIT), commercial systems were developed by some farmers[3] and the term "agrivoltaics" was born. Agrivoltaics is the combination of agriculture and PV, to share sunlight, share land, produce crops and generate electricity.

Revenue from electricity under FITs was more than from farming not just in Japan but also in other countries, including Canada and prevented some farming bankruptcies. Since then, researchers have experimented on many different designs with a variety of crops in a range of climates. They have not found a silver bullet showing how to make such systems profitable in to-day's post-FIT world, but they have identified many effects of such systems and many factors that impact their profitability, which we now summarize, first for field agriculture and then for greenhouses.

Field Agriculture

Benefits to Solar Industry

- Agricultural land is relatively flat and does not need grading prior to installation of solar modules.
- Agricultural land has previously been tilled, reducing the cost of installing supports for solar modules.
- Crops transpire during the day, cooling the surrounding air and the modules above them, thus increasing electricity generation.[§§]
- Modules can be mounted close to the ground over grazing land and sheep and goats eat grass, preventing it from shading the modules.

Benefits to Farmers

- Solar electricity brings a new revenue stream and can also power agricultural equipment such as irrigation pumps and desalination systems.
- Any crop responds to sunlight up to a certain point beyond which there are only marginal increases in yield. For some shade-resistant crops, this point is lower, allowing more sunlight to be used by solar modules. Leafy vegetables and berries are shade-resistant and have done well in combination with solar, as has shrimp farming in Vietnam. The spacing between the solar modules can be chosen to suit a particular crop.
- Solar modules cool the crops during the day and trap some heat that would otherwise be lost at night, thus maintaining an even temperature that increases crop yield.
- Shading by solar modules reduces evaporation from the soil, which reduces costs of irrigation.
- Solar modules protect farmland from wind, thus reducing soil erosion.

[§§] Energy yield from silicon solar modules is increased by 0.45% for each degree Celsius decrease in temperature.

Issues

- Electricity distribution lines to farms have a capacity suited to the needs of the farm and may not have sufficient capacity in the reverse direction to carry electricity generated at a farm.
- Solar modules need to be mounted high above the ground to allow agricultural equipment to pass underneath. This increases the cost of installation, because of the extra height of the supports and also because the increased wind load on the modules means that stronger supports are required.
- There is an increased cost of insurance for solar modules because of the risk that agricultural equipment may cause damage.
- Government regulations may protect farmland from being converted to non-agricultural uses. Such regulations may require that agrivoltaics does not reduce crop yields by more than a certain percentage, for example, 20%.
- Public opinion may be very vocal against agrivoltaics, claiming that solar modules spoil the appearance of the countryside and because of the perception that it reduces food production at a time when the world's population is not only growing but also demands improved nutrition.
- Not many crops are shade-resistant.
- Shading by solar modules causes increased humidity in some climates, thus increasing the number of insects and the cost of insecticide.
- Farmers are not able to burn the stubble after harvest as fire invalidates the warranty on the solar modules.

To take these many factors into consideration, it is necessary to analyze each project on a case-by-case basis. Preliminary experimental work may be needed to quantify the impact of agrivoltaics on crop yield and quality, before the internal rate of return from an investment in solar modules over agricultural land can be estimated.

Greenhouses

Greenhouses are the most energy-intensive form of agriculture, presenting an incentive to develop agrivoltaic systems to offset high electricity bills. Internet of Things applications monitor temperature, humidity, CO_2 concentration, lighting levels, etc. and control heat pumps, ventilation systems, fogging systems, CO_2 generators, LED lights and shading curtains. A survey of agrivoltaics in greenhouses[4] shows the annual electricity consumption per square meter ranging from 2.0 to 26.5 kWh/m^2 with some exceptional greenhouses that needed a lot of heating between 120 and 165 kWh/m^2.

Silicon PV solar modules installed on greenhouses with a coverage[¶] be-tween 10% and 25% generated between 13 and 81.5 kWh/m^2, sufficient for most applications. Hydroponics is increasingly used in greenhouses since it improves crop quality and its additional energy cost makes solar energy particularly attractive.

Mounting regular solar modules on greenhouses is, however, not without its problems. Greenhouses made of glass with metal frames may be able to support the extra weight of silicon solar modules, but polycarbonate is one-tenth the weight of glass and is often used instead, thus reducing the cost of the metal frame. That cost can be reduced even further by using flexible polythene sheeting mounted over metal hoops. Greenhouses using polycar-bonate or flexible plastic are not sturdy enough to support the weight of silicon PV solar modules without costly reinforcement. Enter thin-film PV.

Four types of thin-film PV were described in the previous chapter: cadmium telluride, perovskites, organics and dye-sensitized solar cells. Cadmium tel-luride is toxic and not suited to use near food crops. The other three can be glued to glass, polycarbonate or polythene on the roofs of greenhouses and supported without changing the existing support structure; see Figure 14.3. This reduces the cost of installation, compared with the situation in field agriculture where there is an additional cost of mounting solar modules high enough for agricultural equipment to pass underneath.

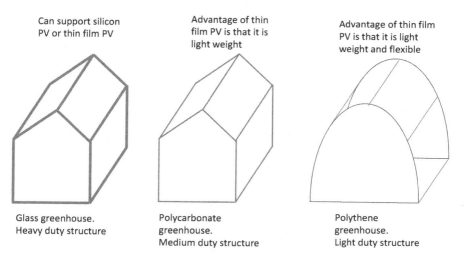

Figure 14.3 Three types of greenhouse showing appropriate type of PV.

[¶] Coverage is based on projecting the area of solar modules on to the horizontal ground and dividing it by the floor area of the greenhouse.

PV Protects Peppers

In a Greek study, organic PV covering 22% of a greenhouse actually *increased* yields of pepper plants by 20% and the plants grew 22% taller. The authors attribute this to the organic PV absorbing ultraviolet light, thus protecting the plants.

Each type of thin film PV can be made of a range of materials that can be tuned to absorb at some wavelengths and be transparent to others. This is a particularly important property in agriculture since photosynthesis in plants uses certain wavelengths and not others. The thin-film PV should be transparent to the wavelengths needed for photosynthesis, and Figure 14.4 overlays those wavelengths with the solar spectrum. The remaining wavelengths are available for generating electricity, and using ultraviolet light in this way can protect plants;[5] see the results of a study from Greece in the sidebar. Researchers are selecting material for perovskites, organics and dye-sensitized solar cells to match these requirements.[79] Lead, a common ingredient in perovskites, should be avoided because of the perception that it could contaminate food crops. The rapid degradation of thin-film PV is not necessarily a disadvantage in applications on polythene-covered greenhouses, since the polythene itself degrades and needs replacing after a few years.

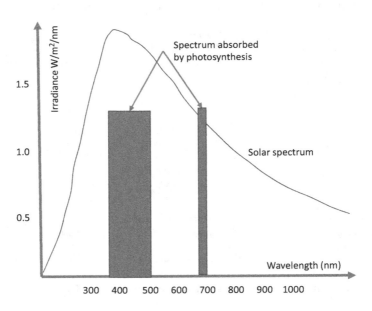

Figure 14.4 Approximate ranges of the solar spectrum absorbed by photosynthesis. Thin-film solar cells on greenhouse roofs should be tuned to absorb the remaining wavelengths.

Avoiding the Electric Utility Death Spiral

This chapter has described a diverse range of emerging applications of solar power, some of which are behind-the-meter (BTM) and others are in front-of-the-meter. BTM applications are designed to reduce customers' electricity bills, which implies less revenues for the distribution company and other players in the electricity industry. However, the equipment in the electricity grid needs to be maintained at the same cost even if it is delivering less electricity. Electric utilities cannot survive if their costs stay constant but their revenues decline and a natural solution is to increase the prices at which they sell electricity to customers.*** This provides an incentive for more customers to install BTM solar, again reducing revenues ... This "death spiral" is illustrated in Figure 14.5(a).

An extreme way of escaping from the death spiral is for the distribution company to charge a flat rate for customers to be connected to the grid independent of the amount of electricity they use. The flat rate could be tiered according to the maximum power that can be delivered over the customer's

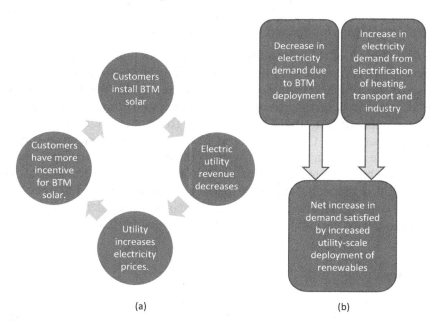

(a)   (b)

Figure 14.5 (a) The electric utility death spiral. (b) How to fix it.

*** This is what happened when customers switched from incandescent to fluorescent and LED lighting, although the effect was small since lighting is a small component of most customers' electricity bills. The change in lighting reduced electricity demand (kWh) but not necessarily electricity costs to customers ($).

access line, a tariff similar to those from some Internet service providers and mobile phone companies. However, unlike the telecommunications analogy, customers could choose to go off-grid completely by installing a microgrid, an option that is becoming increasingly profitable with declining battery and solar prices. When a customer goes off-grid, the distribution company not only suffers a reduction in revenues but also ends up with stranded assets on the customer's distribution line.

We do not need such drastic action. The proliferation of new applications of solar described in this chapter implies increased demand for electricity from the public grid, which could easily compensate for the reduction in demand due to BTM applications, see Figure 14.5(b). The electrification of heating and transport that many countries are planning to fulfill their climate change commitments implies a vast increase in the amount of electricity that needs to be generated from renewable sources, the most rapidly growing of which is solar. The industrial applications illustrated in Figure 14.2 would be hard pressed to fill their electricity needs from BTM solar or wind. A steel plant or an ammonia plant simply does not have enough physical space for wind turbines or solar modules. They may have enough room for electrolyzers to generate hydrogen, but the electricity needs to come from the grid.

The death spiral of the electricity industry is in no one's interest and can be avoided by government planning. At what rates does the government want transport, heating and industry to switch to renewable electricity? At what rates do electricity tariffs incentivize residences and commercial and industrial customers to install BTM renewables? To what extent do the electricity markets described in Chapters 11 and 12 incentivize customers to stay connected to the public grid? The answers to these questions vary from country to country, but each government needs to plan the answers so that some increases in demand balance decreases in demand from BTM renewables over the coming decades. Moreover, increases in net demand should be manageable with planned deployment of solar, wind and other renewables.

Summary

We can use solar electricity for anything that we would use regular electricity for: recharging a phone, powering the cooling system of an office building, running a conveyor belt in a mining operation. These are no-brainer applications. In this chapter, we have focused on applications that are emerging because of governments' commitments to mitigate climate change, such as manufacturing "green" steel, or because of developments in solar technology such as "integration" of photovoltaics into buildings and agriculture.

We have seen hydrogen from solar electrolysis to be a key enabler for the former and thin-film PV to be a key enabler for the latter.

Takeaways

- Green Hydrogen
  - Green hydrogen can be produced by solar electrolysis of water for about the same cost as by reacting steam and methane and using CCS to capture carbon emissions.
  - As the world transitions from fossil fuels, the natural gas pipeline and liquefaction infrastructure needs upgrading before it can be used to transport hydrogen.
  - Green hydrogen can be used in industry to manufacture green steel and green nitrogenous fertilizer, and to provide heat, for example, for rolling steel into sheets.
  - It can be used in jet engines for air transport and in hydrogen fuel cells for marine and rail transport.
  - It can be used to power boilers and furnaces for space heating.
  - It can be used as a store of energy to compensate for the intermittency of solar energy and a hydrogen pipeline is a lower-cost method of transporting energy than an electricity transmission line.
- Building Integrated Photovoltaics
  - Thin-film solar cells can be integrated into roofing materials, vertical facades and windows of buildings.
  - BIPV can be regarded as a way of contributing to the architectural design of a building, by adding reflected color to the exterior and transmitted color through windows to the interior.
- Agriculture Integrated Photovoltaics or Agrivoltaics
  - Sharing land and sunshine between food and electricity production is an emerging application of solar power.
  - Many factors affect solar mounted above crops in field agriculture: increased costs of tall supports to allow agricultural equipment to pass underneath, solar creating a microclimate for crops and vice versa.
  - Thin-film solar on the roofs of greenhouses can be designed to be transparent to the wavelengths needed for photosynthesis and convert other wavelengths to electricity.
- Avoiding the Electricity Utility Death Spiral
  - BTM solar reduces revenues for electric utilities, but their costs are relatively fixed. To maintain an adequate operating margin, they may increase prices, encouraging more customers to install BTM solar, requiring a further increase in prices.

- This death spiral can be avoided by increased electricity demand from the emerging applications discussed in this chapter.
- Governments need to provide incentives for new applications to be developed at a sufficient rate to compensate for lost revenue from BTM solar modules.

Probe Deeper: The Why?

Why develop emerging solar applications?

- Electricity Industry Perspective
  - To expand the market for electricity, compensating for reductions due to BTM deployments
- Climate Change Perspective
  - To use solar electricity to produce green hydrogen, which reduces emissions in hard-to-decarbonize sectors (e.g. heavy industry, transport and heating).
- Solar Industry Perspective
  - To develop markets (e.g. hydrogen) that are resilient to solar intermittency.
  - To develop markets (e.g. agriculture) that can share land with solar.

Process

Hydrogen

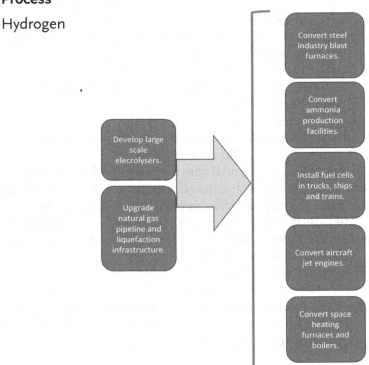

BIPV

Agrivoltaics

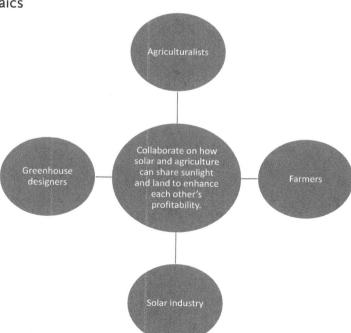

Notes

1 Bloom, Robert, Clean Hydrogen Database, Delta-EE, https://www.delta-ee.com/hydrogen

2 Hydrogen Council and McKinsey, 2021, Hydrogen Insights a Perspective on Hydrogen Investment, Market Development and Cost Competitiveness.

3 Movellan, Juko, 2013, Japan Next-Generation Farmers Cultivate Crops and Solar Energy, Renewable Energy World.

4 La Notte, Luca, Giordano, Lorena, Calabr`o, Emanuele, Bedini, Roberto, Colla, Giuseppe, Puglisi, Giovanni, Reale, Andrea, 2020, "Hybrid and Organic Photovoltaics for Greenhouse Applications," *Applied Energy,* 278:115582, https://doi.org/10.1016/j.apenergy.2020.115582

5 Zisis, C., Pechlivani, E.M., Tsimikli, S., Mekeridis, E., Laskarakis, A., Logothetidis, S., 2019, "Organic Photovoltaics on Greenhouse Rooftops: Effects on Plant Growth, Materials Today: Proceedings," 19, Part 1, 65–72, ISSN 2214-7853, https://doi.org/10.1016/j.matpr.2019.07.658.

15
Profitability Analysis for Emerging Solar Technologies

Introduction

The purpose of this chapter is to describe two methodologies, together with illustrative examples, that can be used to analyze the profitability of emerging solar technologies, which are at an early stage of development so that capital costs are not yet known. We give examples of these methodologies by applying them to two emerging technologies, which illustrate how they could be applied to similar future technologies.

Up to now in this book, we have used the lens of a solar developer and YieldCo to analyze the economics of building and operating a solar project. We now take one step back in the supply chain to take the viewpoint of companies producing solar cells using some of the emerging technologies described in Chapter 13. How can they ensure that their new designs will be attractive to developers and YieldCos? Clearly developers and YieldCos might want to work with them to answer that question, particularly since the answer depends on how their profits from the new technology compare with their profits from silicon photovoltaics (PV).

This book has emphasized that the profitability of solar depends very much on its capital cost. However, when a technology is new, it has never been manufactured at scale and therefore those costs are unknown or, at best, early estimates that may change as the manufacturing process matures. So, if the capital cost is the main determinant of profitability and we do not know the capital cost, what should we do? Before we answer that question, let us also recognize that, even if our new technology turns out to be profitable, it will not necessarily get deployed. It must be *more profitable* than the incumbent technology, silicon PV, which has ruled the solar business for decades. This provides the clue as to how to look at our new technology: compare it with silicon. Below a certain capital cost, it will beat silicon.

DOI: 10.4324/9781003262435-19

What is that target capital cost that our new technology *needs to have*? In this chapter, we show how to answer that question for two examples.

If our new technology is a flat plate, similar to a silicon cell, then it will receive the same amount of solar irradiance as our silicon competitor in any given geographic location. If silicon modules use single-axis tracking, then, so can our new modules. If the silicon module needs to be combined with wind and/or a battery, then the same is true of our new module and the optimal schedule of electricity flow into and out of the battery will be the same. In this case, there are only two main differences between our new technology and silicon: cost and the efficiency with which it converts light into electricity. We therefore do not have to do the microgrid optimization that we described in Chapter 10. All we need to do is calculate the cost of the new technology cells that result in an installed capital cost less than the corresponding silicon cost. This is a relatively straightforward analysis and we illustrate how to apply it to perovskite/silicon tandems.

When solar modules sit out in the sun, they not only generate electricity but they also get hot. Another "combo" technology is to make use of this "waste" heat, either converting it directly to electricity using a thermo-electric generator, or using it, for instance, for district heating. The above method can be applied to this situation and a review of the advantages of this technology is available from Shakeriaski et al[1].

If, on the other hand, our new technology involves two-axis tracking and we are comparing it with silicon modules that are fixed or one-axis tracked, then we need to do the microgrid optimization from Chapter 10 and then calculate the internal rate of return (IRR) from Chapter 5 for both technologies. We can then investigate a range of possible capital costs for our new technology and select those that give a higher IRR than silicon. This is a more complex analysis and we illustrate how to apply it to microtracked concentrating photovoltaics (mCPV).

Perovskite/Silicon Tandems

For the past couple of decades, silicon solar cells have done the world a great service, producing renewable electricity at successively higher efficiency and lower costs. Their efficiency is now approaching the theoretical maximum limit. Costs of manufacturing silicon cells have also been squeezed so much that only marginal improvements can be expected from now on. Their cost ($/W) has declined so much that it is now only 21%, 12% and 7% of the installed cost of utility-scale, commercial roof-top and residential projects, so that further reductions in cost will have little impact on total project cost. So, has silicon come to the end of its road, ready to be replaced by something more efficient, much less costly or both? Not if we combine silicon with another semiconductor that complements it. Enter the perovskite/ silicon tandem.

Silicon generates electricity from a certain range of wavelengths, and perovskites can be designed to use other wavelengths. A thin film of perovskite on top of a silicon cell could absorb some wavelengths while passing other wavelengths on to the silicon. Such a tandem would clearly cost more than silicon alone, but the increased efficiency could make it a winner in comparison with a regular silicon cell. Although some perovskites are already commercialized, they constitute a whole range of chemical compounds and new perovskites are always in the works. Moreover, as experience is developed, manufacturing costs and efficiencies can be expected to improve. Our approach is therefore to identify a range of target efficiencies and manufacturing costs for perovskites that will allow a project based on perovskite/ silicon tandems to have a lower installed cost ($/W) than silicon alone. It also needs to be lower than perovskite alone, and we will check that out too.

In Chapter 13, Table 13.2, we compared the total installed cost of a silicon PV system with that of a perovskite system. The total cost ($/W) consists of two components, the cell cost ($/W) and the module, racking and installation cost ($/W). This latter cost depends on the surface area needed to produce a watt of electricity, which, in turn, depends on the efficiency of the cell. We now extend that calculation to include the costs of a silicon/ perovskite tandem, for which we need a couple of assumptions:

1. *Efficiency of Tandem.* Since the perovskite is a thin film on top of the silicon cell, it absorbs light from some wavelengths first and passes the remainder to the silicon. Life isn't perfect and in practice, perovskites eat up some of the wavelengths that the silicon could have used. We assume that the silicon is left with only 50% of its wavelengths to work with. This percentage depends on the design of the perovskite and is in line with the 47.3% used by Yu et al.[2] A tandem consisting of 24% efficient silicon plus 21% efficient perovskite would therefore have an efficiency of 21% + 0.5*24% = 33%.
2. *Cost of Tandem.* The cost of the tandem *cell* is the sum of the cost of a silicon cell plus a perovskite cell. The cost of the tandem module, racking and installation depends on the area, which depends on the efficiency. These costs are $0.9/W for utility-scale installation of 24% efficient silicon. For a 33% efficient tandem, they are therefore 0.9*0.24 / 0.33 = $0.65/W.

The result is given in Table 15.1 from which we can see that the total installed cost is less for the tandem than either the silicon or the perovskite alone. The tandem cell costs more than either the silicon cell or the perovskite cell (in fact it is the sum of them) but its increased efficiency means that the area-dependent costs of module, racking and installation are reduced so much that the total installed cost of the tandem is the lowest of all three.

The calculation in Table 15.1 is an example of a situation in which we know the cost and efficiency of the perovskite cell. In the case of a new perovskite, those items are not necessarily known and the purpose of this chapter is to deal with that situation. We do that by establishing ranges of values of perovskite efficiency and cost for which each of the three options has the lowest cost. The result is given in Figure 15.1. There is no point in developing perovskites falling into the top left of the diagram and we should combine

Table 15.1 Cost comparison of silicon PV with a perovskite and with a perovskite/silicon tandem for utility-scale installation

	Silicon PV	Perovskite	Tandem
Efficiency	24.0%	21.0%	33.0%
Cell ($/W)	$0.20	$0.15	$0.35
Module, racking and installation ($/W)	$0.90	$1.03	$0.65
Total ($/W)	$1.10	$1.18	$1.00

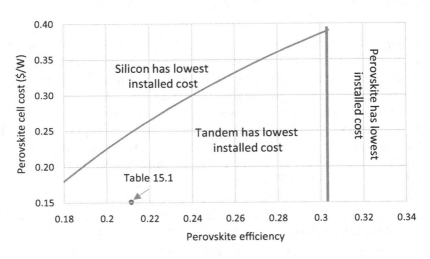

Figure 15.1 Range of values of perovskite efficiency and cell cost for which the total installed cost is lowest for silicon, perovskite and tandem.

them in tandem with silicon at the lower left. If we can develop a perovskite with such a high efficiency that it comes to the right of the diagram, it can go it alone, beating both the silicon and the tandem on total installed cost of our utility-scale solar project.

Optional Math Box

Assuming the data in the table for silicon are known, we seek ranges of values of the efficiency and cell cost for perovskite such that the total cost of the tandem is less than the total cost of (i) silicon and (ii) perovskite.

	Silicon	Perovskite	Tandem
Efficiency	e_s	e_p	$e_t = e_p + 0.5e_s$
Cell cost	c_s	c_p	$c_t = c_p + c_s$
Area-dependent costs	A_s	$A_p = \dfrac{A_s e_s}{e_p}$	$A_t = \dfrac{A_s e_s}{e_t}$
Total cost	$c_s + A_s$	$c_p + \dfrac{A_s e_s}{e_p}$	$c_p + c_s + \dfrac{A_s e_s}{e_p + 0.5e_s}$

The values of the parameters for silicon are known and we are investigating ranges of the perovskite parameters e_p and c_p.

i. The total cost of the tandem is less than that of silicon if:

$$c_p < A_s - \frac{A_s e_s}{e_p + 0.5e_s},$$ corresponding to the lower left of Figure 15.1.

ii. The total cost of the tandem is less than that of perovskite if:

$$c_s + \frac{A_s e_s}{e_p + 0.5e_s} < \frac{A_s e_s}{e_p}.$$ This equation is independent of c_p,

corresponding to the right of Figure 15.1.

We note that the results in Figure 15.1 depend on the cost and efficiency of the silicon cell. We have used an efficiency of 24%, lower than the latest cells in research labs[3] since the efficiency of cells from a bulk manufacturing process are slightly lower than those developed in ideal lab conditions.

We have used \$0.9/W for the area-dependent costs, which corresponds to all the other costs for utility-scale installations. These will be higher for commercial and residential installations (see Chapters 2 and 3) and will be lower if some of the items do not depend on area.

We also note that the results in Figure 15.1 do *not* depend on the geographical location of the project. In sunny locations, we will get more electricity from each of our three options. Nor do they depend on whether our PV is combined with a battery in a microgrid, since the hourly variation in electricity generated is also the same for each option. We do not therefore need to do the microgrid optimization described in Chapter 10.

The above analysis can easily be adapted to other tandems such as perovskite/organic and perovskite/perovskite by changing the corresponding costs.

Manufacturing silicon solar cells is a low-profitability business because of intense cost-based competition, so manufacturers are glad to have a new technology to give them a competitive advantage. Companies in the forefront of the commercialization of perovskite/silicon tandem cells are Helmholtz-Zentrum of Berlin and Oxford PV, a spinoff from the University of Oxford where useful photovoltaic properties of perovskites were established in 2012.[4]

A key contribution of the University of Oxford was to make perovskites stable; however, long-term stability in moist environments is still a challenge and the technology is too new for degradation to have been measured over the decades-long life of silicon. On the bright side, the term of power purchase agreements is dropping from 20–30 years to 10 years; therefore, solar power needs to demonstrate an acceptable IRR over a shorter period. If perovskite/silicon tandems can last ten years out in the wind and weather and indicate an increase in IRR compared with silicon alone over that period, they may be more attractive to institutional investors than silicon even with its 30-year warranty.

Until long-term degradation data on perovskite/silicon tandems are available, the analysis above, based on \$/W costs is the most appropriate. If it turns out that the degradation rates of perovskite and silicon are very different, then an IRR calculation will be necessary to determine the most profitable technology; see Chapter 5.

Microtracked Concentrating Photovoltaics

When we introduced concentrating photovoltaics (CPV) in Chapter 13, we emphasized that it needs two-axis tracking, which has been provided by mounting an array of modules on a central pedestal about which it rotates; see Figure 15.2(a). Such an arrangement is costly because the pedestal needs to be very rigid to withstand wind load on the modules and because of the motors and gearing required for two-axis tracking. In utility-scale applications, silicon PV is less costly and CPV installation halted in 2016. Also pedestal-tracking is not suitable for roof-mount installations because the pedestal imposes undue stress on the roof.

The past decade has seen great cost reductions in PV, not just in the cost of the cells, but also from efficiencies in the design of modules, racking, supports and the installation methods. One way of CPV becoming commercially viable is for it to make use of these developments that have taken place in the PV world. If CPV could have the same form factor as PV, it could be mounted in the same modules, and use the same racking, supports and installation methods. It could then be installed anywhere that PV can be installed, particularly on rooftops. To achieve this, not just the CPV cell and concentrating optics, but also the tracking mechanism needs to be compressed into about 2 cm of thickness, a far cry from the tall pedestal in Figure 15.2(a), which angles the concentrating optics so that the sun is focused on the cell. We achieve micro-tracked CPV (mCPV) by keeping the optics fixed and moving the cell behind the optics so that the sun remains focused on it.

One mCPV design uses transparent polymer cylinders, running north–south, which focus the sun on a CPV cell on the opposite side of the cylinder; see Figure 15.2(b). As the sun moves across the sky, the cylinders rotate to maintain focus on the cell.[5] The cylinders are less than 2 cm in diameter and fit into a standard frame for assembling into a module.

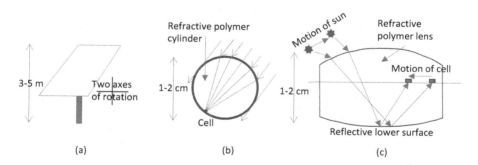

Figure 15.2 Three tracking options for CPV. (a) Conventional pedestal-based tracking; (b) refractive cylinder focusing light on cell on opposite surface and rotating to maintain focus; and (c) refractive polymer combined with reflective lower surface focusing light on a horizontal plane in which the cell moves to maintain focus.

Another option is to design concentrating optics that focus sunlight at different points on a two-dimensional plane and to move the CPV cell across the plane to maintain focus; see Figure 15.2(c). Again, this can be done within a 2 cm thickness[6] and a module contains an array of many such lenses.

These are innovative designs coming out of research labs and are not yet commercial products, so that their manufacturing costs are unknown. To determine their commercial viability, we aim to establish a target cost for mCPV, below which it will deliver a higher IRR than PV.

The mCPV lens in Figure 15.2(c) cannot accept sunlight less than 20° above the horizon, whereas silicon PV can. Differences like this between PV and mCPV affect both the total amount of irradiance available for conversion to electricity and also the hourly pattern of the available irradiance.

To compare the profitability of mCPV and PV, we therefore need to perform a complete analysis for PV to establish the IRR that it delivers at a specific location. We then perform complete analyses for mCPV for a range of capital costs and estimate the mCPV capital cost that delivers the same IRR as PV; see Figure 15.3. This becomes our target mCPV cost. If it is possible to produce the mCPV design for less than this target cost, then it can compete effectively against PV. The end result of this analysis is the same as we described for perovskite/silicon tandems but the methodology is more complex since it involves the microgrid optimization from Chapter 10 together with the IRR calculation from Chapter 5. It also needs to be repeated for different geographic locations, using the corresponding irradiance patterns.

We now present a case analysis for the mCPV design in Figure 15.2(c), for a behind-the-meter (BTM) solar project on an office building in Modesto, California.[7] Following Figure 15.3, we first estimate the electricity generated by PV and our mCPV design. For PV, this is a standard calculation for which commercial software is available. For mCPV, we need to take into account the specifics of our design. The solar generation shown in Figure 15.4 for July illustrates the fact that mCPV does not generate when the sun is within 20° of the horizon, so that the range of hours during which electricity is generated is wider for PV than for mCPV. This is the opposite of what one would expect from pedestal tracked CPV, which can follow the sun as it rises and sets slightly north of east and west in July. However, pedestal-tracking is not suited to BTM installations, whereas mCPV can be used.

The microgrid optimization result is also shown in Figure 15.4 for a 270 kW solar microgrid with a battery capacity of 200 kWh and a stylized load of 400 kW during the working day and 140 kW at other times. Modesto

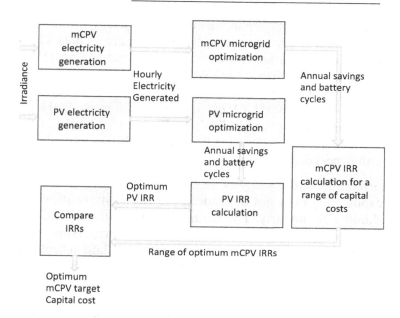

Figure 15.3 Methodology for obtaining target CPV capital costs at which CPV has the same IRR as PV.

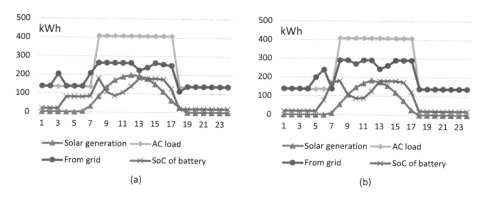

Figure 15.4 Microgrid optimization for (a) PV and (b) mCPV, showing more electricity drawn from the grid for mCPV than for PV. SoC: State of Charge.

has both time-of-use charges and demand charges for businesses customers, giving some incentive to flatten the hourly profile of electricity from the grid, which is evident in the results in Figure 15.4. However, the lack of mCPV generation early morning and late evening results in more electricity being drawn from the grid for mCPV than for PV.

The savings, compared with purchasing all electricity from the grid are increased if we use a larger battery as shown in Figure 15.5(a). However, the increased cost of the battery reduces the IRR, and Figure 15.5(b) shows that the optimal battery size is 200 kWh for PV giving an IRR of 21.4%. We now choose an mCPV capital cost that matches the PV IRR for a range of battery sizes and find that mCPV can match PV if it uses a 200 kWh battery and if it can be installed for $1.07/W; see Figure 15.5(b). The fact that the optimal battery size is the same for PV and mCPV is a coincidence. In general, we can expect different optimal battery sizes for different technologies.

We performed the above analysis for other cities and found that the target mCPV capital cost does not depend on the electricity tariff, which affects both technologies similarly. The main difference between mCPV and PV is that mCPV only uses the direct beam of solar irradiance, whereas PV also uses the diffuse light from the whole sky and light reflected from the ground. The proportion of direct beam to total irradiance is higher in Lancaster, California and in Las Vegas than it is in Modesto. The target capital cost for mCPV is therefore higher in those cities, so that we can see that competition between PV and mCPV depends on the geographical location. This is in contrast to the analysis of perovskite/silicon tandems earlier in this chapter, which was independent of geographical location. Also, in our mCPV analysis, we have optimized the battery capacity in our microgrid, whereas that was not necessary for the perovskite/silicon tandem analysis, which is independent of whether microgrids and batteries are used.

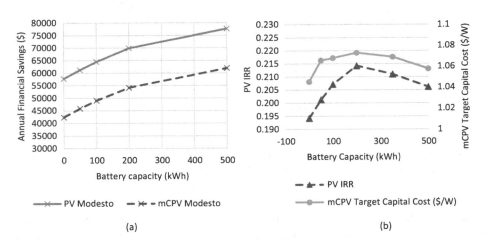

(a)

(b)

Figure 15.5 (a) Increased savings obtained with increased battery capacity, for PV and mCPV. (b) Optimization of IRR for PV at 21.4% and optimization of mCPV target capital cost at $1.07/W.

The above analysis is for installed costs. Since mCPV is more efficient than PV, it occupies less area and hence less structural equipment and other installation costs. Taking this into account, using an analysis similar to that in Table 15.1, we calculate a target mCPV module cost of $0.25/W in Modesto.

Summary

The cost of solar cells contributes to the capital cost of a project, and their efficiency determines how much electricity we can generate in a given area. The cost of the cell is a small proportion of the total cost and therefore attention focuses on improving efficiency so that the area-dependent costs (supports, racking, installation labor) are reduced. Silicon is reaching the limits of its efficiency potential, and volume manufacturing costs for more efficient semiconductors are not available. We therefore estimate *target* costs for two emerging technologies below which they are more profitable than silicon PV. First, an efficiency and capital cost comparison is made among silicon, perovskite and a perovskite/silicon tandem, establishing target tandem cell costs for a range of perovskite efficiencies. Second, mCPV is analyzed, in which a tracking mechanism behind the focusing optics moves the cell to maintain focus. A silicon PV cell and an mCPV cell receive different irradiance because of the limitations of the focusing and tracking mechanisms, so that a complete microgrid optimization and IRR calculation must be done for each case. We calculate the PV IRR and then the mCPV target capital cost, which will give the same IRR. Target capital costs for mCPV are higher in locations with a high ratio of direct beam irradiance to total irradiance.

Takeaways

- Total Installed Capital Costs
  - Reduced costs of new solar cell technologies do not contribute much to the total installed cost of a project since they are a small proportion of the total.
  - Increased efficiencies of new solar cell technologies can contribute to the total installed cost of a project by reducing the area-dependent costs.
  - Silicon is approaching the limit of its efficiency so let's try other semiconductors.
- Perovskite/Silicon Tandem
  - A layer of perovskite on top of a silicon cell can improve the efficiency compared with silicon alone.
  - The tandem cell cost is higher than silicon alone.

- We can calculate ranges of perovskite cell cost and efficiency for which the installed tandem is lower cost than silicon or perovskite alone. This can be done by simulating tandem costs or by using formulas provided in the Math Box.
- Microtracked CPV
  - Microtracked CPV maintains focus by moving the CPV cells behind focusing optics so that everything fits into the 2 cm depth of a standard PV module frame.
  - This allows mCPV to be installed on rooftops as a distributed energy resource.
  - Target mCPV costs that give the same IRR as silicon PV can be calculated by (i) estimating electricity generation from each technology, (ii) performing a microgrid optimization for a range of battery capacities, (iii) estimating the optimal PV IRR, (iv) optimizing the mCPV IRR for a range of capital costs. The target mCPV capital cost is the one that has the same IRR as PV.

Probe Deeper: The Why?

Why use perovskite/silicon tandems and mCPV? Because they have the same form factor as PV, fit into the same module frames, use the same racking and supports and can be installed without retraining the installers. They can therefore be used wherever silicon PV can be used including commercial and residential rooftops. Their high efficiency reduces the costs of modules, racking, supports and labor since the area required is less.

Process

Perovskite/Silicon Tandem

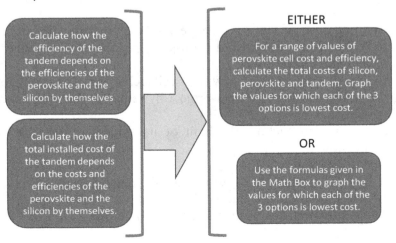

Calculate how the efficiency of the tandem depends on the efficiencies of the perovskite and the silicon by themselves

Calculate how the total installed cost of the tandem depends on the costs and efficiencies of the perovskite and the silicon by themselves.

EITHER

For a range of values of perovskite cell cost and efficiency, calculate the total costs of silicon, perovskite and tandem. Graph the values for which each of the 3 options is lowest cost.

OR

Use the formulas given in the Math Box to graph the values for which each of the 3 options is lowest cost.

mCPV

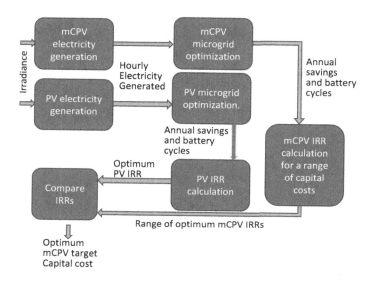

Notes

1 Shakeriaski, F., Ghodrat, M., Salehi, F., 2021, Integrated Photovoltaic Thermal Systems, Their Applications and Recent Advance on Performance Improvement: A Review, *International Journal of Environmental Studies*, 78(5), 838–864.

2 Yu, Z.J., Carpenter III, J.V., Holman, Z.C., 2018 Sept. 3, Techno-economic Viability of Silicon-based Tandem PV Modules in USA, *Nature Energy*, 747–753. doi.org/10.1038/s41560-018-0201-5

3 NREL, Best Research-Cell Efficiency Chart, https://www.nrel.gov/pv/cell-efficiency.html

4 Gallucci, M, "Perovskite Solar Outbenches Rivals", *IEEE Spectrum*, 2021.

5 Lee, T., Kim, J., Cho, S., Pyo, S., Song, K., Lee, J., 2020, "Planar-type Concentrating Photovoltaics with Cylindrical Lenses Directly Integrated with Thin Flexible GaAs Solar Cells", *Progress in Photovoltaics*, 28(1):71–78, https://doi.org/10.1002/pip.3209

6 Price, J.S., Grede, A.J., Wang, B., et al., 2017, "High-concentration Planar Microtracking Photovoltaic System Exceeding 30% Efficiency," *Nature Energy*, 2(8):17113. https://doi.org/10.1038/nenergy.2017.113

7 Wright, David, Liu, Lauren, Parvan, Laura, Majumdar, Zigurts, Giebink, Noel C., 2020, "Economic Analysis of a Novel Design of Micro-tracked CPV", *Progress in Photovoltaics: Research and Applications*, 1–14, DOI:10.1002/pip.3379.

Epilogue

Energy in the form of sunlight lands on a solar cell, maybe set up in a desert or maybe integrated into the architecture of a building. The light energy is converted at low cost into electrical energy, which then runs through wires to power electric heaters and appliances in our homes, offices and factories. Some of it is used in electric arc furnaces to melt scrap iron and make steel. Some of it is sent through aluminum oxide where it tears aluminum atoms away from oxygen atoms to give us the pure metal. Some of the solar electricity is stored for future use, for instance, in electric cars and trucks.

Yes, solar electricity works many wonders such as these, but that is not all.

Some of our electric energy is also converted to the chemical energy of that highly reactive element, hydrogen, by shattering water molecules into their component hydrogen and oxygen atoms in an electrolyzer. Oh, how that hydrogen yearns to be reunited with oxygen! Just make a spark in a hydrogen powered jet engine and the hydrogen will grab the oxygen out of the air in a burst of energy powerful enough to thrust a plane into the sky. We can slow this reaction down in a fuel cell and recover some of the original electrical energy and use it to power ships, cars and trains. Even when the oxygen is bound tightly to iron in its ore, hydrogen snatches it away, leaving metallic iron from which we can make steel. And we can also trick the hydrogen into combining with nitrogen from the air instead of oxygen and put the resulting ammonia to use, making fertilizer for crops to feed the world.

Solar power does not therefore just *replace* fossil-fuel generators of electricity. Its clean credentials and ever-declining cost attract greenhouse gas emitters from across heavy industry and fossil-fuel powered transport to invent and implement new ways of doing things. Not only clean and low cost, but also abundant, solar power provides humanity with an audacious new world, powering profitable innovations that promise to transform our economy over the coming decades.

Geographical Index

Note: **Bold** page numbers refer to tables, *italic* page numbers refer to figures and page numbers followed by "n" refer to end notes.

Comprehensive Index

Note: **Bold** page numbers refer to tables, *italic* page numbers refer to figures and page numbers followed by "n" refer to end notes.

Printed in the United States
by Baker & Taylor Publisher Services